A
YORKSHIRE
GIGOLO

An Anthology of Recollections

Fantasy

&

Myths

By

Melvyn Walker

ISBN-13: 978-1539688723

ISBN-10: 1539688720

Conditions of Sale

This is dedicated to my mother
Alice Fallowfield, nee Walker, who gave me my life.

FORWARD

Sometime in the early 90's I saw a man known as Wolfgang Neuss, an actor and satirist on a late night talk show from NDR, the regional TV station for the North of re-united Germany.

I can clearly recall when he lit a joint and said *'Es darf nie wieder ein Joint aus Deutschland jemals wieder ausgehen!'* A pun on the German edict that Germany will never again start a war.

I took this act of rebellion against the Overlords to heart and have lived monk-like in my contribution to oppression; like a tangent on the periphery of polite society and a thorn in the side of authority – a plague on the House of Nations.

This is not intended to be either Pro or Contra for the consumption of any substance that has a perturbing effect on one's CPU, more a recollection of life experiences over the past 40 years of the use of Cannabis Sativa, and other variants well known by aficionados. The first contribution is by my mother.

IN SERVICE

I left North Cliffe School when I was 14, at Easter time. My mother was already working at a farm in South Cliffe. She used to go every Monday to do the washing and ironing for 2s/6d. I was hired out on this farm for 4s/6d a week (paid annually). I never had to go to any hirings because I already had a job to go to before I left school. The hirings held once a year at Martinmas (23rd November) in various market towns - Driffield, Market Weighton and so on. Deals were done in the streets and in pubs. Lads from Hull would come to some of these hirings, especially those near to the city. It was not an easy way to make a living! The day started at 5.30 am and stretched through to nightfall. At my first job I had every other Wednesday afternoon off when I used to walk to Market Weighton, which was three miles away.

My first morning job was cleaning and black leading the kitchen grate. A big job was scalding out and cleaning the milking things - churns separators, etc. The redbrick kitchen floor had to be scrubbed with a strong soda solution, no rubber gloves, as did the stone floors in the sleeping quarters. The only floor coverings were corn bags round the beds. All this washing and scrubbing played havoc with your hands, especially in wintertime. I rubbed "Snowfire" ointment on my hands at night and then wore cotton gloves, which my mother gave to me to keep the grease off the sheets. 0h, those sheets! They were so rough and the blankets were no better. I cannot bear blankets even to this day. Friday afternoons we had to scrub the earth closet clean and then cut up newspapers to serve as toilet paper.

Another cutting up job was of material to be used in making clip rugs. The tool for making the rugs was often just a wooden clothes peg pared down to shape. On one farm at North Cave they ran a coal business as well as a milk round. I had to deliver milk from a one gallon can into people's jugs door-to-door. I also delivered butter, cream and eggs. Collecting these eggs gave me many a dreary walk round hedges, in Stack yards - wherever these "free range" hens decided to lay their eggs! I tried to get these delivery duties to let me off from the Sunday morning Epsom salts dosing! However, I not often successful. Saturday night was bath night. This meant heating the wash-house boiler and bringing out the zinc bath in front of the fire. The family followed the same routine on Friday nights. I remember going to the picture house in Market Weighton - Jack and Rosie Garforth's Picture House - 6d a time. We had to go to the matinee because we had to be in by nine o'clock on Saturday nights. Two things made me feel very smart! One was a velvet (or, perhaps it was velveteen) dress made for me by Edith Davies for 10/-. The other was having my first perm when I as 17 years old. My hair was straight as pump water and the 10/- Eugene perm lasted a year!' (*Alice Fallowfield, Holme-upon-Spalding Moor WI 1999*)

A

YORKSHIRE

GIGOLO

OED definition: A man who is kept by a woman, especially an older woman.

Little Tommy Tucker sang for his supper What shall we give him?

Brown bread and butter How shall he cut it, without a knife? How shall he marry, without a wife?

Who, or what, was a Little Tommy Tucker?

Little 'Tommy Tucker' referred to in the words of this nursery rhyme was a colloquial term that was commonly used to describe orphans - Little Tommy Tucker.

The orphans were often reduced to begging or 'singing for their supper'. The reference to Little Tommy Tucker marrying and the lack of a wife reflects the difficulty of any orphan being able to marry due to their exceptionally low standing within the community. The first publication date for Little Tommy Tucker was 1829.

I have to confess, there have been times when I did indeed sing for my supper to win the attentions of women, both young and old. More of that later.

MY DAD 'S e-mails....

From: E-mail from mel@web.de

To: Maeve walker@yahoo.com Time: 11/07/2018. 18:30 GMT Re: Your 18th Birthday.

Dearest Maeve,

I know it's an important day for you, however, once again, I was unable to be there on your birthday, but it's only four weeks since Arwid's fourteenth birthday party and I'll come and celebrate my seventy fifth with you all at the beginning of September. As you know, the reason why I couldn't be there with you and the family was to come back to the UK when my Mam' had to go into the nursing home, indefinitely. She died, as you already know, last December, just before Christmas.

Most of my brother's, sister and various partners and close family and friends turned up sooner or later to help clear the bungalow. As it transpired, I was able to take over the tenancy of the one-bedroom bungalow. In addition, there was as in addition, a ten strong delegation from the village W.I., and half of the twelve-strong, Cross Keys Ladies' Darts team turned up. One day whilst sorting and disposing of her belongings I came across a large, reinforced A4 envelope. Inside was a thick, leather bound, loose-leaf folder with;

PERSONAL DIARY
(Hand written on the cover) Alice Fallowfield; nee Walker.

I've spent the last two weeks reading the diary and scanning it into my PC; correcting, formatting etc., and as well as including some of my own adventures. I'm sending you a copy as an attachment so you can read it before it becomes a 'Remainder', or you pick up a copy at the airport. To make it more understandable I have written some of the essays in German. Now I know what brought me to Thuringia in the first place. Ever since my divorce in 1978 I have spent the best part of the last forty years moving ever eastwards. And now I know

4

where my father lived and worked. Not the 18-year-old tenant farmers' son, as she had told me for the last 30 years. She also wrote and told of her love affair with a German POW as well as the name of the 25-year-old *Oberfeldwebel* (Air gunner, Christian Fischer). I'll tell you more when you've read some yourself. I look forward to seeing you and Arwid in four weeks' time. Take care and say hello to everyone in Vieselbach.

CU soon, BFN, Opapamel.

***

15th. AUGUST 1944.

I've just started working for the 'Land Army', a battalion of women from all over the country to help on the farms all over Britain. And I saw a nice lad today when I finally got there. We were getting the last of the harvest in from the 12-acre field at Bursea Hall farm. I found out that he's a German POW interned in Holme upon Spalding Moor. He's really good looking, like a young Cary Grant...

17th. AUGUST 1944.

The Germans came to 12-acre field again today. Twelve of them turned up this time in an army lorry with six home guard soldiers equipped with WWI 1 rifles under the command of a regular army sergeant. Apart from him there was nobody under 60 in the squad. I found out that the lad's name is Christian, good job me Mam makes me go to church on a Sunday morning. He came over at dinnertime with two of the other German lads to give us a loaf of bread that they'd baked in the Nunnery kitchen. It was very nice, a lot firmer than our bread. In return we gave them some tea from our flasks and one of the other lasses smoked, so she offered them her Senior Services. Next week there's a dance in the village hall and the POW's will be allowed to go under armed escort. However, I've promised Alain, my boss's 18-year-old son that I'd go with him, that is, meet him there inside the hall so that he doesn't have to pay for me; he's a skinflint like his dad. Along with other captured aircrew

5

Christian was interned in a walled nunnery on the outskirts of a small village until the end of the war in the East Riding of Yorkshire called:

HOLME ON SPALDING MOOR.

This survey was carried out to commemorate European Architectural Heritage Year 1975, the aim was to record the buildings and other features of architectural and historic interest in our village.

Holme is one of the largest parishes in Yorkshire containing according to ordnance survey, over 11,500 acres. It is widely scattered, stretching from the Foulness River which bounds on the west and the south, to a little beyond the Market Weighton Canal. The surface is generally level and until the Enclosure Act in 1773 the nature of the land was very dangerous, consisting of marsh and bog land (the situation of which was known to only a few). Geographically Holme is situated on the high road from Market Weighton to Selby, 5 miles northwest of the former and 14 East of the latter. Its longitude is 54° North and its latitude is 3/4° west. The railway came to the village in 1848 the line being the Selby one and it was closed in 1965. Part of the Station house was demolished in 1977.The area is mainly agricultural, in which a number of the villagers are employed. The Dale Farm Foods Creamery is another source of employment and also the Hawker Siddeley Aviation Company, which is situated on the old Airfield. *16/01/1945.*

It's me birthday t'day, I'm twenty-five and I'v just missed my period, so it looks as though I'll have to go and visit my aunt in Halifax until I've had the baby. My mother told me once, that if I got pregnant, and when the baby arrived, I should give it away for adoption. Now I've told me Mam and I think she suspects who the real father is. However, she seemed to believe me when I told her that the eighteen-year-old son of the tenant farmer, where we both work, was the father... And that's what I've been telling you all these years. In reality your father is/was an air gunner with the Luftwaffe. His aeroplane was hit by the Flak, which they encountered over Hull in 1944. Their mission was to drop incendiary bombs on the docks.

SCHEHERAZADE

The story goes that every day Shahryar (Persian: ر, "king") would marry a new virgin, and after doing so would despatch the previous day's wife to be beheaded. This was done in anger, having found out that his first wife was unfaithful to him. He had killed 1,000 such women by the time he was introduced to Scheherazade, the vizier's daughter.

In Sir Richard Burton's translation of The Nights, Scheherazade was described in this way:

"[Scheherazade] had perused the books, annals and legends of preceding Kings, and the stories, examples and instances of bygone men and things; indeed, it was said that she had collected a thousand books of histories relating to antique races and departed rulers. She had perused the works of the poets and knew them by heart; she had studied philosophy and the sciences, arts and accomplishments; and she was pleasant and polite, wise and witty, well read and well bred." Against her father's wishes, Scheherazade volunteered to spend one night with the king. Once in the king's chambers, Scheherazade asked if she might bid one last farewell to her beloved sister, Dinarzade, who had secretly been prepared to ask Scheherazade to tell a story during the long night. The king lay awake and listened with awe as Scheherazade told her first story. The night passed by, and Scheherazade stopped in the middle of the story. The king asked her to finish, but Scheherazade said there was no time, as dawn was breaking. So, the king spared her life for one day to finish the story the next night. So the next night, Scheherazade finished the story and then began a second, even more exciting tale which she again stopped halfway through at dawn. So the king again spared her life for one day to finish the second story. And so the King kept Scheherazade alive day by day, as he eagerly anticipated the finishing of the previous night's story. At the end of 1,001 nights, and 1,000 stories, Scheherazade told the king that she had no more tales to tell him. During these 1,001 nights, the king had fallen in love with Scheherazade, and so he spared her life, and made her his queen.

EMAILS VON MALA

Betr: Sie haben eine Grußkarte erhalten.

Von: babuschka@web.de

An:schnellmel@web.de

Datum: 22.09.09 07:56:02

Hi, Mel,

I could open the pix. The kitchen looks like the one you had in EF. I've just finished my Sunday morning class. I'm really happy to teach only AUA. It suits my working rhythm. I've been writing quite a lot in the last three days. As it turns out, I'm writing about myself. Kind of funny. Like my own therapy: how did I become who I am now? A long way to go. And I want a new beginning, so I better get over with the past...I'm going to Payam on the 18th!!!!!!!And tonight Friederike is embarking on her flight to bkk. So, I'll have superb company, merry Xmas to you, too BB

Hi, I already returned the post box key. It was exactly one year after you rented it. So, don't send anything here. I'll see you soon anyway.

Sorry to hear about your mom. If she is having a good stay where she is, why worry about her mind? Maybe her world gets more and more interesting or colourful or whatever. Who can tell...Gotta go. Final exams...CU, BB

Beautiful!

How's everything? I'm still struggling with writing. I have some topics on my mind and my laptop but I'm kind of missing the thinking time to develop something.

Meanwhile, Chain is making amazing things with the most primitive tools. I'm making stuff, too - however, when I have time. I'm gonna send you some pics next time the internet works and I have my laptop with me. AUA class is waiting...Take care! P.S.: Still no ticket, because no bank account yet, because my work permit has expired and they need a pic again and a health certificate, and, and, and... Sooooon

Btr: Butterfly Love
Von: babuschka@web.de
An: schnellmel@web.de
Datum: 11.08.09 14:33:40

Von: satanimala@web.de
An: schnellmel@web.de
Re: whereabouts

Hey Mel

I'm fine, too. I'm back in Surat teaching university again. God, I was lucky to get away from that primary school in Ranong... the worst job ever all registers considered I'm slowly working off my debts, so there's no Internet connection soon for teaching. The job is only for 3 months, and then every thing's open again. I'm ready for something new. Let's see what comes my way. I'd like some adventure. Life's so boring in the rat race.......

Talk to you soon. LOL, BB

CANNABIS

My first experience with Cannabis was some forty-four years ago in 1971 in a beach bar near Changi Royal Air force base in Singapore at the relatively tender age of 25. At the time I was a Senior Technician attached to 205 SAR Squadron. A couple of our aircraft took part in War Games with the US Navy at Subic Bay in the Philippines. Of course we beat them at their own game. A couple of the ground crew, and to the best of my knowledge one of the aircrew brought back about an ounce of the weed each.

It was this Radar/MAD specialist, Joe, who introduced me to the delights of 'Mary Jane'. Joe and I were old friends – we'd faced each other on stage at the Base Amateur dramatic club.

It turned out to be a similar epiphany that I'd experienced with the 'Hangover/'Flu' in Yemen (See Arabian Knights and Daze). The next occasion was four years later at the Ideal Homes Exhibition at the Earls Court exhibition Centre. I was, at the time, employed by 'Schloss Boeckelheim GmbH, a German wine marketing company, along with several other reps from all over the UK. In addition, there were two attractive German stand hostesses, Krista and Monika. One evening after a relatively successful day of sales the UK director, Herr Wolfgang Strauss, invited us all for a drink after work in the bar of the Eden Plaza hotel where all of us out of town reps were billeted. Before long the London reps started leaving. The rest of us including the two German girls got down to some serious drinking. It wasn't long before the rep from Leeds, a portly, jovial northerner, who we nicknamed 'Baconman' because he used to sell Danish bacon before starting to work for Schloss Boeckelheim, produced a spliff. By the time it got to me I was deep in conversation with Krista, who had already told me that she was 23 years old, had grown up on a large farm 20 kilometres from Ingolstadt and was studying drama and journalism at Munich university.

After preliminary Intel and reconnaissance, I had the feeling that maybe Krista would not be averse to some 'exploration into the possibilities of finding a mutual conclusion', in single syllable words, she wasn't averse to some Techtel Mechtel, that's German for, How's your father? so I took a couple of drags and passed it to her. She did the same and turned back to me and said,

"I think I've too much drunk back to Richards flat to drive. May I in your room sleep?"

Richard was a chubby mid 20's rep from London – an 'attempted moustache'- at the time I had just turned 30 and wore a full beard. In retrospect I had an uncanny resemblance to a young Osama, who hadn't yet shown up on the CIA's radar.

"Sure," I replied. To avoid gossip, I told Krista my room number after we'd finished our drinks and went up in the three-man lift to my room.

I'd just taken off my jacket and tie when Krista tapped gently on the door. I let her in and we hugged and kissed briefly until she said that she was not only tipsy but that she was also dog-tired. When got ready for bed she surprised me by taking off her bra without removing her T-shirt. After she'd extracted herself from her jeans she hopped under the bed covers in the one-metre-wide bed. I undressed and slipped in next to her. We snuggled up and when she felt JT straining in his Budgie smuggler, she said patting him, "We'll take care of him in the morning," and immediately fell into a deep slumber.

Krista was at least 5 cm taller than me. She was a well-built, stereotypical Deutsche Fraulein, blonde hair, blue eyes with an infectious laugh and my first German lover. The next morning, I woke up with the usual 'morning glory', which was pressing unmistakably between her ample buttocks. She stirred and mumbled something, so I started to get out of bed. Her eyes opened and she grasped my hand and said," Don't go!" and pulled my hand to her Mons Veneris, "Liebkoese Mich, bitte!"

Without further ado I fulfilled her wish and she was soon writhing and moaning under my administration. She then ripped off her t-shirt so that I could kiss and nibble her large well-formed breasts until she couldn't take any more and wanted to take the game to the next level. She slipped out of her pants and releasing JT from his restraints pulled him towards her' docking portal' and said throatily,

"Komm, ich will Dich in Mich spuren!"

"What about contraception?" I grunted with J. T's helmet between her labia Majoris,

Pulling him deeper she gasped, "My period last week finished so it should be OK!"

(Insertion)

Not being a gentleman who declines to offer assistance to a young woman in distress, I concurred. And after ten minutes of 'Flying United' she came with a loud cry, almost breaking my back and crushing my ribs in the process. I, of course, was denied relief as anyone one who has been afflicted with 'Morning Glory' can testify. We had a couple of return bouts; once before the end of the exhibition when she invited me to dinner in Richard's flat. And once more several years later on the farm near Ingolstadt, and again at her sister's flat in Munich when I arrived unannounced from Athens. Baconman gave me a nugget of hashish on the last day of the exhibition. So when I got home late on the Saturday evening I told Lex, my wife and we enjoyed a couple of Spliffs together and we both had a more pleasant DNA exchange. However, she was a bit worried in case our two young sons, Jake and Lucas found the rest of the dope by accident. We finally decided in the tea caddy on top of the cupboard adjacent to the kettle.

Until I went to Saudi Arabia in 1976 I/we enjoyed the occasional spliff with friends and acquaintances. One of the most memorable was when I was stand manager for Schloss Boeckelheim at the first Ideal homes exhibition in Cardiff. Theoretically I could have driven home every evening because I only lived a forty-minute drive away in Yate, an over-spill town for Bristol. However, I chose to stay at the Bed & Breakfast in Penarth during the week where Baconman was also staying. On the second night we were walking back to our digs when Baconman spotted a young woman sitting in a Mini at the kerbside a few metres from our B&B.

He was a bit of a Don Juan so he stopped and engaged her in conversation. I continued to our B&B and ten minutes later he turned up grinning like the proverbial Cheshire Cat. He told me that he had a date with her the following evening and that her name was Janet and she had a four-month old baby. She was going to tell him more when they met. It wasn't to be. The next day I got the order from Herr Strauss to cut our losses, and to send Baconman back to Leeds to work because we weren't getting enough custom at the exhibition. He took it with aplomb and gave me all the info for the rendezvous.

Sure enough at 20:30 the following evening Janet was sitting in her Mini just below the B&B. I introduced myself and told her about Baconman being called away and told her that if she liked I could take his place. I'd taken a couple of bottles of our best Mosel wine for the occasion. So I asked her if there was somewhere we could go to drink it and talk. She suggested the cliff tops above Lavernack Point. After she'd locked her car we got into mine and she navigated us to the aforesaid cliffs. We sat on a bench overlooking Cardiff Bay and drank the best part of the first bottle of wine and smoked a spliff while she told me of her needs. It seemed that her husband had lost interest in her as a woman since her baby was born. But he didn't mind her going out with a girlfriend, Sylvia, who was her alibi for that evening's assignation. It started to get chilly so I suggested that we got back in the car. Janet immediately chose the back seat because she said we would have more room to stretch out. It didn't take more than a few minutes before we got down to the nitty-gritty. Under her button-through dress she was wearing a teenager's wet dream, stockings and suspenders and a half-cup bra that strained to contain her plump white breasts. When I released them from their captivity and nuzzled them I was greeted by the taste of mother's milk, which oozed from her engorged nipples as she was still breast feeding her baby. By this time, she had freed JT from the confines of my trousers and proceeded to engulf him in her apparently hungry mouth. She was well versed so I leant back and enjoyed the experience. After I had reluctantly sprayed her tonsils with my gene code I returned the compliment as she lay stretched out on the bench seat. We finished the wine and I drove her back to her car where we had one last cuddle and exchanged telephone numbers since the exhibition finished on Saturday evening. I told her that I would call her the next time I was in Cardiff, which would be soon because I'd been given the task by Herr Strauss of developing the business in the Valleys, and I had already made a connection in Cardiff, Hilary, who was an attractive 18-year-old trainee dental nurse. Hilary had turned up on the first day of the exhibition with her mother. But that's another story.

Between 1975 and 1978 I was employed by BAC, the British Aircraft Corporation, now known as BAE, British Aerosystems. As a Technical trainer with the Royal Saudi Air Force. So I had little opportunity to enjoy the pleasures of Mary-Jane.

When I returned to the UK in late spring in 1978, after the break-up of my 12-year long marriage I lived in a shared house in Bristol. I spent my evenings drinking with my house mates and alternatively visiting the several Casinos around Tower street in order to supplement my savings from Saudi Arabia, (see Arabian Daze and Knights). During this period of re-evaluating my purpose in life I had several occasions to once again to savour the joys of Weed (See Buggsy).

The next occurrences took place over the next five months, (see The Summer of '78).

THE LONG AND COSTLY ARM OF THE BRITISH JUSTICE SYSTEM

This all started when I was arrested in Portsmouth for possession of a small quantity of a so-called class B drug, namely in Police jargon 'Herbal cannabis' at Ca. 15:00 on Thursday the 5th April 2012. When the police officer at the house where I was staying asked me if I had any of the aforementioned substance I handed him my tobacco tin with a couple of grams of the illicit material.

We then drove to the main police station where I was duly processed, i.e. photo, dabs and DNA swabs. I was then released on police bail with a document telling me that I had to appear at Portsmouth magistrate's court at 09:45 on the 27th of April to answer to the charge.

After I inquired about the location of economical 'Back-packer' hostels one of the officers said he would drive me to a homeless shelter. This turned out to be quite hospitable, even though it meant sharing a dormitory with 4 other men and 2 women. The regular residents had a wide screen TV, as well as tea and coffee making necessaries. The following morning, I got up early and took the first available train home.

On the following Monday I wrote to the court and told them that as I had already admitted to the possession, and the fact that it would cost me around £ 200 to attend the court hearing, would the court accept my postal statement of guilty as charged? I didn't hear anything further until 17:45 on the 29th of May. See following entry. 29.05.2012 As usual I was woken by the 'dawn chorus' so I got up had a quick wash, made fresh coffee and went back to bed and read and smoked until around 07:30. Got up had my breakfast – yoghurt with honey – watched the news, checked and answered my e-mails.

Ca 10:35 I went and bought some groceries.

When I got home I made my midday repast, 'Zanzibar chicken'- last night's dinner micro-waved. From two until four I played cards at the village social club without any success.

Ca 17:45 I was washing yesterday's dishes prior to making my evening meal; poached salmon fillet with broccoli, new potatoes, and a spicy parsley sauce, when I heard a knock at the front door. Drying my hands, I went to see who it was my door to find an attractive young police officer, who was in the process of calling her colleague, on his way around to the back of my bungalow.

After she had shown me her ID and warrant for my arrest, because of my no show at Portsmouth magistrate court on the 27th of April, I was allowed to pack some necessary items as I would be spending the night in a holding cell in Goole police station before being transported to Portsmouth by a security company the next day. On arrival I was duly processed, i.e. photo, dabs and DNA swabs. I was then shown into my abode for the night until my departure the following morning. Dave, the charging officer, asked if I would like a cup of tea and something to eat – coffee wasn't available – too expensive; he rattled off a list of micro-wave meals. I chose Cottage pie, which was delivered piping hot, however the mashed potato had the appearance and texture of wallpaper paste. Nevertheless, it filled me up and after I'd eaten I was questioned by the police nurse about any illnesses or medication. During and after this examination I chatted and joked with the station staff. I asked the young police woman if she had been selected for the Olympic reinforcement 'gravy-train', which brought a round of jeers from her fellow officers. When I returned to my cell I drank some more tea and read until I'd finished the penultimate chapter in my current book. I buzzed the front desk and Dave came and asked if I needed anything to which I asked him to turn down the light, which he did and wished me a pleasant night's sleep.

Thursday 29.05.2012 I was woken by the sun and the sound of the early morning traffic. The night officer brought me a cup of tea around 06:00 and asked me what I would like breakfast. The choice was micro-wave beans, potato and sausages, or scrambled eggs and bacon. I chose the former; the beans were OK, the sausages appeared to be made of sawdust soaked in Soy sauce. Shortly after 07:00 I was released from my cell and handed over to the two security officers from GEO-AMEY.

They immediately handcuffed me and one of the guards attached himself to my right wrist with a second set of 'cuffs for the three metres to the transport vehicle. It was fitted out to carry up to six prisoners from jail to the courts and vice-versa. Before getting into the van I asked one of the guards if I could have a smoke before we left. He said no, but he would make me a roll-up as soon as we got on the road.

We drove 4 hours non-stop and arrived at Portsmouth Magistrates court at 011:20 where I was handed over to the court security personnel with the same procedure I endured on departure. The security supervisor asked me if I would like the services of the duty solicitor, to which I replied, 'Why not?'

As in Goole I was given something to drink and a short while later I was cuffed and escorted to an interview room where I met the aforesaid lawyer. She already had my file and said we should play it as it transpired. Cuffed again I was taken back to the holding cell. At approximately at 13:00 as far as I could estimate I was given another micro-wave meal; Thai red curry with rice which was piquant as a poor Lancashire Hotpot.

Just after 14:15 I was once again cuffed by a rather jovial magistrate's prison guard and escorted to the dock, which was a wooden cage with triple-layer bullet proof glass facing the bench with its three 'worships 'in the courtroom. The current hearing was coming to an end as we entered the chamber and the guard removed the cuffs and told me to be seated. The chairman of the court then called my name and the solicitor indicated that I should stand and answer. He then informed me that if I pleaded not guilty the case would be passed to the crown court. I thought briefly, 'Is it worth the hassle and expense to the taxpayers to show how stupid the law can be.' But then, having paid the piper several times, I have frequently called the tune' so I responded, 'Guilty, as I had done when first arrested five and a half weeks ago.' The duty solicitor then told me that I shouldn't say anything unless asked. She then presented my case. The panel went into a huddle for a couple of minutes and the Chair told me that they had considered every aspect of the case and the court would fine me £ 100, which was commuted because I had already spent over twenty hours in custody. He then said that there was a 'victim surcharge' of £ 15, and did I have the means to pay this?

Before I could reply the clerk of the court said that this also could be commuted.

I'd paid my debt and was once again 'a free man'. The guard looked at me and grinned, 'Wher've yow come from?' as we made our way back down to the holding cells. When I told him he said, 'Yow'll be needin a travel warrant, then? He told me to sit in the reception cell, which was furnished with a table and two utility chairs, while he got my belongings and a travel warrant block. He gave me the warrant and told me that the station was five minutes round the corner. I acquired a ticket to York for £150 at the ticket window. 14:50 and I was on a train to Waterloo.

17:25: I was on an East coast train to York with amicable fellow travellers and arrived in York, where I had time for a pint and a spliff before catching the last bus home. Got home shortly after 21:00 and went to bed at 23:00.

BTW; I ate the salmon for dinner on Thursday.

THE BEGINNING

GROUND ZERO AT KILNWICK PERCY

DATE: 11.11.2020

TIME: 20:00

LOCATION: St. Mary's church hall Kilnwick Percy.

AGM K-P Parish council meeting

AGENDA:

Parish Autonomy Proposal

Present; the regular members of the K-PPC where all present as well as sixty per cent of the remaining 210 odd parishioners.

As the last peal of the church clock resounded the village rector, the Right Reverend JBH, dressed in the manner of a country vicar, i.e. dog-collar, braces and dreadlocks, stood up on the rostrum where the K-PPC were seated, as current chair of the K-PPC and with the appropriate gestures subdued the whispered, curious chatter. After welcoming the assembled congregation, he said in an East Yorkshire dialect, tinged with Caribbean patois,

'Brethren, citizens of Kilnwick Percy, I would like to introduce you to the first speaker and proposer of tonight's agenda. I've known him for almost 30 years, a few of you have known him even longer, but for the newcomers among you, please welcome Alain Percy Jackson!'

The slight man leaning on the left side of the small proscenium arch at the edge of the small stage stood and made his way up the three steps at the side of this front-room sized podium. He was somewhere between 60 and 70 years of age, his shoulder length salt & pepper hair was somewhat unkempt. However, his matching beard was a neatly trimmed spade. Under his multi-pocketed DP (Disruptive Pattern) Gilet he wore a pale silk tunic with an open Cossack collar and rolled up sleeves. Round his neck he sported a 'Guhtra', the scarf made famous by Yasser Arafat. His jeans had seen better times as well as his mud-caked gardening boots.

'Tanks, Mon. Good evening ladies and gentlemen. Thank you all for coming on this foggy November night. For those of you who do not know me and who have heard my name for the first time this evening I will give you a brief resume of my life until today. I am the illegitimate son of a scullery maid and a German POW. They exchanged DNA early on January the 1st 1945 and nine months later I entered this dimension.

I never got to know my father because he was moved to a holding camp near Richmond before he was repatriated to Germany at the end of WWII. Countless years later my mother told me that he was an Air Gunner with the Luftwaffe. His Heinkel 110 was shot down over Hull on a raid on the docks in early 1944. She also told me that he was the son of a state forester in a small village called Steinach in the mountainous south of Thuringia.

K-P was my home until I joined the Royal Air Force two days before my sixteenth birthday. Three years later I qualified as a Junior Technician so I applied for pilot training and was accepted. After basic flying training at RAF Cranwell I converted to Jets at 8 FTS Swinderby and after six months at 229 OCU Chivenor I was posted to 43 Squadron (Fighting Cocks) base at Khormaksar, Aden. Our task was to give air support to the Army units trying to root out the freedom fighters in the Radfan mountains. However, that's not what I would like to propose this evening. You will notice from the booklet you were given when you arrived, that, even the title may shock and surprise you, or maybe an absurd farce.

The words, SOCIAL EXPERIMENT alone, are most likely stir up unhappy thoughts of the past. Simply put, what I am suggesting, is that we declare the parish of Kilnwick Percy a free, autonomous, neighbourhood Republic, with allegiances to now; the future and not the ill-advised past. My aim is to make Kilnwick Percy into a Zero Energy community within five years. We can do this by converting the redundant limestone quarry, the ridge above it and the slope below it into our powerhouse, giving us warmth, light and food provider. The technology for this already exists. I won't go into technical particulars, or facts and figures and projections, that are all laid out in great detail in the booklet. However, the first step in this voyage into self-sufficient, steady state economy is to petition the government of the United Kingdom of our intentions. Before we continue this meeting I would like to ask you to cast your eyes on the hand-out that you received this evening. Thank you....'

THE BEGINNING I

19.01.91 06:45 It was a cold winter's morning as I waited at the crossroads leading to the Autobahn access road in Hofheim/Taunus. I still had the scent of the previous night with Ingrid in my nostrils. I was waiting to be picked up by Barbara and Michael, my future business partners and sponsors, who operated a small language and prep school in Kronberg/Taunus, a small town just over the hill from Kelkheim where I lived. They were relatively punctual – a plus point in their favour.

In November 1990 I had answered their Ad for English teachers in the Frankfurter Rundschau. It was for a language school project in the Neue Bundesländer (The new Federal German states).

When you are free-lancing you are always on the lookout for work for the future. As it turned out, I got the task to help them set up a school after they had found suitable premises in the ex DDR.

The reason I got the position was partially due to my experience, plus the bonus that I am a native speaker, and I had a second arrow in my quiver; I am also a technical translator. Moreover, I did not demand the financial security that the other applicants wanted, who were all German born, English teachers. I even made the commitment to mortgage some of my meagre savings and invest in the project myself. Originally they had targeted Leipzig, because Barbara had relatives there. However, they were not interested in helping her. A short while later another friend off theirs found potential partners for the school project who were willing to look for suitable premises in Erfurt, the State capital of Thuringia. Moreover, this was the reason we were driving to Erfurt on a cold and frosty morning. The reason for the early start was the fact that there was no direct Autobahn link at the time between Frankfurt /Main and Erfurt. It took us 4 hours to drive the 300 odd kilometres to Erfurt, including a brief stop for a pee etc., We arrived shortly before the designated meeting time and met Kris, who was to become my future partner in the joint venture, and her husband, Helmut in the Cactus Bar in the foyer of the Erfurter Hof, the hotel facing the Haupt Bahnhof (main station) where Willi Brandt made his famous appearance at a second floor window in 1970. After coffee and the preliminaries Kris and her husband showed us two prospective premises. However, they were both too far from the centre of town. They promised to look for other locations and we said goodbye to them at about 17:00 and drove back to the Taunus where Barbara and Michael dropped me off at my garden flat around 21:00. I say garden flat, when I looked out of the windows I had a worm's eye view of the lawn!

ACCORDING TO ALICE

It must have been late summer according to Alice, me Mam. We were living in one room with shared kitchen and bathroom in Beechwood House on the outskirts of a small market town called Market Weighton on the edge of the Yorkshire Wolds. When I say we, I mean Mam, Basil, my new Dad, three-year-old me and my new brother Kenneth who was six months old. He was in his cot sleeping; Mam and Basil were in the brass four poster bed, which had squeaky springs and a horse-hair mattress, and I was half asleep in **my** bed, the bottom drawer of my Grandmother's Biedermeier chest of drawers, when I heard Basil whisper, 'Do you feel like a bit of 'How's your father!', or something similar. My ears pricked up in the early evening gloom and I piped up without hesitation, 'What's that taste like? Can I have some, too? 'Basil replied gruffly,' No you can't, it's for grown-ups only. Now go to sleep!'

JUST ANOTHER MONDAY?

Monday 11.04.05 06:45. I woke up a little later this morning because I'd watched TV with Bastian, one of my young cohabitants in our three person WG, until about 23:30 last night. He's a young high school student from Steinach in the mountainous deep south of Thuringia.

As usual I got up and went to the kitchen to microwave the left over coffee from the previous evening. Anna, the other member of our humble abode, was already having breakfast before leaving for work at the local seed company. We exchanged greetings while my coffee was running its cycle in the microwave. I made a roll-up and took them both to my still warm bed and read my latest book until 08:30, occasionally getting up to replenish the coffee and make another spliff. I got up and had a bath, loaded the washing machine and switched it on, checked my e-mails and Ryanair flights to Stansted next week, ate my yoghurt, made a couple of phone calls and tried, to no avail, to make Petra change her mind about access to our daughter. She would only agree to the date we'd agreed on last Friday. I played Blackjack against my PC for roughly speaking an hour, and as usual I finished with a small gain, unfortunately only a virtual profit – I have better uses for my meagre pittance than tempting fate with money I need to live, although the system I play does give the player a slight edge on the casino (see Blackjack). Over the past ten years I have learnt that it's better to invest any surplus cash in commodities!? In the meantime, the washing was done so I hung it to dry on the washing line on our three square metre balcony. When I'd finished I took the empties to the supermarket and caught the number 2 tram to the Anger, went to the bank and drew some money and got the number 3 tram to BB's. Drank a Bud, smoked a couple of Spliffs, and chatted to Andreas, the son of K-D, the proprietor. However, it was in vain none of the usual merchants turned up so I made my farewells and decided to take a stroll to one of my favourite spots in Erfurt, the Krämerbrücke.

KRAEMERBRUECKEN FEST
(THE TINKER'S BRIDGE FESTIVAL)

My first visit to the Krämerbrücke Fest was in the summer of 1991. I had recently arrived in Erfurt to help set up an educational training business. At the time I was living in a WG, (commune) and one of the other co-habitants, Katrin told me about the festival, which usually starts on the last, or the penultimate Friday in June and continues until Sunday afternoon. She said it's easy to find the festival, even if you don't know the town. Head for the town centre and just follow the throng.

It was the first weekend I had spent in the city since moving here at the beginning of the month. I had nothing to do and as it was a beautiful warm, sunny day so I put on my Bermuda's, one of several silk T-shirts, my battered old Panama and took a stroll after lunch to take in the atmosphere of Erfurt, the state capital of Thüringia. The original festival has been organised by the inhabitants of the medieval, timber-frame houses and businesses on the bridge since 1975, which is the oldest bridge over the river Gera, dating back to the 15th. Century and has no fewer than six stone arches. Back in 1975 the festival was mostly confined to the bridge itself. By 1991, however it had been extended to take in the island, which forms the foundations for the central arches, as well as the adjoining cobblestoned square known as Wenige Markt (Lesser Market). On the island a jousting tournament, archery contests, musical activities and other medieval activities, were in full swing.

Access to the island was either from the steps leading down from the new bridge, which runs parallel to the old one, or from a timber gangplank from the steps on the other side of the Krämerbrücke. To get on to the island and enjoy the show I had to pay 5 Taler, i.e. 5 DM, which also gave access to the Wenige Markt. This was fenced off, and inside this stockade a medieval market place had been created. Straw was strewn over the cobblestones; dogs, cats, chickens and barefoot children ran underfoot. Stalls offering medieval wares and delicacies were set up all around the market place. A blacksmith, with a real forge demonstrated his skills and falconers showed of their proud birds. The latter filling me with fond memories of *Rasham,* the falcon that I had briefly owned in Saudi Arabia.

The multitudinous smells of mulled wine, beer, herbs, freshly baked bread, and burning meat filled the hot summer air. Right in the middle of the market place a side of beef was slowly turning on a spit over a huge charcoal fire. A muzzled, fully-grown brown bear on a chain was standing guard close at hand to the roasting beef. The smell made my mouth water and I could not withstand the temptation. I strolled among the crowds soaking up the warm afternoon sun and absorbing the ambiance with a roast beef sandwich, the size of a baseball catcher's glove in one hand and a pint of the local beer in a plastic beaker in the other.

A medieval hot tub was located to the left of the main entrance. This was half a three-metre wide barrel full to over-flowing with hot suds, in which 6 to 8 people could sit comfortably and drink beer or wine whilst enjoying a soothing warm bath. It also cost 5 Taler, but the wine or beer was included. I confess, as soon as I had finished my late lunch, I also succumbed to these delights! Outside this market, this little island of voluptuous, medieval indulgence, countless beer and wine stalls had been set up by the local breweries and taverns, and every-where the omnipresent smell of Thüringia Bratwurst and Brätel grills! As the afternoon turned into evening I was so full of food, beer and impressions that I just sat down on the steps behind the bridge, smoked a Spliff and listened to one of the live bands performing until dozed off.

I woke up to the laser show on the island after the sun had set.

THE EARLY YEARS

I was born the eldest son of a scullery maid and a tenant farmer's son in a small village in East Yorkshire, whose name is Danish for Island. I already had four brothers by the time I left home at sixteen to join the Royal Air Force as one of Trenchard's 'Brats' at Nr. 1 School of Technical Training RAF Halton; a sister and two other brothers (twins) arrived before I graduated as Junior Technician when I was nineteen.

It was during my last six months at the training camp when I met my first wife, Alexis. She was the only daughter of Milan, a Polish Air Force Air Gunner, now a housing inspector at RAF Halton, and civil service clerk, Jacqueline, originally from Wallsend in Newcastle on Tyne. A year and a half after I had graduated with accelerated promotion to Corporal Technician, we got married, with all that it entailed (see Photos); white wedding in the Wendover parish church, reception at the Shoulder of Mutton inn just two minutes' walk to the station. In addition to the wedding gown Alexis had to have a coordinated going-away outfit, a la Coco Chanel. From there we took the train to London where we spent our wedding night in a B&B Hotel near Paddington station because our two-week honeymoon was a package tour to the Costa Brava with an early morning flight from Heathrow. It was once again the 'silly season', i.e., the French air traffic controllers were on strike again. This meant that instead of landing at Perpignan we diverted to Barcelona airport and were bussed for two hours via the early morning suburbs of Barcelona to Estartit our honeymoon destination. Alexis couldn't resist wearing her newly acquired bikini. This turned out to have a somewhat negative effect on our two weeks of marital bliss. If you can remember the fashions of the early sixties, you'll know that bikini tops were under wired half-cups. This meant that even a stroll on the beach an hour before sunset can have catastrophic results; burnt shoulders to say the very least! On the 6th January 1963 I was posted to 8 FTS at RAF Swinderby halfway between Newark and Lincoln as a nineteen year, old freshly qualified, Junior Technician. The main task of the unit was to convert the pilots to Jets. We were operating De Havilland Vampires, a single-engined gas-turbine trainer, with a balsa wood nacelle for the pilot and twin booms. The unit was closed down in March 1964 and I was transferred to 229 OCU RAF Chivenor in North Devon on the Taw estuary. The pilots here were converting to operational fighters, Hunter F6's, PR 9's and T7's. It was during my posting here that I got married.

We had less than one year to get to know each other because I got posted to MEAF at RAF Khormaksar in Aden. This was a one-year unaccompanied posting. So Alexis went to live with her parents during my absence.

Because of my experience on Hunters I was posted to 43 Squadron 'Fighting Cocks'. In addition to our trades we had to do 12-hour guard duty once a month and 24-hour duty every 3 months or so. When I came off one graveyard shift, 04:00 – 06:00 I received a very pleasant surprise. The guard commander told me to secure my weapon and ammo and go to the terminal building as my wife, Alexis was waiting for me. She'd saved up her holidays from the hairdressing salon where she worked and got a forces special discount ticket and flown to Aden to spend Christmas and the New Year with me. So we had something like a second extended honeymoon....

THE LAND OF SMILES

For those of you who don't know where I'm referring to; it's Thailand, previously known as Siam and it's one of the world's largest producers and exporters of rubber and cement, as well as having a flourishing tourist industry.

I've just returned from almost three months there, away from the beaten tourist track. What took me there, and why did I leave the UK with such haste? The answer is quite simple; on the 16th of June 2008 I received the following e-mail, one of several, from Bianca, from Erfurt where we met when she was studying Anglistik, who I have known for many years; she went to Thailand in April 2007 to take up a post with the Goethe Institute (The German equivalent to the British Council) – and with whom I'd been mailing ever since her departure last year.

Von:cosmo@web.de

.06.08:07:57

: schnellmel@web.de

: Re: whereabouts

Ciao Bello, got some good news: The Uni I'm teaching at is interested in meeting you. They are looking for teachers and they said that age doesn't matter at all. You know, some places here they are a bit funny about that. About an overnight stay in Bangkok? There are some hotels near Don Muang airport, but they are quite pricey. I suggest taking a shuttle bus from the airport to Bamglamphu - this is a nice area near the crazy Kao Saan Road. Accommodation there is cheap and it's got a nice atmosphere. I think it's OK to just show up there and ask for a room.

Where to meet in Surat? I'm still looking for... and I'll look for a house that we can share. Bis Bald, BB

What would you have done in my circumstances? I had offers for employment that summer from two Summer Schools in the UK; my current commitments terminated at the end of the month and I had my winnings from on-line Backgammon and Blackjack (See Blackjack and Backgammon).

The cherry on the cake was, so to say, the £7,500 I'd been awarded by the DWP tribunal that upheld my claim.

This meant that I could live like a prince for a long time in Thailand, if not like a king, taking into account my impending State pensions in Germany and the UK. So I struck while the iron was still white-hot. I called Bianca the next day and asked her if she was serious about her proposition.

She said, yes, she was very sincere, and would love to see me. As she was already looking for suitable accommodation for herself she just changed her search mode to include the two of us, so I set the ball rolling. The very next day I went, on a tip from the Bangladeshi owner of the internet/ telephone café, to the Explorer travel agency. The representative there found me a one-year open ticket to Bangkok's, new international terminal, Suhvarnabhumi, including a domestic flight from there to Surat Thani, where Bianca lives and works for only Euro 650.

As I intended to stay more than 30 days I acquired an 'O' visa from the Thai Consulate General in Hull, which meant that I could stay for a year, only having to leave the country every 90 days to renew it. This turned out to be a mistake, but more about that later.

Two weeks later Bianca mailed me that she had found suitable accommodation for us. It was a large, two-part house at the end of a *Soi,* lane that ended in dense jungle. The rent was only 4000 Baht/ month plus 300 for electricity; about £ 75/month, in addition we would have to buy our own water, which we would share, because we would also have to share with the owner, Pee Moo, literally, Older brother Pork, a successful restaurateur in Surat Thani. The house was surrounded by a two-metre high masonry wall. Entrance to the premises was via two large metal sliding gates, which meant that two large SUV's could be parked in front of the house in the small half-roofed courtyard. There was a small side door in the right-hand gate. From here pale marble steps led up to the 20 square metre marble tiled foyer. To the left was the door to the owner's side of the house and steps leading up to a large roofed veranda, which was furnished with a huge solid mahogany table and matching chairs. Our quarters were on the right: double-doors led onto a large parquet tiled area, off which were our kitchen, my bathroom and a wide tiled wood-panelled corridor cum anteroom. This led to my bedroom, which had three doors on two sides to the small courtyard that was full of rubber trees, banana trees, Frangipani and other dense tropical foliage.

There was a flat-pack wardrobe large enough, she said, for my belongings, and a 2 by 2 metre mattress. All I would need to buy when I arrived was a mosquito net and a fan. Bianca's part of the house was two rooms with en-suite bathroom, with a hot shower and access to a large covered veranda from her bedroom. As my flight to Bangkok was from Nürnberg via Vienna, I flew to Germany to make my farewells to my children and grandchildren as well as seeing friends in Erfurt.

On Wednesday the 6th of August I took the 12:49 from Erfurt to Saalfeld and from there a connecting ICE to Nuremberg. Then 10 minutes in the S-Bahn (Metro) to the airport. My flight to Vienna wasn't until 17:30 so I checked in my bag at the Tyrolean Airline counter and went to the open-air rooftop restaurant. I had a sandwich, a beer, and a Spliff and read until the flight was called.

The Bombardier DHC 8, a twin turbo-prop, Tyrolean Airline commuter aeroplane took off on time, and after a pleasant journey, which was only an hour and 10 minutes we landed in Vienna. My bag was checked through to Bangkok. This meant that I had four hours to kill until my flight to Bangkok. However, Vienna airport was still not a smoke-free zone, so I passed the time with a coffee, a couple of beers and my book, and a final Spliff and James Patterson novel that I hadn't read. The flight to Bangkok was ten hours in a Boeing 777 wide-body. A three-course dinner was served after we'd reached our cruising altitude at about one am. I tried to sleep after watching one of the available films on the in-built DVD screen on the seat in front. With the help of a couple of whiskeys I obtained whilst chatting with the 2 stewardesses in the aft galley I managed to doze for an hour or so. About an hour before we landed breakfast was distributed in the usual in-flight manner. The travel agent had told me that I wouldn't have time to make it across Bangkok in time for the evening flight from Dom Muang airport to Surat Thani so I took a taxi to Bamglamphu and found a cheap hotel, 120 *Baht* (About £ 2) for the night. After a quick shower I tried to sleep.

However, after four hours I woke up and decided to explore the area and get something to eat. After I'd called Bianca and told her that I had arrived in Thailand and would be landing at Surat Thani airport at around 11:25 the next day I had another shower and dressed more appropriately for the climate - still 35 C and 90% humidity. There was a bar and restaurant on the ground floor equipped with 2 TV screens suspended two metres above the tiled floor. On one there was a DVD film running and the other was showing some sports channel. I ordered a *Gao Pahd Gung,* Prawn fried rice. I was feeling courageous, so I told the waitress that I'd like it with 5 chilies. It didn't kill me, but I promptly downed two large bottles, 650 cl of Singha beer, a bit oily, which was served with *Nam Gaeng* (ice cubes), literally hard water.

After I'd eaten I went for a stroll around the area and stopped at another bar and tried a different beer, Leo, which was better. The owner/manager of the bar was a Farang – foreigner from the USA, who claimed to be the nephew of Walter Mondale, Jimmy Carter's vice president.

My flight to Surat Thani where Bianca lives and teaches wasn't until 09:50 the next day so I set my alarm for 07:00 and went to bed. I woke up about 04:30 and couldn't get back to sleep so I made a coffee and read until 06:00. the hotel café didn't open until 06:30 so I got dressed and had another turn around the square, which was slowly coming to life; the night smells mingled with the odours from the street kitchens that were setting up for the day's business. Several dogs roamed around the square looking for tit-bits the night revellers had discarded. Occasionally one of the dogs would wander across the road seemingly oblivious to the various vehicles regardless of their shape or size. The sun was already up by the time I got back to the guest house and the mercury was already nudging 30 0 C as I had my breakfast. I caught a Tuk-Tuk to *Don Muang* airport and checked in for the Thai Airways flight to Surat. Once in the departure lounge I got another coffee and enjoyed the intimacy of the 5m by 5m smoking 'shed' with several other passengers until my flight was called. When we boarded I was somewhat puzzled to see a Buddhist monk sitting the 1st. Class.

The flight to *Surat Thani*, the regional capital of the province went without mishap. It lies about 25 kilometres east of the airport on the *Tapi* River. After I'd retrieved my luggage I followed Bianca's instructions – "Find a taxi then call me and I'll give the Taxi driver directions to our house". We set off and 25 minutes later I spied Bianca sitting astride her 125 cc Yamaha motor scooter at the roadside. My backside would make intimate acquaintance with the pillion of the said scooter over the next few months. I tapped the driver on the shoulder and indicated that he should pull over. When we'd come to a standstill she came over and grinned a wide "Hi." at me and told the driver in Thai to follow her. Two minutes later we stopped in front of the gates she'd told me about in her e-mail. After I'd paid the driver Bianca and I hugged intensely for a couple of minutes, we hadn't seen each other for over a year, until she broke away and said, "We have to buy a mosquito net and a fan for your bedroom. But first we'll have a coffee after I've shown you your part of the house."

While she was making us an instant coffee I had a shower and provisionally unpacked. We drank it on her veranda and she brought me up to date on her lifestyle. Later on after she'd done her karate *Haka*s and I'd caught up on my jet lag we drove to Tesco on her motorbike to buy the aforementioned mosquito net and oscillating fan. Yes, there is one in Thailand, one of many I suspect, albeit it's called Tesco Lotus. While we were there I went to a bank and found that if you don't have a work permit you can't open a bank account. However, they were quite willing to exchange my sterling and Euros; for 1 Euro one got 51 *Baht* and for £ 1 sterling I got 60 *Baht,* which meant with the money I had with me was enough money to live for 4 months without having to draw on my reserves. Don't forget my share of the rent and utilities was only 2200 *Baht*. We also bought fresh vegetables for a salad and I bought a rucksack – it survived 4 weeks before it disintegrated! On the way back from Tesco Bianca stopped at a roadside restaurant where we ate *Gao Sen nam sup* (chicken noodle soup), which we washed down with bottled water with *Nam Gaeng*. When we got back to our *Soi* (lane) we made a big bowl of salad, iceberg, carrots, shallots, tomatoes, mild green chillies, Thai Basil and a tin of tuna. We sat on B's veranda and ate whilst listening to the jungle sounds outside our garden wall; frogs croaking their everlasting love, crickets condemned to always playing second fiddle and the omnipresent courtship of the fireflies interspersed with the chatter of the geckos that inhabit the ceiling and walls of our house. After we'd eaten Bianca suggested that she introduce me to Bik's café/bar where several '*Farang*' (foreigners) tend to congregate. It turned out to be a treasure trove; he had about a thousand paperbacks, mostly in English. *Bik*, the Thai owner was conjugated with Susie, an over-sized Canadian woman. Bik is about 1.65 metres in his socks and probably weighed 50 kg. On the way home B stopped at a 7/11 and bought a bottle of local rum, six bottle of club soda and a bag of *Nam Gaeng* to end the day. Saturday 09.08.2008. I woke up late today. I still don't know where I am.!

THE LAND OF SMILES

PART II

The following evening Mala, (Bianca) took me to an open air restaurant next to the main road into town. I was very impressed with Bianca's command of Thai; thankfully she could even interpret the plastic-coated menu which didn't have an English translation. She ordered for the two of us, including four bottles of Leo with Nam Gaeng; grilled Carp, Sticky rice, followed by *Gow pad Gung* and finished with *Kanom mor gaeng,* (baked custard pudding), not unlike non-burnt Crème Brule. We drank two more Leos and a nightcap of the local brandy with Nam Gaeng.

I slept like a baby.

BACKGAMMON
OR
CUSHTIE!

It must have been late summer of '77 because I was teaching Technical apprentices at the King Feisal Aviation Academy in Riyadh, the capital of the Kingdom of Saudi Arabia; average daily temperature fluctuated between 40 and 50 degrees Celsius. As usual I was in the tutor/trainee rest room doing the daily assessments on my 3 students when Omar bin Khalidi; the best of the three came in and greeted me with ''Marhaaba, Saihd Jake, sabaahul noor,' (Hello Sir Jake. Good evening.). After further niceties he got down to the nitty-gritty: His cousin Tariq, who was a student at the university studying 'Double entry book-keeping'. He'd just returned from a holiday in Crete, where he had been bitten by the Backgammon bug and had acquired a Backgammon board. Whilst waiting for tasks at the academy we often played the game in the common rest room with the students, which meant that I was a fairly accomplished player. Would I be willing to teach his cousin to play well? He could come and pick me up that evening at 19:00 because his cousin's house was only two kilometres from our family compound. I declined and suggested the following evening at the same time, to which he agreed. I'd already put on my Guhtra (headscarf), because of a minor sandstorm when he arrived promptly at 19:00 in his Cadillac. Two minutes later we pulled into the courtyard of his cousin's villa, set in an acre of desert. After he had introduced me to his cousin Tariq he left. Tariq was a chubby 20-something young man wearing the typical Arabian Thob, (night dress!) and a lace prayer cap. He was very polite and his command of English was excellent. He asked if I would like something to drink so I said I would like Gowa (coffee and cardamom), quite pleasant, if somewhat medicinal. We went into the spacious living area, in the middle of which was a large chrome and glass coffee table on which sat the purpose of my visit; a large hardwood back gammon board was standing open, its playing surface a zigzag of Carrere and Alicante Rosso marble inlays, the stones were also marble as well as the five die. When Tariq's servant, a young Egyptian had brought the coffee pot; the traditional beaked copper jug with coconut hair as a filter in the spout, he told me that he wanted me to show him how to play skilfully. He then dropped the bombshell and said,' we can play for money! 'To which I demurred and said that I didn't have that much money with me. This was not quite true as I usually had at least 1000 Riyals at any time in order to take advantage of any 'special offers' that occurred from time to time, i.e. frozen meat from a cold storage warehouse that had electrical problems. Digging into one of his pockets he pulled out a bundle of 100 Riyal notes and split it roughly in half, saying,' Maalish', (Never mind.) handing me the smaller bundle as though it was monopoly money, 'You can play with this.' 'OK,' I replied, 'but first I will show you the best way to play and win.' He agreed and for the next 45 minutes I explained the best tactics and strategy for every possible combination at all stages of the game. After a top up of the Gowa we started to play in earnest: 100 Riyals per game, three points for the set and five sets for the match. About ninety minutes later he won the deciding set so I said that we should finish as I had an early start the next day. He reluctantly agreed and told his servant to drive me home after a final medicinal coffee. I then picked up the bundle of notes and tried to hand them to him. Once again came the response, 'Maalish, Habib, (Dear friend), now I can beat my friends.' We made our farewell salutations and he kissed me on both cheeks, a sign that I was now part of the Khalidi family. When his driver/servant dropped me off at our compound I gave him a 100 Riyal note. When I got to our bungalow I took the roll of banknotes from my pocket and counted them. In total the evening had increased my wealth by 1400 Riyals; at the time the official exchange rate was six riyals to one-pound sterling. The average annual income in the UK in 1977 was £1800/ annum! "Luvely-jubbly".

CARPE DIEM

15.07.2006. Standing on the ledge above the urinal - where I was emptying my liquid waste receptacle before my flight to Stansted from Altenburg – was a business card bearing the words:

'DO YOU WANT TO BE A MILLIONAIRE, OR OWN ONE OF THE OBJECTS PICTURED BELOW?' (A large house, a luxury car and holidays, etc.).

It caught my attention because it was in English with a 0044 country code followed by a 7833... Mobile number. So I picked it up and stuck it in my breast pocket.

Several days later while I was visiting my mother I came across it whilst looking for my stylus. After we'd had our tea I called the number on the card only to get an answering machine message; 'Blah, blah, blah, please leave your name and number after the beep'. I duly concurred and the following afternoon the distributor of the card, Malcolm Wilde, a representative of a US catalogue company, who had been in Leipzig to try and develop the German market, returned my call. He asked me if I would be interested in being the regional sales manager for the 'Neue Bundesländer'. Having worked in sales for a number of years I told him I'd have to think it over. He agreed and said he would send me some info, including the Dutch version of the catalogue and several German leaflets with a promotional DVD.

When these arrived a few days later I almost wet my pants laughing when I read the German leaflets. I called him that evening and told him that not only was German incorrect but was also ludicrous, and would only be laughed at before it ended in the waste bin. He said that the translation had been done by one of the company's Dutch managers. However, I told him that I could provide him with a perfect German Translation and give him a quote within 24 hours. He agreed immediately. After I'd scanned the leaflets I mailed them to a friend in Erfurt, Babushka. She mailed back with a quote within an hour and told me she couldn't stop laughing when she read the leaflets. She said she would need 5 hours to do the work. I immediately mailed the quote to Malcolm Wilde and then had tea with my Mam. He called a while later and agreed to the conditions; 20% up front payable to my UK bank account and the remainder on completion. The following day the aforementioned deposit was on my account, so I gave B the green for go and to do the translation within 24 hours. She duly did this and I mailed the completed task to Malcolm.

Four days later I returned to Germany and the final payment was on my account so I gave B the money for the task minus my commission. It didn't make me a millionaire and I didn't get any of the luxury prizes. Nevertheless, I'm still happy!

US DROPS BOMB ON HOLME UPON SPALDING MOOR

A US fighter-bomber dropped a dummy bomb on an industrial estate in East Yorkshire, the US Air Force admitted today. An F-15E Strike Eagle, flying from its base at RAF Lakenheath in Suffolk, released the 25lb dummy munition during a routine training mission on Thursday evening. It landed on private land used by the Allied Grain plant on the Holme Industrial Estate in Holme upon Spalding Moor, East Yorkshire, according to witnesses. An investigation into the cause of the incident is under way. First Lieutenant Augustine O Ekpoudom, an RAF Lakenheath spokesman, said:

"At approximately 5.15pm January 8, a 25lb BDU-33 training munition from an F-15E Strike Eagle landed in a sparsely populated area near Howden and Market Weighton in Northern England. There were no injuries, limited property damage, and the inert munition was recovered."

The F-15E Strike Eagle was conducting a routine training mission at the time of the incident.

Trained and experienced base personnel including Ministry of Defence, and local constabulary authorities responded to the scene and an investigation team is determining the cause the incident. A spokeswoman for Humberside Police said officers had helped in the search for the bomb. Des D'Souza, a spokesman for Allied Grain, said:

"An inert object fell to the ground in an area where we have some grain stores in East Yorkshire. It caused no disruption to our business whatsoever, apart from when they came to retrieve it. It scratched the surface of the concrete but that was all. No real damage."

One woman, who lives close to the industrial estate but asked not to be named, said she saw lines of police scouring the area where the device landed on Thursday. There was no sign of any damage from the perimeter fence today. Lt Ekpoudom confirmed the dummy bomb crashed. Asked whether the "bomb" had been released by accident or had missed a target, he answered unapologetically that this was a matter for the ongoing investigation.

After I read the above headline and the accompanying article in the Pocklington Post on the 12th January 2004, it reminded me of one of my teenage escapades, so I wrote the following.

A PHEASANT PLUCKER'S SON

Without a doubt I often watched my mother plucking pheasants, geese, ducks, pigeons and occasionally chickens. Not only did she pluck them, she also drew them; i.e. she removed the intestines. In addition, I watched as she skinned and gutted rabbits and hares for the family table. I also learnt these and other skills in my secondary school, then a brand new secondary modern and today a Comprehensive?

Supervised archaeological digs, visits to local historical sites were two of the extra-mural activities at primary school. Making explosives and rockets were a couple of self-initiated 'Home Projects' that I undertook with two or three classmates Robby, Dave, Rolly and Frankie after we'd had a chemistry class in the school in Market Weighton.

Don't forget this was long before Moslem terrorists and the Internet information explosion. We found the formula for gunpowder in a book in the school library. Ten ounces of Sulphur and Saltpetre were easily obtained from the local pharmacy - even though we were only 14 years old. We made the charcoal ourselves by burning wood the way it is normally made, i.e. in a charcoal pit.

Our first controlled explosion, i.e. Smarties tube full of our gunpowder with a model rocket engine fuse placed in the entrance to a rabbit burrow.

The results were impressive, the whole tunnel system collapsed for a radius of two metres.

After a few more tests we decided to build a rocket.

This was simply a cigar tube about 20cms long and 3 wide to which we fitted the nozzle from a model rocket engine. On the sides at the back we attached fins made of cardboard.

The Guinea Pig for the first flight was a Newt that we caught in a local pond behind the school. Its cockpit was a test-tube that we had 'borrowed' from the school science lab. This was taped to the nose of the cigar tube and the rocket was launched ceremoniously with a NASA countdown. We'd aimed the rocket so that it would splashdown in the pond, which it duly did. However, we never found the rocket or the Newt again!

LIN FOUT

Friday 14.01.1981. 1200 hrs. I'd done it. I'd defied the old adage - Last in - First out. I went of my own accord and left the Pan-Am personnel department in the main terminal building at Ff/M airport and took the airport shuttle bus to the Pan-Am maintenance area where I'd been employed as an FAA approved A&P Mechanic since the summer of 1979. At the time Pan-Am was providing, along with British Airways, Air France and Air Canada, flag carriers of the occupying forces - the IGS, Internal German Service between the Bundes Republic and the allied airports in Berlin.

I got into my Citroen Visa, which was nothing more than an aerodynamic, 2CV 'Ugly Duckling ', much loved by French farmers and students throughout Europe because of its economy and the ability to keep up with the high speed motorways of central Europe, with an egg shaped streamline body and about 40 PS, if my memory serves me well.

What it meant was that I had the weekend to relax with, and help J. and L, my two sons settle into their new environment before taking up my new job as Applications Technician in the plastic processing department G.M, which was responsible for the polyurethane and fibre glass coating equipment at the Ransburg Corporation in Offenbach/Main, whose core product was paint spraying equipment for the auto mobile and other industries that require surface treatment for their products. When my contract with Lufthansa finished in December 1978 I decided to stay in Germany because I had been living with a novice Lufthansa stewardess, Angie since November. In fact, we even got engaged in May 79. The first thing I did after we got back from the festive season at A's parents in Wildeshausen was to apply for a residence permit, get a German driving license and look for work.

I got my first job as night porter in a small hotel close to Rhine-Main Airbase through AFN, the American Forces Network. It was easy work. I got paid DM 100 cash per night to check-in and out any servicemen and their families on arrival or departure to their next postings. In addition, I had to drive them to the main commercial airport on the south side of the main runways when required.

However, the job only lasted three nights because Angie didn't like spending the nights alone in our two-room mansard (attic) flat when she was home between flights.

My second job was Housing Inspector for the US Air force at Rhine Main Airbase, also thanks to AFN. All this entailed was checking for wear and tear on furniture, fixtures and fittings and wilful damage in the married quarters when the American servicemen and their families "marched in or out". This usually took place in the mornings and the afternoons were occupied with writing up any changes onto special graph paper and giving these to the punch-card typists on the ground floor. The final duty of the day was to "park up and hose down" the two ton, Air Force blue pick-up truck in the Motor pool. The job also had its advantages - I could use the base library, cinema and the German-American canteen where one had to pay in dollars. However, the PX wasn't accessible unless you knew someone who was willing to get you duty-free goodies. In addition, I could use the Rod and Gun Club restaurant where one could get US style cuisine where you also had to pay in US $.

However, I only stayed here for two months because when Angie agreed to marry me I applied for one week's holiday at the beginning of May, as that was the only time Angie could fit our honeymoon in with her flight schedule in the next two months. Later in the year she requested a flight to Mexico City with a 4-day layover in Nassau, Bahamas and I flew on a 10% standby ticket. What it meant was we had two days together until she took over for the 5-hour round trip to Mexico City and a further two days until she took over the return leg to Frankfurt/Main.

The CO of the Housing unit told me that it wasn't possible to take furlough during the trial period of three months and unpaid furlough didn't exist, so I quit. We got married as planned and had a very brief honeymoon in Bournemouth in the UK. When we got back we moved into a two-bedroom apartment in Unterliederbch only ten minutes from Ff/M airport. When Angie went on her next flight I went to the main Arbeitsamt (the Federal Employment Agency) in downtown Frankfurt on the last Friday in May to sign on as a job seeker. The clerk there told me that I should contact the

Landesarbeitsamt (the Hessian State Employment Agency) because they were responsible for aviation jobs. He also gave me the telephone number and the name of the clerk for aircraft mechanics. It was already 11:30 hrs. by the time I got back to our flat. Nevertheless, as one who believes in striking while the iron is hot, I called the number and the man asked where I lived. As it turned out his office was only ten minutes' walk from our flat and he asked me to come round after his lunch break at 13:00 hrs. I arrived punctually and he spent the next 30 minutes calling various airline personnel departments at the airport. On the sixth he struck lucky and he made an appointment for me on the coming Monday at 1800 hrs. with the DCE, Deputy Chief Engineer, a certain Herr Pikes in the Pan-Am Base Maintenance hangar at the west end of the main terminal. I arrived on time for the interview and Herr Pieksch; the DCE gave me a quick rundown of the Base maintenance facility and duties. The hangar was large enough to carry out 100 and 1000-hour checks, as well as major structural repairs on Boeing 727 100 and 200 series that Pan-Am was operating on the IGS flights. The work schedule entailed 24-hr coverage from Monday to Friday. It appeared that an aircraft was due in at 1900, so he sat me at a vacant desk in the tech control office at the back of the hangar and gave me an aptitude test to complete. It only took me ten minutes to finish the test so I handed it back to him and he said that the personnel department would be in touch. The following Friday they called and asked me to come to the office in the main terminal building to complete the documentation on the following Monday. The reason for me leaving my well-paid job with Pan-Am started back in September 1980 when my two sons, J. and L. came to me for two weeks in their summer holidays in the UK where they went to school and lived with their mother Lexi. At first I was surprised and confused when I picked them up at Ff/M airport because both of them had two large suitcases, rucksacks, shoulder bags and plastic shopping bags. The reason for their excess baggage was made clear when we got back to the two-bedroom flat I was sharing with my new wife Angie, the Lufthansa stewardess, when J. gave me the letter from his mother. Basically what she wrote was that she had had the two boys since our divorce in September 1978 and it was now my turn to look after them; and it was of no use trying to contact her because she was on honeymoon with her Lebanese husband S.

JOYCE

When I was unlawfully given the sack from my well-paid job at Glass-Mate GmbH, (Private limited company) at the beginning of November 1986, I successfully challenged the sacking at the Offenbach Industrial Tribunal and was awarded DM 10,000 compensation and the right to unemployment benefits from the 1st of January. At the end of January, I started working as a free-lance English teacher for a private language school in Frankfurt am Main. Within a couple of months my income plus my benefits meant that I had time on my hands even though I was also fulfilling the role of single parent and 'Hausman'. So I decided to use the opportunity to explore my creative talents.

Whilst working for Glass-Mate I had often taken a sketchpad and a box of water-colours with me on my numerous 'business trips' to the Middle East, which included Baghdad, Basra, The United Arab Emirates, Kuwait, Bahrain etc. It was a way of passing the time in one's hotel room after a hard day's negotiation and training at 350C, when you'd eaten and watched all three in-house videos.

However, now my orientation was to writing and acting/directing plays and short sketches, a la Monty Python, the Two Ronnie's, etc. At the time I was living with Heidi, who I mentioned in Liz's story and my two sons, Jacob and Lawrence, who were attending a local Gesamtschule (Comprehensive).

The first step in this direction was to join the aforementioned local amateur theatrical group in 1987. After this disastrous excursion into German amateur dramatics I concentrated my free time and creative energy writing, producing, directing and performing 'AN EVENING OF ENGLISH HUMOUR AND DRAMA' in the Gallus Theater in Frankfurt at the end of June 1988. It was shortly after this theatrical event, which attracted two full houses, mid-week in a 'Frauen Theater Woche' (Women's Theatre week). Unfortunately, I forgot to invite the press. Shortly after this first excursion into writing and directing I went to Spain and once again over the holiday season. When I came back I bought my first PC.

It was an Amstrad/Schneider 'Joyce', i.e. Alan Michael Sugar.

WINTER 1990/1991

December 20th 1990. I have just finished my last class for the year and the rehearsals for my production of A Sleep of Prisoners" by Christopher Fry, a modern day language master, are going well. Only six weeks to the premier on January 30th. All that remained now was for me to eke out the heat from the electrical night storage heaters in my garden flat in the Taunus foothills, as I would be spending the better part of the days there until my classes start again on January 5th.

December 21st Ingrid called to tell me that she'd got the letter I'd written in response to her Ad in the 'Bekanntschaftsanzeigen' - (Contact Ads in the Frankfurter Rundschau).

Since Liz gave me my final marching orders at the end of May, I'd been replying to, and also posting "Wanted" posters in the local newspaper, with some success!

After six weeks of being in the desert of despondency, I'd finally called Liz and she agreed to meet me one lunch hour in a bistro near the publishing company where she was the head of the in-house photo studio.

She said that it would be no good if they started again from square one, because everything would take the same direction as before, and she didn't want that, Basta!

Ingrid had said that she had liked my letter and the photo I'd sent with it, and that she would like to meet me, but we would have to postpone it until the Yew Near, because she had a lot of end-of-term assessments to write; she's the senior art teacher at a well-known Gymnasium (Grammar school) in Hofheim, the regional administrative centre for the Main/Taunus/Kreis, and she is also interested in theatre!

December 24th. I stayed in bed and read until midday to conserve the warmth coming from the heaters, which were set at minimum, otherwise the heat would be used up by mid-afternoon. This meant either freezing, or using a hot air blower fan - normally a relatively expensive way of heating. However, my rental agreement also includes electricity. Late afternoon I took the train into town and went to give Liz and her kids, Daniel and Julianne their Xmas cards. I only stayed long enough to drink a couple of glasses of wine with them. I got back home about 21:30. I'd only been home five minutes when Astrid, who also lives in Kelkheim, called to ask if I was also alone on this eve of Christian celebration. She's the ex-girlfriend of the owner of the school where I still teach the occasional client. I said that I was indeed contemplating opening a tin of soup and drinking a bottle of wine alone. To which she said that she'd be at my place in five minutes and pick me up, and that we could spend the evening together at her flat as she had more than enough to eat and drink.

Could I say no?

December 25th Xmas day. I left Astrid's at about 11:00 after we'd had a long lazy breakfast and a cuddle in her big double bed. Called my sons, Jason and Luke to wish them season's greetings. Later on I went into town and had coffee and dinner with Petros, one of my cast and his girlfriend Gundi at her flat, which was very convenient for the Süd Bahnhof (South station). I could catch the S Bahn (local commuter train) to the Taunus from here. On public holidays it operated on Sunday schedule, i.e. once an hour. I caught the penultimate train home and as there was 30 minutes to wait for the last bus I had a last pint in WunderBar, a pub and eatery near the station. Got home at 00:20 or thereabouts and went to bed.

December 26th. Stayed in bed most of the day reading and watching my black and white TV that could only receive 3 channels. What luxury! The shops are all shut anyway and I'd enough provisions to last a couple of days. Nothing much of interest happened until the 30th when I went into town around midday for some reason or another. The pretty young woman, who I'd smiled at once or twice when getting on the train in Kelkheim returned my smile and indicated that I should come and sit next to her. She always occupied the same seat on the train coming from Königstein, the up-line end station, her name is Doris and she is older than she looks because she is very small, only 1.52 m in her bare feet, as she told me later. I had estimated that she was in her mid-20's, but she was in reality 10 years older. The train wasn't crowded at that time of day so we were able to talk all the way to Hoechst, where we had to pick up the S5 from Niedernhausen into Frankfurt. We chatted all the way into town and exchanged telephone numbers with the promise that we would call in the Yew Near, and parted company when I got out at the HBF (main station).

31.01.1991. Yew Near's Eve. I went to a party with Alex, a young guy I know from WunderBar, and his girlfriend, Grit in her flat. Crashed out on the sofa at sometime between 02:00 and 03:00 and slept like a baby until the sun woke me around 10:15. I got up, washed my face and left without waking the other bodies scattered around the flat. Had a coffee and a roll-up while I waited for the train to Kelkheim where I spent the rest of the day recuperating from the excesses of the previous night.

***

Wednesday 02.01.1991 Mike, my English friend called to invite me to a fry-up at his place in town. He's the ex-neighbour from the time when I lived in a 2 man WG (shared flat) just across the corridor from his flat in Frankfurt.

He's also a free-lancer like me and has been operating "Behind enemy lines" just as long. He's a self-taught graphic designer/ photographer, and an ex Royal Navy rating.

I went into town late afternoon to Mike's and had a good old English fry-up: bacon, fried eggs, sausages, that were a Bratwurst cut in half, grilled tomatoes, baked beans and toast etc. we washed it all down with a couple of pints of Binding beer. While I was there Katerina, Mike's Polish wife, who is a theatrical make-up artist, told me that she had worked in the Mousson Turm on Yew Near's eve and had seen a huge photo of me there.

The Mousson Turm is a converted soap factory that was now run as a cultural centre with a cinema, a theatre, a cafe and restaurant, as well as offering artist's studios at very reasonable rates. My curiosity was aroused because I knew the picture could only originate from one source, and it wasn't Liz. Earlier in 1990 I had posed as a model for the draft design for the dust cover of a new edition of 'Journey to the East' by Heinrich Heine.

It had been for one of the artists who rented a studio there. With another man, who was a dentist by trade, I was the motive for the cover design. We were simply dressed in blankets. The artist paid for our lunch and a couple of pints instead of a modelling fee because he was also running on a shoestring. He also sent me an A4 photo of his final design photo. I never did find out if his submission had been chosen or not.

When I left Mike's I was still curious so I changed trains at the Opernplatz (Opera Plaza), took the U 4 to Bornheim and went to the Mousson Turm instead of taking the S 4 or 5 to Hoechst. Sure enough, there we were, larger than life hanging inside the cafe-bar over the doorway. In a fit of self-adulation, I decided to have another beer and take a later train home. After I'd got my beer I was able to get a table with a good view of the picture, and also of the patrons as they came and went. I'd just settled down and rolled a Spliff when two women came into the cafe. The younger and smaller of the two, who appeared to be about my age, looked at me intensively and gave me a half-smile as they passed my table. At first I thought that she had seen the picture and had recognized me. But then I realised that that wasn't possible because they had only just come in. The puzzle was solved some twenty minutes later as they were leaving. The younger of the two stopped at my table and said questioningly,

"Alain?"

"Yes? Have we met somewhere before, or did you recognise me from the picture up there? "I replied, somewhat taken aback.

"Now we have met! You wrote me a delightful letter and it was easy to recognise you from the photo you sent with it. And that picture on the wall up there is really a very good likeness. I'm Ingrid!" She replied holding out her small slender hand. I stood up and took her hand, and all I could say was, "Nice to meet you." because I was flabbergasted. She could have been Doris' older sister! The same child-like body with an over-proportional head, and really quite charming!

"I have to take my mother home now." she said, as she turned to leave. "And it's already late, but you've got my number. Give me a call on Friday, maybe I can find some time at the weekend so that we can meet properly."

"OK, I'll do that. Take care. "I answered as they left. After they'd left I finished my beer and was able to catch the last S 4, connection with the last train to Kelkheim. Got home about 23:20 and went straight to bed.

"OH HAPPY DAYS"

Thursday 03.01.91 nothing much happened over the past few days until Doris called in the afternoon to ask when I have time to meet. My first classes start next week, but I have intensified the rehearsal schedule for the upcoming play, so I suggested that we could meet in WunderBar at 21:30 the same evening, as I would be on my way home from rehearsals. We had a very productive rehearsal. All the actors and crew arrived on time at the church where we are performing the play on the 30th & 31st of January and the 1st of February. I was very lucky to get four different nationalities performing in English. My cast and crew: Doug, who is also from GB, he's about my age, in banking, I think and a member of the Taunus English Theatre Club, who performed an English pantomime in one of the local schools in the Taunus last year. Petros is from Athens, he's a music/ photography student. Gundi, his girlfriend, who is a graphic design student usually tags along to rehearsals and she will also be the prompt at the performances. N'dako is originally from Namibia, but he trained as a lab technician at the Hoechst chemical company and is also Reggae musician. Gerd, the German member of the acting cast, is a steward with Lufthansa, the German national airline. Andreas, our technician and sound-man is a delivery driver for an electronics shop. Mechthild, a dancing teacher is my assistant director, and she is taking on the job of stage manager, properties, costumes etc. I got to WunderBar for my tryst just before 21:30 and waited for Doris to arrive. As I expected she'd taken the penultimate shuttle train from Königstein and arrived within five minutes. We spent the next couple of hours drinking Ebbelwöi (apple wine - cider) and finding out about each other. She told me that she had an inferiority complex because of her size and that she was currently attending a re-training course as an upholstery craftswoman in Offenbach. We caught the last bus together to Königstein via Kelkheim just after midnight because the last rail connection was just before 23:00. In the darkness of the bus we chatted and joked until my stop in Kelkheim. When I got up to get out she gave me a goodnight kiss that was full of promise.

Friday 04.01.91. I had a lazy day at home, did my weekend shopping and did some writing and preparation for my classes next week. I called Ingrid late afternoon and she said that they would have to postpone our meeting for another week as she still hadn't finished her assessments and they have to be done before the middle of the month, and she didn't want have to do it at the last minute. I watched some film on my B&W TV and had an early night. Couldn't get to sleep immediately so I had a double Bushmills and fell asleep at once.

"OH HAPPY DAYS II?"

Saturday 05.01.91. I did my weekend shopping and hung up my clean laundry that my landlady had so kindly washed for me, and thought that I must remember to buy her a bunch of flowers on Monday. I called Doris after lunch and asked if she would like to go to the theatre or cinema with me in Frankfurt that evening. She said no, but if I wanted I could visit her as she had a couple of bottles of wine left over from the Yew Near. She also asked if I could bring some recreational substances. Now I remembered why I went into town on the 30th. It was to get some recreational substances!

I spent the afternoon cleaning and airing my flat. Had a shit, shower and a shave, in that order in preparation for my evening's tryst with Doris.

I caught the 20:13 up-line train to Königstein. Doris' one room apartment wasn't even 5 minutes' walk from the station. She welcomed me warmly with a hug, dressed in a tabard, woollen tights and knee-length, Norwegian winter socks. We sat at her dining table under the window, and while she opened a bottle of Montepulciano D'abruzzo, I skinned up the first Spliff of the evening. We toasted each other with the wine and exchanged brotherhood customs; I.e. linking arms and drinking while looking each other in the eye, as is the custom in Germany. I then ceremoniously lit the Spliff, took a deep draw, gave it to her and said,

"Here's to a very pleasant evening together Doris?"

"I hope so, too, Alain!" She replied, and taking a draw on the Spliff, she leant over the table and kissed me tenderly on the cheek as she handed it back to me.

"The thief exchanged hands a few times and the moving finger having writ, moved on." (Omar Khayyam).

After one or two more draws on the Spliff she said would like to lie down on her bed and would like me to join her there. It was only 2 metres away behind a half-open curtain. We took the wine and the ashtray with the remains of the Spliff to the bedside table and lay down. She cuddled up to me and we started kissing almost immediately.

Within 15 minutes we were down to the bare essentials.

It was incredible!

Doris, who as it transpired, had the body of a 16-year-old and the head of an attractive woman of 34 took a condom and slipped it deftly over my tumescent penis after moistening the glans with her lips and tongue.

She then lay back on the bed, opened her legs and guided me to her quim, at the same time saying,

"Be gentle with me, but fuck me long and slowly!"

JT slipped into her like a finger in a jar of hair-gel and her vaginal muscles gripped him tightly almost immediately. After half an hour - and halfway through the Karma Sutra and back we took a break - drank the rest of the wine and finished the Spliff. She then asked me to take her from behind, but this time she said without a condom, because she knew that by now I was feeling pretty much drained! She rolled over and knelt on the bed with her petite buttocks stuck in the air. It didn't take long for her to reach another climax, her quim clamping my semi-limp penis and massaging him until he was hard again as I entered her from behind - forcing an involuntary dry ejaculation and whimper from me as she cried out as she had another orgasm. We collapsed exhausted, and a short while later we fell asleep in each other's arms.

Sunday 06.01.91. 06:30 Doris woke me at around this time by rubbing the erect nipples of her pert breasts on my Morning Glory. She looked up at me demurely and said, "May I have an early morning canter?

"Yes, of course." I answered, thinking that maybe my reserves had been topped up in the meantime and I would have to be careful. Her quim was dripping wet when she straddled me and impaled herself on JT. He went in without touching the sides. When she was settled in the saddle she started a slow bucking motion just like when you go horse riding. I picked up her rhythm and started my own sideways movements, and caressed her tender, half-orange sized breasts. Within 10 minutes she reached a climax and collapsed sweating on my chest, biting me as I released a dawn salvo into realms unknown! We fell asleep again and at about 08:30 she got up and made some coffee and breakfast, including Buck's fizz, which we drank in bed. Her brother and his wife came at 10:15 to take her somewhere and I caught the next train back to Kelkheim. As I didn't have any special to do for the rest of the day I decided to take the train all the way to Hoechst and have lunch and a beer in WunderBar. And spend the rest of the day recuperating! Lazy day in bed.

Monday 7th January. My classes in Offenbach start again today. Monday to Thursday, 2 school hours per day from 16:30 till 18:00 in the company's premises in an industrial estate in the south west of the town. It takes almost an hour and a half to get there by train and bus and the same time to get back, but it's worth it because I have a total of 8 hours per week, in addition to the hours I'm still doing for Martin, and as I acquired the contract himself there is no middleman or agent to take a cut of my fee. More often than not one of the course participants will drop me off at a convenient U or S Bahn station for Frankfurt, so I'm sometimes home relatively early. Now I usually stop off in Frankfurt on the way home and have a rehearsal in the church, as we are now past the reading and characterisation stage. It went well; we had the first sound effects try-out today. After rehearsals we went across the street for a drink to Troika, a bar run by a Russian woman. I caught the last through train to Kelkheim.

Got home about 23:20, went to bed and fell asleep immediately.

Tuesday 8th January, ditto Monday except no rehearsals.

Thursday 10th January. This morning I went with Christopher, my landlord and retired bank manager to his friend's. And for a reasonable amount I managed to get four chipboard panels and some off-cuts that I can use as legs and enough screws to do the job. Christoph's friend said he would pre-cut the off-cuts to size. So that all I would have to do would be to screw them on when needed and he would bring the material to my flat next Monday morning. Otherwise, ditto Monday. Another good rehearsal, although Gerd turned up more than half an hour late.

Friday 11th January. I had a cleaning, airing day at home. Called Ingrid in the afternoon and she said she could meet me for lunch on Sunday at about 13:00. When I suggested WunderBar she agreed immediately. Went to bed about 02:45

Sunday 13th January: Didn't wake up until 10:15, had breakfast, showered and caught the 12:17 train to Hoechst in time for my first rendezvous with Ingrid. I was halfway into my first beer when she arrived.

We spent the next couple of hours getting to know each other while we ate lunch. She told me that she had practically finished the assessments, and the other reason why she hadn't had time to meet. Her father had died at the beginning of December. In addition, she told me a little about her past. When she had been a newly qualified art teacher she had an affair with one of her Abitur students who was quite a bit younger than her and was forced to leave the school where she was teaching at the time. Later she got married to the student but the marriage only lasted five years. Perhaps this was the reason my letter had interested her so much?

After we'd had coffee she drove me home to Kelkheim and said that if I liked I could visit her on the coming Friday as she should have finished her school assessments by then. I spent the rest of the evening watching TV.

Monday 14th January Christoph's friend turned up at around ten o'clock to deliver the wood I needed for the theatre production in two weeks' time. Ditto last week as well as rehearsals.

Tuesday 15th January. Ditto last week, rehearsals as well.

Wednesday 16th January. Ditto last week, rehearsals as well. Ingrid called this morning to say that if it was all right by me, I could come and visit her at her flat in Hofheim on Friday evening.

I agreed because I knew that on Saturday morning I had to get up early.

Thursday 17th January. Ditto last week, rehearsals as well.

Friday 18th January I woke up just after 08:00. No classes, no theatre performance and no rehearsals, just the day to fill in and keep warm until I went to see Ingrid at her flat in Hofheim at about 20:00, according to how the trains were running.

I stayed in bed until about 09:45, drank coffee and watched the breakfast TV programmes. Got up, had a quick wash and went to the supermarket to get some food for lunch. It was a bright sunny day so I took a walk through the park on my way to the shops. Maybe a good omen for my rendezvous that evening!

After I'd had lunch I made some notes about some changes I wanted to make at the rehearsals next week. I just had a light snack for tea because Ingrid had said that she would prepare some food for us. Then I had a shit, shower and an extra close shave, because for some reason I had a hunch that Ingrid preferred smooth cheeks. I caught the 19:25 train to Hoechst and I only had to wait five minutes for a connection to Hofheim, just one stop up-line. It only took me a couple of minutes to walk from the station over the railway bridge to her flat in a three family apartment house. In fact, it was two minutes to eight when I rang her doorbell. The entrance was on the first floor and round at the back of the house. She opened the door to welcome me dressed in jeans and a loose red cardigan over a plain white T-shirt and I gave her a hug. She returned it with a warm peck on the cheek.

Her two-room flat was quite sweet and cosy because it was also very tastefully decorated, and every piece of furniture seemed to be designed for a Lilliputian, which indeed she was, in a manner of speaking. She told me later that she was only 1.52 m tall. She had the body of a petite 14-year-old and her head was that of a person of normal growth. After I'd taken my shoes off she showed me into the living room, which had a thick pile, real wool carpet stretching from wall to wall and many paintings on all the free space on the walls. They were mostly all her own work as she told me while she poured out two glasses of a light Italian dry white wine. We toasted each other in the usual German custom and after she'd taken a sip she said that she had a confession to make. She hadn't finished all her work. And if I wouldn't mind making the dinner with the food she had bought she could finish off the last of her work, and then we could eat and the rest of the evening was ours. I agreed immediately and told her that I had to get up early the next morning to go to Erfurt. After she'd shown me the food and where everything was in her small, but ergonomically functional kitchen, she disappeared into her study after putting on Vivaldi's 'Four Seasons' on her reel-to reel tape deck - the reels of which were almost as large as her head. She'd bought Dover Sole fillets, fresh spinach and potatoes. I got to work at once. First I peeled the spuds and put them in a pot of boiling water with a good sprinkling of salt. I then washed the spinach and the fish fillets. When the potatoes were boiling I turned them down to a medium heat and put a deep plate on top of the pot as a lid. Into this I placed the fish fillets, after seasoning them with salt, pepper and some dried chilies.

Then I poured about a quarter litre of milk on the fish and some fresh herbs, mint, basil and chives and a few knobs of dairy butter. I then covered them with the pot lid and left it to cook for fifteen minutes. Ingrid had said she would prefer it if I didn't smoke in the flat before we had eaten as she is practically a non-smoker herself.

So I rolled a Spliff, re-filled my wineglass, waved to Ingrid in her study, and went and smoked the spliff on her small veranda. By the time I had finished my smoke the fish was ready and the potatoes only needed a few more minutes, so I washed the spinach. And without draining it put it in a pot with a lid and put it on to cook at a medium heat. Meanwhile I poured off the juice from the fish, which I left to keep warm on top of the potatoes. Then I put the juice in a small sauce pan, added a good 100 ml of single cream and a couple of teaspoons of cornflower, seasoned it, brought it up to the boil and let it thicken for about a minute. Poured off the water from the potatoes. The spinach, by this time was cooked so I turned everything off, set the table for dinner for two and went to tell Ingrid that the food was ready. She met me halfway to her study with her wine glass in her hand and said,

"I'm ready, would you fill me up, please?" as she held out her glass. "Sure! Dinner is served, Madam Stein."

I replied, taking the proffered glass at the same time showing her into the dining area of her kitchen. We sat facing each other after I'd served up the food. She told me that she was indeed finished with her work and that she was as hungry as a horse. I too had a good appetite after smoking the Spliff, so we practically licked the plates clean.

When we'd cleared away the dishes we retired to her living room where she lit up a cheroot and I made another Spliff. I sat on the carpet and she on the sofa near me so that we could share the ashtray on the glass-topped coffee table, while we made inroads on a second bottle of Soave.

It was then she told me how old she was and asked me directly if this was a problem. By this time, I was full, feeling pretty mellow and somewhat laid back. So I replied that I was, after all in my forty-ninth year, only three years younger than her, and that, regardless of the difference in ages that I would still like to nothing more at that moment than to make love with her.

"That is what I wanted to hear, Alain! Because I want you too! Ever since I got your letter and picture, and then meeting coincidentally in the Mousson Turm. I've been almost like a teenager on her second or third date. And I haven't slept with a man for almost a year since my last relationship came to an end."

She then slid down from the sofa and sat next to me and put her head on my shoulder. I put my arm round her child-like shoulders and caressed her back and naked neck. She started purring like a cat almost immediately and her slender arms encircled my waist. Stroking her thick, greying hair back from her forehead, I kissed her gently on her closed eyelids.

They opened at once and she looked me in the eyes and kissed me on the lips with her full red lips, the hint of her tongue scraping my bottom lip. I returned the gesture and stroked her upper lip with my own. Within seconds our tongues were communicating by themselves while we turned our attentions to the current dilemma – who could get rid of their outer garments the quickest?

She won because I was wearing a pullover over my shirt. We lay down on the thick pile carpet in our underwear and started exploring each other's bodies with our hands and tongues. Her skin was still smooth and soft, her lemon sized breasts sitting high and firm on her child-like chest, her small rosy nipples already aroused. When I pushed up her T-shirt and kissed and nibbled them her purring intensified, and when my fingers made a preliminary excursion to her Mons Veneris, her pants were dripping wet as I slipped my fingers underneath. I caressed her outer lips prudently before dipping my finger into her quim while I gently rubbed her clitoris with my thumb.

In the meantime, John Thomas was straining at the leash because her dainty, manicured fingernails were playing hell with the underside of my swollen balls. Hoarsely I said, "What about contraception?

"Don't worry; I've already had my menopause. Just take me now!"

She sat up, pulled off her T-shirt, rolled over on her back, slipped off her panties and opened her legs. I did the same and knelt between them as she took JT in her tiny hands and guided him into her quim. I don't know if it was because JT was especially big on this occasion, or that she was very tight even though her quim was oozing, because it took a while until she opened up sufficiently to accommodate his size. The moment he was fully embedded she started to thrust against my movements, started to gasp as though she was in childbirth and within a few minutes she started to have an orgasm. When her first spasms had subsided I wrapped her legs around my back and sat up with her impaled on my lap. Then I was able to kiss and nibble her breasts again as she rocked forth on JT until her second climax triggered mine and I filled her with my gene-code. We came down slowly and just lay there cuddling for quite a while, occasionally kissing and sipping wine from each other's mouths until she reached down and started stroking JT to semi-hardness. She then took a mouthful of wine, turned round and knelt between my legs, took JT in her tiny hands again, held him up to her lips, pulled back the foreskin and sucked him in until her lips were just behind the ridge of the helmet. The coolness of the wine seemed to increase the flow of blood so that JT was soon once again in all his glory. She then started a rocking motion, slowly taking him deeper with every movement until he was at the back of her throat and ready to blow again.

"What do you want? "she said throatily, letting him slip out and taking him in a spanner-like grip at the base with both her hands.

"Everything! "

I gasped, not really under-standing the question. She then turned round, and without releasing him, she impaled herself on him once again, this time with her back to me. She held on to my knees and started rocking her pelvis to and fro until we climaxed together again. This time after we'd come down she told me that this position was known as the Russian sleigh ride and that she had always wanted to try it. By this time, we were starting to feel a little cold. She suggested that we take a shower, and I asked her if I could spend the night at her flat. She kissed me again and said that she was an early riser.

I called Michael to inform him of the change in pick-up point.

We showered together and she gave me a thick towelling bathrobe to wear. After she had set the alarm for 06:00 we got into bed and cuddled some more. I returned the compliment, and played with her clitoris and pussy lips with my tongue until she came again and she fell asleep in my arms. Ingrid made me a coffee before I left for my pick-up 06:30.

DONS, DANS & LEDS

30.05.07 My receptors have arrived at saturation point - that is their tolerance has reached the limit of their sensitivity. The only thing that can make them return to a more controllable state of insanity is at least one week of total withdrawal. Don't get me wrong, the amount I consume during my waking hours is about the same as young pothead inhales in one or two Bongs.

There are all kinds of Dons & Dan's; Oxford and Cambridge Dons,

Redbrick Dons, Spy master Dons, Mafia Dons and of course the Dan's, exponents of martial arts, eaters of Cow pie in the Dandy or Beano. Then of course there's me, the original Little Erfurter Don, sometimes known as LED, or Imam to my Moslem brothers. 'Allow me to introduce myself. As you already know my name's Alain Jackson. I'm a British ex-pat who's been living and working in the green heart of Europe for the last quarter century. I've just turned 60 and I have two grown-up sons who live with their partners and my three granddaughters just a couple of hours' train ride from where I am at this moment in time. In addition, I have a 15-year-old daughter and a son who is 11 years old. They only live a ten-minute tram ride - also from where I am now. I try to see them all as often as my workload and their mother, Petra permits.'

"Why do I give myself the accolade of Don? It's quite simple really. Today is the 30.05.07. It's just turned 14:00 and I've just got back from BB's after picking up 100g's of 'Skunk' from my friend at the Hauptpolizeirevier (Main Police station)."

The weed is for me and my flat mates to see us through until I harvest next week. However, there was a time, not too long ago when I was supplying half of Erfurt with recreational substances. I stopped trading when my daughter was born ten years ago. At the height of my criminal activities an average of five kilos of Ganja a week were passing through my hands, and on one or two occasions, 10 Kilos. The commission on such medium sized quantities is not on a par with any of 'Howard Marks' numerous enterprises."

Nevertheless, it did help me to enjoy a relatively comfortable life in times of low income from my legitimate occupation.

I don't have any qualms about making a small profit because of certain information that I possess, regarding access to material that is sometimes difficult to come by. After all, we all traded in school - whether it was marbles for chocolate bars, cigarette cards, and conkers - or as my eldest son did when he was eight or nine. He swapped his prize bag of marbles for a Belgian Giant, complete with hutch. For those of you who are unfamiliar with rabbits, a Belgian Giant is the size of a small to medium sized dog and weighs anything between ten and fifteen kilos. We soon found out why the parents of his playmate and trading partner were OK about the swap! My son was a little bit wary when he opened the door to give it fresh food the day after the Monster, as it became known over the next few weeks, was installed in its hutch in our back garden The beast jumped as high as it could and banged its head on the roof of the hutch. My son dropped the water bowl and fell about laughing because the rabbit was lying semi-conscious and dazed at the bottom of the hutch. Over the next few weeks we became used to its antics and it seemed to have learnt its lesson because it no longer jumped so high when we opened the door.

When we let it run in the garden while we were mucking out the stall it would, without delay, start burrowing in the flowerbeds next to the fence separating our back garden from the neighbours'. One day whilst my son was pre-occupied with cleaning and putting fresh food in the hutch it even succeeding in tunnelling under the fence and surfaced in next door's vegetable plot where it immediately started making short work of his carrots and lettuce, much to our neighbours' displeasure!

On another occasion a poodle from down the street had the impudence to squeeze through the gaps in our wrought-iron garden gate and ran up to the Monster yelping, the way over-strung poodles tend to – a bit like Odie in the Garfield comic. The Monster took one look at the poor dog, sprang three feet in the air and landed on the dog's back. The poodle squealed more in surprise than through injury and took off the way he had come at a speed that would have made Wyatt Earp blink. Two weeks later we gave the Monster his freedom in the woods just north of the new settlement of terraced houses in Yate, just 10 miles north-east of Bristol. I felt sorry for foxes and badgers in the neighbourhood.

Shortly after that in 1975 I was dispatched to Saudi Arabia as technical instructor to teach trainee aircraft mechanics for British Aerospace, who had a billion-pound deal to train the pilots, technicians and logistic personnel of the Royal Saudi Air Force how to operate and maintain their aircraft.

What it entailed was living and working and relaxing in a practically all male society. Alcohol was illegal and forbidden. Anyone caught by the Saudi authorities dealing in, or consuming it was automatically guaranteed a 'window-seat', the euphemism for a one-way ticket back to the UK. It happened to a colleague who had spent the afternoon in the bachelors' bar on the Base. He had the misfortune on his way back to the family compound, to run into the back of a car driven by a Captain in the Saudi police force. He landed in the nick at the down town police station in *Sharah Wazir* – colloquially know as Shit Street. Less than one week later he and his family were on their way back to England.

It was a long time before I got involved in making and running WL 'White Lightning'.

As it turned out the company provided ample leisure activities for the all employees ranging from three films per week, tennis and Squash courts, a swimming pool, stables where you could keep a horse, a social club where home-made beer, wine and Sideki, as the above-mentioned 'White Lightning' was called by the Saudis, if they could get their hands on it, could be safely consumed. I started off by brewing Saki (Rice wine), rice, sugar, a hybrid yeast and lukewarm water in a plastic dustbin covered with muslin and left to ferment for a couple of weeks until the alcohol level had reached its maximum around about 16 %. All that one had to do then was to siphon off the semi-clear liquid and let it settle for another week before bottling it for consumption.

All of the yeasty beer available in the bar was made by fellow employees who were supplying the social club for a small fee. Another syndicate was supplying it with WL. Before arriving in Saudi I had not spent much of my free time in the pub culture in the

UK, because prior to taking this contract I had been a wine merchant. For this reason, I didn't become one of the regular clients of the social club bar. This was only open after lunch on Thursdays for two hours and again in the evening, as well as Friday lunch times and evenings. Instead I played squash every other day after spending a couple of hours at the swimming pool, swimming when it got warmer and trying slowly to acquire a rudimentary tan. Quite a good time to do so actually because at the beginning of March the sun is not so strong, even at midday.

I also experimented with a sketchbook and water-colours. I even took up Macramé to pass the time until my first leave. So when a fellow trainer, who'd arrived on the same flight as me, told me at the end of April that one of the admin staff was leaving soon to retire after working in Riyadh for some 6 years. And he'd made his nest egg making and selling WL and was looking for a buyer for his 10year-old Arab stallion.

So when Dave, my colleague suggested going halves for the horse, I agreed immediately. After all he was only asking 1200 *Riyals*, which at the time was about 300 Sterling and the stabling charge was only 200 *Riyals* per month and included fodder. I'd already bought a Yamaha off road bike – much to the chagrin of my wife, Lex back in the UK - with the money I'd made on the favourable exchange rate. I'd opted to draw the maximum allowed for married men and every last Thursday of the month I'd pick up an envelope with around 800 sterling in *Riyals*. The rest of my salary was paid into the joint bank account in Yate. Like a lot of my co-workers, until I went home on leave after 14 weeks in country, I took the company bus into town after dinner to buy a cheque at one of the money-changers, drawable on the London branch of the money-changer's bank. This meant that I was able to save enough to afford the aforesaid bike. The cheque I posted with my weekly letter to Lex and my sons. As compensation, or revenge my wife bought an MG Midget from a fellow social worker. The reason I'd so readily agreed to co-own the horse with Dave was because the fact was that, until then at the age of thirty-three, the only thing I'd ridden, apart from donkeys on the beach in Bridlington, were various bikes and a 50 cc Suzuki in Aden and a 125 cc Yamaha in Singapore.

70

I'd grown up with a digest of cowboy comics, films and TV series, so it was somehow natural to see if it was something that would occupy my free time and learn something new. My first home leave was due in a couple of weeks which meant I wouldn't be able to help Dave for the first two weeks with the daily exercise regime that was necessary because '*Tariq*' was a 10-year-old retired race-horse. To appreciate why such a young horse should be put out to pasture you have to know that in Saudi Arabia most horse races are short distances up to a maximum of about a mile. The long-distance races are the domain of the racing camels, ridden by jockeys as young as 10, who are literally strapped to the camel with duct-tape so that they can't fall off!

When I got back the situation had changed. During my leave in the UK Lex and I decided that I should apply for family accommodation when I returned to Riyadh. This was because my eldest son, Jacob had been causing disturbances in class. Lex had taken him to the schools' child psychologist, who had diagnosed that Jake, my eldest son was missing me, his father. On my return I kept up my part of the deal with Dave and on alternate days I took Tariq for a ride in the cooler air about an hour before sunset. At the end of June, we changed to hot season working hours 07:00 – 13:00, or as long as the training flight operations were flying. If we were hit by a sandstorm we sometimes went home at 10:00. It was a long hot summer but by the end of August I'd been allocated a three-bedroom furnished villa in its own walled-in 'garden', 100 square metres of sand, only two klicks from the base where I worked. Lex soon forgot her anger about my extravagance when she realized that she could go riding whenever it took her fancy, especially since she'd got a job within 3 weeks of arriving in Riyadh, working in the office of an American drilling company, even though she had never worked in an office. Jake and my youngest son Paul were picked up every morning and taken to the company school at Banda Sudairi, the family compound at the other side of town and Lex was picked up by a driver from the company she worked for. It was during the horse ownership that we made friends with a Dutch couple, Wim and Theo, who worked for Ballast-Needam, a Belgian road construction company. They also kept a horse at our stables, which they shared with another Dutch family who lived in the Dutch compound that backed onto our villa. By now it was late autumn and we were soon socializing, i.e. barbecues, riding, tennis, and swimming when it was warm enough etc.

It was at one of the barbecues in their compound when Theo put the proposition to me. He said all you needed was a large pressure cooker; these were readily available for a reasonable price in the down town market. The minimum economic version could hold 40 US gallons and there were enough single guys on the base who had the skills to convert the said PC's by removing the pressure regulator and replacing it with a copper tube, which fed a spiral that was cooled by water from our cistern in the garden. In addition, the safety valve had been fitted with a thermometer because it was important to control the temperature of the mash. He didn't want to do it in his compound because of the other families living there. So we commissioned one from the base and the guy who supplied and delivered it to my villa also gave us a copy of 'Blue Flame', a leaflet describing how to operate a pot-still. This apparently had been put together by some American Moonshine specialists at Aramco, the Saudi-American oil company. Basically to check that all the ethyl alcohol had been removed you simply set light to a teaspoon full of the distilled alcohol and if it burnt with a clear blue flame it was palatable. So from 40 gallons of mash we would get about 6 gallons of 90 % alcohol on the first run, which meant that after 3 similar batches of mash we ended up with around 20 gallons of 96% alcohol after we'd run it through a charcoal filter, just like Jack Daniels, to remove the toxic ethyl, which can cause permanent blindness. We could sell this at between 700 – 1200 Riyals per gallon depending on the time of year. For example, the French would pay premium price just before Bastille Day. Some enterprising guys from there, who were helping set up the Saudi TV stations, even bought it to make a Pernod substitute. The alternative was to cut it two to one with still mineral water to bring down the potency to a more palatable strength between 40 and 45 % and sell it in the 1.1/2 litre bottles that the water came in for between 50 and 70 *Riyals*. Because our raw materials, rice and sugar were subsidized by the Saudi State our operating costs were less than 100 Riyals for the 20 gallons. This may sound like money for old rope; however, it was a very time-consuming leisure activity, but a very profitable one. One distilling run lasted about two hours because a close watch had to be kept on the temperature and the cooling water during the whole process. It all came to an end when we were allocated a three-bedroom bungalow in the family compound. I sold my half of the still to Theo and concentrated on distributing for a couple of big-time moon shining co-workers in the compound who were fully automated and could turn out in one day what took us a week. With a couple of other colleagues, we formed a syndicate to buy the first illegal load of brand name alcohol, i.e. Johnny Walker, Hennessy Cognac, Gordon's Gin, Smirnoff Vodka, etc. This was delivered late at night by an Austrian truck driver with a false bottom in his articulated trailer. My share was an assortment of 10 twelve-bottle cases of this first load, which I stored in the built in wardrobe in our bedroom. Lex went ape! However, I was able to calm her down as the whole batch was gone within three days because it was just before the Christian festive season and the asking price for contraband spirits almost doubled. The asking price for standard 75l. bottle of JW red Label could be anywhere between 80 and 120 Riyals and we were paying 500 Riyals per case of 12. You don't need to be rocket scientist to work out that the profits on the deal were very lucrative. Unfortunately, it was a one-off deal because we later heard that the truck driver had been picked up at the border with large quantities of counterfeit Dollars, Swiss Francs and Deutsch Marks'.

***

Sunday 20th. January. Lazy day in bed.

Monday 21st. January. Ditto last week. Crisis! Gerd didn't come to rehearsals again. So when I got home I called ´him and he told me that he couldn't, or wouldn't be able to play his role in my play in 10 days' time.

Tuesday 22nd January Ditto last week. Told the rest of the cast and crew the situation. In my opinion, we either call the whole thing off, or I take over the role and with their help, I thought we could pull it off. After all, we would only be able to put on a dress rehearsal, to which I had already invited the local press, and two performances. We had a beer in Troika and I caught the last S-Bahn, which connected with the last local train to Kelkheim.

Wednesday 23rd January I went into town after lunch and rehearsed with Petros at Gundi's flat until I left at 16:00 to go to my class in Offenbach. I got back to the church at 19:00 and we rehearsed until 22:00. I took the next S-Bahn to Hoechst, had a beer in WunderBar and caught the last bus to Kelkheim.

Thursday 24t January Ditto Wednesday. Called at Mike's and picked up the posters he'd done for me. Rehearsals went well and I was able to catch the last local train to Kelkheim and had an early night.

STUDIEN TREFF ERFURT

Saturday 15th June 1991. Open day at our school, 'Studien-Treff''
I had been in Erfurt since Wednesday putting the final touches to the
rooms, cutting up fliers that Kris's husband Helmut had photocopied
for the school from the design that Gundi and Petros had done for
me, and sticking up posters advertising their start-up. I'd already
moved into the WG (commune) that Chris had recommended when
I arrived at the school on Wednesday midday. It's only five minutes'
walk from the school in Johny-Scherstr.

When I asked Elizabeth, my new landlady and mother of two
young children, how much she wanted for the ten square metre
room, with a loft-bed and a small stove I was confused when she
said thirty-five DM. Did she mean per night, per week, or per
month? It was resolved when I said that I would pay five DM more
if I could use her washing machine and spin dryer occasionally. She
had meant per month! Apart from her and her two kids there was
one other occupant in the large, five room, first floor flat, Silke, a
trainee kindergarten teacher. Elisabeth said that I would get on with
Walter, the father of her two kids - Rachel, who was almost six and
Clarence, who was almost four – because he is also interested in
theatre.

My friend and ex neighbour from Frankfurt, Mike had driven over
in the morning with Linda, the woman I'd met through Ingrid and
who was now interested in me as more than just someone to satisfy
her physical needs. She needed a pilot was Mike's opinion! Barbara
and Michael had also driven over for the opening day and had
brought some additional chairs and an office desk, which I had to
put together as neither of them is practically inclined. After I'd
finished assembling the desk Mike and I walked into town
distributing leaflets advertising the school. When they were all gone
we had lunch somewhere and then went back to the school in
Friedrich Engel's Strasse, only to find, what at first impression
appeared to be an alcoholic who had wandered in from the street.
He appeared to have made inroads into the bottle of Tullamore Dew
that I'd bought for the occasion. In addition, he was trying to chat
up Linda. However, it turned out that it was Roland, a friend of

Helmut's who wanted to sign up for an English course with us, and who later became one of my students and best friends in Erfurt. Quite a few people turned up during the course of the afternoon that appeared genuinely interested in our project. At the end of the day we had two courses that Kris had brought with her from ENAG, the local energy Kombinat. They would both start after the school holidays, this year starting early and finishing in the middle of August. I had a group of four women and one man and we were to meet on Saturday mornings. They wanted to start at 07:30, I suggested 09:30 and we agreed on 08:30. Barbara and Michael left around 17:00. When we'd cleared up and washed the glasses I went with Mike, Linda and Thomas our landlord, whose wife had inherited the building, to find some place to eat. At the time there were not as many eateries as there are today. However, we found one next to a tram stop on the Boyneburg Ufer called 'Johannes Klause'. The food was very good and very cheap compared to West German restaurant prices. Thomas drove us all back to my WG in Johny-Scherstrasse. Mike had brought his sleeping bag and he slept in Silke's bedroom as she was away for the weekend.

Friday 25th January 1991. Lazy day at home. Called Doris and she told me that she was going to the cinema in Frankfurt with a couple of girlfriends in the evening, and if I liked I could go with them. I thought, was I being vetted, or is it just that she maybe wants to cool down a bit after their first intimacies. Nevertheless, I agreed and she said that they would pick me up around 20:00 because one of her girlfriends had a car. Maybe they would have a replay of their recent encounter so I did my usual ablutions.

They arrived on time and they were able to get reasonable seats for the film. It was some action – horror bullshit. After the show we went to a cocktail bar. They drank the typical cocktails that were on offer, I couldn't remember the names. I just had a glass of dry white wine.

When we drove back to the Taunus her girlfriends dropped us off at my flat.

However, by this time it was after 01:30 and as we were both pretty tired we cuddled and fell asleep with her bum in my lap and JT nuzzled between her legs.

76

Saturday 26th January 08:00. I was woken by Doris who was sucking and nibbling on JT, who was already displaying his full 'Morning Glory'. I reached down and pulled her face up to mine and kissed her on the lips that tasted of pre-come. I asked her if she would like to ride me because I knew that in my current state of engorgement that I wouldn't be able to come before I'd had a piss. She said that there was nothing more that she wanted at that moment. I quickly turned her round and slipped my tongue into her quim only to find that she was already dripping wet so I lifted her onto JT and she started rocking to and fro.

As she started to orgasm I lifted her gently so that she was riding side-saddle, which allowed JT to penetrate even deeper and the sinews on my legs could stimulate her clitoris. This made her flood my balls with her juices as she came again. When we were back to normal I got up, put the kettle on, went the bathroom and had a piss and a cat-lick. When I'd done my ablutions I made us a cup of instant coffee, which we drank in bed. She said that she didn't usually eat anything for breakfast so we cuddled a little and she was soon purring like a contented cat. She rolled over, stuck her sweet backside in my face and said,

"Take me again, please Alan. I'll do anything you ask!"

By now JT had lost his 'Morning Glory' but was still semi-tumescent so I knelt between her thighs and licked her vulva from her clitoris to the beginning of her quim and nibbled her inner lips occasionally slipping my rigid tongue into her depths until JT was ready to enter her. I wiped her juices with my hand and rubbed them on JT and then I gently nudged her quim with my glans and he slid in like a ferret down a rabbit hole. It didn't take long for us to reach a mutual climax, her quim massaging a small barrage from JT. She left Just after 10:00 to catch the train to Königstein with the promise that she'd call me soon. I went shopping and spent the rest of the day learning my text for the play, and recuperating.

Sunday 27th January the full dress rehearsal is only five days away and the premiere six. Laid in bed and read my text until 10:30, got up, had brunch and went into town to rehearse with Petros and N'dako in Gundi's flat. Had dinner with them and went home in time to catch the last train to Kelkheim and had an early night.

Monday 28th January same as last week. I managed to get through the rehearsal with only a few prompts. The sound and lighting cues needed to be tightened up otherwise I was very pleased with everything. We had a couple of beers in Troika and once again I had to catch the last bus to Kelkheim.

Tuesday 29th I got a lift into Frankfurt with one of my student so I was at the church before any of the others and they all turned up on time. Had good rehearsal and was able to catch the last train to Kelkheim.

Wednesday 30th January. Went into town after lunch and rehearsed with Petros and Doug before I went to my class at 16:00. No rehearsal tonight because tomorrow is the dress rehearsal when the press will be there and I wanted them all to be fresh for it. I got to WunderBar early, and as the Indian cook was on duty I had a plate of chips with tomato ketchup, which he always serves up warm in a stainless-steel gravy boat.

Thursday 31st January. Dress rehearsal! I got a lift again with one of my students and at 18:30 all the cast and crew were already in the church so we had a final run through of the sound and lighting. We had rented the equipment for three performances from a theatrical equipment company where a girl worked, who had played a couple of roles in my first excursion into writing and producing in 1989, 'Stop Press', An Evening of English Humour and Drama at Gallus Theater. But that's another story!

The journalist from 'Frankfurter Allgemeine' turned up just before 20:00 and the dress rehearsal went without a hitch, except for the fact that I needed a prompt in one of the dream sequences, but it wasn't noticed by the press, at least she didn't mention it in her review, which appeared in the Friday edition. The main criticism being that not only did the audience need to be well versed in English, in addition they would need pretty good knowledge of the Bible.

After the play was over we adjourned to Troika and talked about the performance. Caught the penultimate train to Hoechst, had a last pint in WunderBar and got home about 00:20.

Friday 1st February. Premiere!! The church wasn't even half-full. Nevertheless, it was great. Several of my students from Eloquia came and to my surprise my sons, Jason and Luke also came with a couple of their friends. I'd decided not to have a party after the first performance but to celebrate after the final performance on Saturday night after we'd cleared away all our props in time for the church service on Sunday morning.

Saturday 2nd February. The second performance didn't go as well as the premiere. I fluffed a couple of lines near the finish, but Petros and N'dako covered up well. The rest of February and March was taken up with teaching in Offenbach and performing 'Oh Happy Days' every other Friday and Saturday for the Theater in der Uni in Frankfurt until the end of February and then we started performing something that was no more than a radio play with pictures. I was also able to visit both Doris and Ingrid once during these two months and on both occasions a good time was had by all. In the meantime, Barbara and Michael had found premises in Erfurt through a friend who was setting up a roofing business. So one Saturday morning, about the middle of March when I didn't have to go to the theatre, I drove to Erfurt with Barbara to have a look at the rooms. They seemed adequate for a small-scale start up. It was a four room flat on the second floor of a large corner-house with three fairly large rooms, which could be used as classrooms and an office. It needed wallpapering and decorating. The fourth room was much smaller and was originally the kitchen. The owner had previously installed new double-glazing, electrics and central heating, etc. Barbara had already signed the rental agreement and all that Chris and I had to do was to come to some form of partnership agreement with her and Michael. We agreed that Chris, her husband and I would do the necessary renovation work and they would give us a start-up loan to buy the necessary furniture and equipment. They decided that I should come to Erfurt on the 1st of April and start and help Kris and Helmut with the renovation work, wallpapering, painting etc. They wanted us to have the school open and operating by the 15th June, one week before the summer holidays started. I agreed to do this against my better judgment.

Easter week. By now I had finished my contract with the 'Theater in der Uni' and my course for the company in Offenbach was also completed. So I only had a few clients at Eloquia, which left me ample time to take on work from Guilliamo, an Italian construction engineer who was my agent for translation work. His rates were rock bottom, but this was more than made up for by the numerous repetitions and in volume. In addition, I was now getting more proficient with Joyce, my green-screen computer, and was seriously thinking of buying a faster model.

Monday 12th April. I called Ingrid and she said that she would love to see me, but she was tied up at the weekend doing the make-up for a performance of the musical 'Man of La Mancha.' in the school where she taught. She said that if I liked I could come to the performance on the Saturday and she would leave a complimentary ticket at the box-office in the town hall in Hofheim, where the play was being performed and that they could have a drink after the show. I told her that I would most definitely come. I spent the rest of the week working on the latest translation from Guilliamo, and writing 'Jake and Friends', my first attempt at writing short stories.

Saturday 17th April. I caught the down-line train to Hoechst and the next S4 to Hofheim so that I was in time in the town hall to have a drink before the play. Ingrid came out during the interval and said that she wouldn't be able to go for a drink with me afterwards because she had a severe attack of 'flu. However, she introduced me to Linda, a very elegant looking woman in her mid-forties, the mother of one of her ex-students, and who as it transpired could speak excellent English. After the show Linda said she would like to go with me to a wine bar and chat about the play. After several minutes searching the back streets behind the town hall we finally found a cosy little Weinstube (wine bar). We sat and drank wine and chatted and I smoked a Spliff until I told Linda that I had to catch the last bus to Kelkheim, which meant I would have to catch the next train to Hoechst. She then told me that she lived in Niederjosbach, a large village two stops down the line from Hofheim in the other direction, and if it was OK by me she could drive me home. This meant that we were able to sit and talk a little longer. The reason she spoke such good English was because she had been married to an American Air Force technical sergeant who had served in Vietnam. For some reason this was like being invited to put your foot in an open door, for the simple reason that I too had been a Crew Chief in the Royal Air Force until I left when I was thirty. We left the wine bar around midnight and walked to where she had parked her car, an almost brand-new, early model Golf. On the way to the car park she shivered as the night had turned cold, so I took off my trench coat that I had draped over my shoulders like a cavalier's cape and wrapped it round her shoulders. We talked all the way to my flat and when she dropped me off she kissed me tenderly on the cheek and we made a date for the following Saturday afternoon.

Sunday 18th to Friday 23rd April. Nothing special to write about except for the fact that now that the weather is warmer I no longer freeze in the afternoons because I don't need to put too much of a demand on the night storage heaters.

Saturday 24th April I got up fairly early, did my weekend shopping and had the usual sh, sh, sh in time for my rendezvous with Linda this afternoon. She's picking me up at the lay-bye at the end of the street where I live at 14:00.

By five to two I was dressed and ready to go so I made a Spliff and walked to the lay-bye. I just had time to finish the Spliff when she arrived at 14:05.

When she got out of the car to greet me her lips were trembling like a young bird waiting to be fed. When I hugged her and gently brushed her cheek and lips with mine her whole body gave a shudder and she relaxed as though she'd just experienced a minor orgasm as her arms encircled me and pressed her lower body against mine. We then drove into Frankfurt and spent the afternoon walking round the Palmengarten talking, and had coffee and cakes in the cafe there. In the evening we went to the cinema and saw the early showing of the original English version of 'When Harry meets Sally', which she enjoyed immensely, especially the scene where Meg Ryan shows Harry how she can fake an orgasm. When the house lights went down her hand found mine so I put my arm round her shoulder and we sat like this throughout the whole performance, occasionally kissing each other exploratory on the lips and cheeks. After the cinema we walked to an Indian restaurant that I knew near the Haupt Bahnhof, and had a very good chicken Massala. When we'd eaten we picked up Linda's car, drove back to Hoechst and had a glass of wine in WunderBar.

It was there that she asked me if I would like to go to her place for a coffee before she drove me home. It only took us ten minutes to drive there.

Niederjoshbach is a village that is built on a south-facing slope in the Taunus foothills. She lived in the upper flat of a two-storey house owned, as she told at a later date, by her father. As it was still early and quite warm we took our coffee and drank it on the balcony. I made a Spliff and Linda, who is a non-smoker, asked if she could try it. I passed it to her and told her what to do, upon which she started coughing and spluttering. I took the Spliff back and when she had got her breath back I told her to open her mouth and relax. Then I took a deep draw on the Spliff, held her face in my hands, put my lips on hers and let the smoke drift gently, but continuously into her mouth. This time she didn't cough, but her tongue probed cautiously at the corners of my mouth. I returned the pre-emptive kiss and our tongues were soon entwined and sending urgent messages to various extremities, including my toes. We broke off the kiss and I said,

"We'd better stop now before it's too late to drive me home!"
"You can sleep here if you like, but I can't sleep with you because we hardly know each other, and I don't have any prophylactics." she replied, using the American term for condoms, as her arms pressed me closer.

"Linda, I don't have any either. Let's just go to bed together like brother and sister. I'm farting to steel tired anyway." I said, pulling her face back to mine and kissing her again this time without the smoke.

"OK, but let's go soon, I'm feeling pretty tired myself." She replied as she led the way to her bedroom where she told me I could hang my clothes on a chair near the window. She disappeared into the kitchen with the empty cups.

I took off my socks, trousers and shirt, went to the bathroom, splashed my face and cooled JT with cold water, went back to the bedroom, got under the bed-covers and closed my eyes.

The bed, which had a mechanism that enabled it to be partially raised so that you could sit up and read in bed, was in the upright position. Linda came in shortly after, wearing a knee-length, floral-patterned, cotton night-dress and a candle, switched off the main lights and got into bed beside me after she'd put the candle on her bedside table. She cuddled up to me on right side so I put my arm round her and she put her arm round my waist. We cuddled and caressed each other for a while until I asked her if I could sleep on the other side of the bed. She said it was no problem as she usually slept in the middle, anyway. After she had lowered the bed to the sleeping position we swapped sides and I put my right arm round her shoulders and leant over and kissed her gently on the lips and whispered softly,

"Goodnight, Linda."

"Goodnight, Alain. What would you like for breakfast?" she replied returning my kiss, her left hand kneading my chest robustly.

"You, roasted, with a white-wine sauce!" I replied, as I gently caressed her small firm breasts through her thin nightdress to find her nipples standing up proudly like twin, undefiled pencil erasers. She moaned with contentment and her hands crept down and freed JT from his confines. I eased the shoulder straps of her night-dress down and I took first one nipple and then the other in my mouth and bit and licked them gently at the same time gently rubbing her quim through her cotton panties, which were already soaking wet, until she could stand it no longer. She sat up, pulled her night-dress over her head, slipped out of her panties, lay back on the bed, her legs wide open as she said, "Fuck me, Alan, but be careful, don't come in me!"

"OK, Linda. I promise you I won't!"

I pulled my T-shirt over my head, knelt between her legs and gently slid JT into her expectant, oozing quim until he was buried up to the hilt. We soon found a mutual rhythm and before very long she cried out as her first climax hit her. Without withdrawing JT, I carefully turned her over until she was on her knees. Her firm buttocks thrust back at me at once so I grabbed her hips and gave her a good seeing to. After her second or third climax she collapsed under me. When I rolled off her she slid down my stomach and grasped JT and fed me into her mouth and gave me a good seeing to until I could stand it no longer and tried to pull her off. She shook her head and mumbled between mouthfuls,

"I want it all! Come in my mouth, please Alan!"

Without further ado I left JT to his fate and rode out the spasms that convulsed me.

After the torrent had subsided she came up again and kissed me on the mouth to let me taste my own seed. It was just at this moment that I had the feeling that I had been recommended by Ingrid. TBC. When she visited me for the School opening day, Linda and I slept in my loft-bed and there was only enough room to sit up and read. However, we nevertheless managed to make up for the time since we had last met at her place the previous weekend. She had told me on our second date some weeks earlier, that she relied on the temperature method of contraception because she hadn't had a regular sex partner for more than a year when we met, and that she didn't like 'prophylactics'. Neither did I. As Mike once said to me, "It's like paddling in the sea with your fucking socks on!"

So on this occasion I was able to forego the doubtful pleasure of having my gene-code extracted orally, because Linda said it was OK to come inside her. Within ten minutes we fell asleep in each other's arms.

"Why don't we get the cushions from your sofa and lie here on the balcony for a while?"

"That's a great idea, Alan!" She answered, jumping up and almost running into the adjacent living room. I cleared away our dinner dishes and made space for the large, thick cushions. She returned promptly with the aforesaid cushions and a quilt from her bed. We laid the four cushions together and we both lay down on them then Linda covered us with the quilt and cuddled up to me.

All I was wearing was the bathrobe and it wasn't long before she started massaging my chest vigorously, occasionally pushing the robe aside and biting me. She just had thin cotton leggings on and a light summer sleeveless blouse with a camisole underneath so I was able to return the favour. I soon freed her from her clothes as she undid the belt of the bathrobe and rubbed and pressed her small, firm breasts and nipples across my chest slowly making her way down my stomach where JT was standing to attention, having attracted hers. She then started rubbing him and scraping him with her aroused nipples and sucking him deep into the back of her throat until neither her, nor I could resist the tension. So I said taking her face in my hands and releasing JT from her lips,

"Gräfin (Countess, my pet name for her because her maiden name is Burggraf), I don't want to come in your mouth. What does your thermometer say?"

"My period finished two days ago, so it should be all right for you to come inside me, and I'd like that, too!" she said still clasping JT in her well-manicured fingers, his helmet glowing like Rudolf's nose. "OK, would you like to ride me?" I asked kissing her and reaching down to squeeze her quim lips gently.

"Oh yes! But can I ride side-saddle like the last time you were here?"

"Sure, just help yourself!" I answered as she sat up without releasing JT from her grasp and straddling my groin fed him into her juicy quim emitting a gasp of pleasure as he sank into his full length, tickling her kidneys from the inside as the old proverb goes. She soon started riding me and JT, rubbing her clitoris on the sinews of my inner thigh. She then changed up to a canter, her firm buttocks massaging my balls with each downward stroke until clasping my knee she cried out in relief as her climax kicked in causing JT to erupt in her quim, my glans knocking on her vulva as the cushions slipped from under us due to our convulsions, depositing us on the still warm balcony tiles ripping JT from her quim - the life-line of our combined juices the only connection now between us.

Linda tried to stuff him back inside her minge, to no avail and I sat up laughing, pulled a cushion under my backside and said as I caressed her slender back,

"Let him recover awhile, Gräfin. Sir John has done his duty for tonight."

"Your right!" she said laughing too. Let's go straight to bed and cuddle." as she stood reaching down to give me her hand. I took it

85

and followed her into the bedroom picking up the sofa cushions on the way. When we were finally in bed she snuggled up to me and she fell asleep almost at once with JT nestled between the cheeks of her bum.

Before I disappeared into the Land of Nod I thought maybe the reason for her maiden name was because someone on her father's side had once worked as a stable boy at the local castle!

SUMMER 1991

By now it was getting serious between me and Linda and the school didn't have much to occupy me, so at the end of the month I borrowed Chris' car and drove to Kelkheim and collected Joyce, my computer and the rest of my belongings, and spent a long weekend with Linda in Niederjosbach, Kucking and Fooking, and generally getting to know each other better and enjoying the free time. I spent the next 10 days in Erfurt doing some last minute decorations and sorting out a bank account for the school as well as doing some preliminary work for our advertising campaign for the upcoming school year.

Sometime at the beginning of august I went to England with Linda in her car. She'd come up with the idea that would mean that she would possibly get a tax rebate for a course of English which would be accepted by the inland revenue when she put in her tax return. All I had to do was write her an invoice for an English language course in England. We split the costs of the ten-day tour. We first drove to my parents in Yorkshire and spent three or four days with them. While we were there I showed Linda around York. Before we left we took Mum and Dad out for a drive to the coast where we had a fish and chips dinner in a seafront restaurant. From there we drove to Bradford and stayed one night at my brother Kens' in Lowmoor. After breakfast next morning we drove across the country to Wales. On the way we stopped and had a picnic in a meadow next to the Wye, that was partially covered with cow-pats – not an ideal place for a picnic, but Linda thought it was great!

It took us almost an hour to find a Bed & Breakfast for the night. We got a room on a smallholding and the landlady told us we could use the washing line, but to make sure to use the prop otherwise the sheep would chew them. The room was spacious and had a large wardrobe with mirrors on two of the doors. After we'd been for a meal and a couple of pints in the local pub we had an early night and went to bed where we started making love and Linda was so intrigued by the fact that she could see us in the mirrors of the wardrobe that she asked me to take her from behind like a dog.

I concurred and we fell asleep tangled in each other's arms and bodily fluids.

The next morning after breakfast we drove to Yate where my ex-wife lived but she was at work so we drove to London and while Linda did some sightseeing, I went to Waterstones' and bought a few books to take back to Germany. The following day we caught the night ferry from Ramsgate to Oostende. In case you don't know, it was a 6 – 7-hour crossing.

While we were on the boat Linda wanted to shag, but all the cabins were taken. I did what I could – but in the restricted circumstances I wasn't able to fulfil her wishes so under the cover of my raincoat and a blanket from her car I frigged her with three fingers in the semi-reclining seats until she came. When her spasms had subsided she bent over, took JT in her mouth and claimed her reward. He was glowing like a red glass ball on a Christmas tree and standing ready for duty like a sentinel at the 'Gate to the Happy Hunting Grounds'. We got to her flat in Niederjosbach and slept until midday. I stayed there for a few days before I went back to Erfurt.

By now it was the end of August and things were picking up at the school. I'd managed to sign up a rock band called Naïve for a 30hour English course. In addition, a 17-year-old student called Dominique, whom I'd met at the French bistro 'Le Cave' on the Fischmarkt where she worked as a part-time waitress, also signed up for this course. She'd come round to the school one afternoon to ask about English courses. And while Chris was out one afternoon we had a necking session in the armchair in what was my classroom. When Chris came back we sprang apart like guilty teenagers. Later that evening we continued our necking session on what I call 'The Scottish Island', which developed into heavy petting, until she said that she had to be home by 23:00. So we stopped in at Rapunzel, a small gallery bar run by a collective of women artists of various ilk's, and had a glass of wine before saying goodbye! Indeed, I shagged one of the said lady artists in September – but that's another story. In addition, we'd landed a Spanish course for Deutsche Bank in Erfurt, as well as a Spanish course in the school. By the end of September things were looking good for the next six months. I was able to get teaching work for both Chris and myself in the mornings at a retraining institute in Erfurt at DM 35 per hour. I'd got into the habit of commuting to Linda's in Niederjosbach at a frequency of every 2 to 3 weeks at the weekends. At the time I could only get a train after my Saturday morning 'English Breakfast' class. This meant that I seldom got there before late afternoon early evening. However, I didn't need to be in Erfurt for my first class until 16:00 on Monday afternoons - and as it was only fortnightly – it was fine. Linda an intelligent, attractive, well-situated woman only two years younger than me, with whom I could communicate in English as well as Deutsch and who loved the way I Fooked and Cucked. In addition, she was open to experimental attempts with the Karma Sutra as 'Leitfaden'. I'd even met her daughter, Wendy, a tall girl of 24 - with an excess of 'Gluteus Maximums' for my taste - who was studying Print Process Engineering at the TU in Berlin. My biological clock system kicked in and I found myself once again in the limbo of existing relationships. At the time I was teaching an average of 30 hours a week, doing the school admin, socialising in Erfurt, as well as commuting to the Taunus once a fortnight to see Linda. The happening took place one weekend when I stayed in Erfurt at the beginning of October, because it was Kris's birthday and her husband Helmut had organised a surprise. We all had to be at their place by 19:00. As it turned out he'd got tickets for the premiere of 'Linie 1', a musical based around the first underground railway line in Berlin. I'll tell you about what happened that evening in the next story.

LITTLE WITCH

On the evening mentioned at the end of Chapter IV, I arrived at Chris' flat in good time as I'd prepared an Indian meal for the party as a birthday present for Chris. Shortly after I'd got there, and was putting the finishing touches to the meal, when a small, petite woman with her long hair parted in the middle arrived. The air must have been electric for the rest of the guests when our eyes met. Chris introduced her as Helen, who was a doctor. We didn't have any chance to talk before we all trooped off to the theatre. And we only had chance to exchange a few pleasantries in the interval. After the show we all went back to the flat and ate the Indian food I 'd prepared.

After we'd eaten we then started to play an inter-personal relationships board game. It wasn't long before the specific question arose:

"Write on a piece of paper which two people in the room you think would like to know more about each other."

When all the slips had been collected and evaluated the unanimous decision was Helen and me, the woman whose eyes had fenced with mine at our first encounter four hours earlier. I later learnt that her letterhead was 'Little Witch'. During the course of the evening I gradually found out that she was divorced and had an eleven-year-old son. The evening came to an end and after taking my leave I walked back to my garret in Johny-Scher-Strasse.

The following Monday when Chris and I were in the office I told her that I found Helen very attractive and would like to get to know her better.

She said, "Why don't you give her a call and ask her if she'd like to go to the cinema or something similar?"

"Do you have her number?"

"Yes, just a minute. Here, it's Erfurt 567840."

"Thanks. I'll give her a call tomorrow." Chris had told me that Helen worked from 07:00 until 16:00 so I waited until Tuesday evening before I dialled her number. She came on the line after three rings, her voice soft and gentle but somehow challenging, as I remembered it from the previous Saturday.

"Hello, Helen hier, Wer ist da?"

„Hi, Helen it's me, Alain. Wie geht's Dir? Do you remember me, we met at Chris' party on Saturday?"

"I'm fine. Sure, of course I can remember you, even though I'm over thirty."

Chris had told me that she thought Helen was in her mid-thirties. "I was wondering if you'd like to go out for a drink or to the cinema sometime this week or next, because I won't be here at the weekend."

"That sounds like a good idea, because there's something I want you to talk about with you. But I've maybe got a better idea. Do you like jazz?"

"Yes, to some degree, as long as it doesn't get too experimental, because I lose track easily as I'm tone-deaf. Why do you ask?" "There's a Jazz band playing tomorrow evening in the E-Burg student's club (Engelsburg). And I was thinking of going. Do you know where it is?

"Only roughly."

"I could pick you up at the school if you like. What time do you finish teaching?"

"All being well, about 20:45. That'd be great if you can pick me up!" "That sounds OK. I'll come and pick you up before 21:00. If that's all right with you, Alain?"

"Sounds good to me. I'll try not to overrun so that you don't need to come up."

"O.K. I'll see you tomorrow around nine. Tchüsss!"

"Bye Helen CU 2, bye."

I'd done it: I had a date with a woman who seems to have been struck by the same short-circuit in her bio-chemical communication system as myself. However, the cards had been dealt and the only way to keep ahead of the game is to keep on playing; even after the

Mafia has broken your fingers.

I'd only been waiting for a minute in front of the entrance to the school when she had arrived in her almost new two-door Peugeot 305. I got in and we shook hands, as is the custom here in eastern Germany, and she drove off to the centre of town.

She knew all the secret parking places and we got into the Engelsburg just as the band were starting their first number. We found seats and I got a couple of beers from the bar, which was manned by the students' union so the beer was subsidised. It was impossible to talk while the band was playing, but we managed to communicate somewhat between sessions. It turned out that she wanted to ask me if I could give her son English tutorials.

I told her that it should be possible to fit him in one afternoon a week for an hour. We were able to communicate better when the band had finished their gig.

At about 23:00 she said that she has to get up early in the mornings and would like to leave. She offered to drive me home and dropped me at the end of Johny Scher Strasse. I gave her a soft kiss on the cheek as I got out of the car with the promise that I would call her again next week.

The following weekend was a long one because the Thursday was 31st. October, Reformation Day, a public holiday in Thuringia. This meant that I was able to catch the penultimate connection to FfM (Frankfurt/Main) on Wednesday evening.

***

Re: whereabouts
johnnycosmo@web.de
schnellmel@web.de
01.12.08 07:20:27

Hi dear,

I missed your calls yesterday. I was on the bike and didn't hear it. The weather here is getting a bit better which means there are a lot of clouds but one can get from A to B now mostly without a rain coat. That's good because both of mine are fucked.

I had a very lazy weekend again, reading, watching movies, exercising. However, I'm looking forward to Friday going to Payam, hurrah. I need a break from my solitude and get some supplies. Looks like rain again! I think I'll go home now!

Take care!

BB

Betreff: Re: whereabouts
Von: johnnycosmo@web.de
An: schnellmel@web.de
Datum: 18.11.08 03:53:12

Hi dear, are you going to write this in episodes? Do you have any propositions yet? I cross my fingers...I miss our conversations, too. My solitude is levelling down to some funny symptoms like not wanting to see anybody. Digging myself into my four walls reading, etc. It's a bit cocoon-like. I'm not in a bad mood, actually, just very remote. So, going to teach - especially the bullshit they decided we have to this term - is APITA. However, I think for my writing it will do wonders. Hope, you get into work soon - maybe in sunny Spain... Sounds nice to me.

Take care, BB

Betreff: Re: whereabouts
Von: johnnycosmo@web.de
An: schnellmel@web.de
Datum: 02.11.08 09:20:04

Hey, I've got something to 'meckern': and old friend and student (?) from Erfurt I didn't know that...In your description it sounds as if I was living in a palace... marble tiled floors, etc. :-)

Well, I like it more and more. It's just perfect for my self-imposed solitude - transformation time...Get back to you later...Take care!

Miss you, too.

BB

Betreff: whereabouts
Von:babuschka@web.de
An:schnellmel@web.de
Datum: 30.07.08 04:07:25 30/07/08 04:07

Hey, that's one of my favourite poems from Buk. It's from his last book published in 1993 called "The Last Night of the Earth Poems" (Black Sparrow Press) I'm still looking for another house. This "house woman" is nosing around and I don't like that. Anyway, got a friend here helping me. However, don't worry, there will be a place to stay for you. It's quite difficult to find a single house so I might go for two adjacent town houses so we both have our space. We'll see. See you soooooon! Take care, B

***

I spent a very pleasant four and a half days at Linda's. Fooking and Kucking. I took the midday train from FfM the following Monday because the connections to and from Erfurt had improved, now I only needed to change trains twice, once in Bebra and again in Fulda. I called Helen on Tuesday evening after my last class and told her that there was a late showing of an English language film in the 'Hirschlach Ufer', a small cinema club in the centre of town and if she'd like to go with me. She agreed, but it would have to be the following evening as she had a lot of paperwork to catch up on that evening.

I said OK and we agreed to meet in the little café/bar in the cinema at 21:00, half an hour before the film was due to start. She was on time and the film was very funny. We had a glass of wine in the café and talked about this and that. We agreed that her son Florian could come to school on Wednesday afternoons when he finished school. Once again she offered to drive me home, even though I could have walked to Johny Scher Strasse in the time it took to walk to her car and drive round Juri-Gagarin-Ring and drop me once again at the end of the street. This time she leant over and kissed me gently one the cheek as I got out and said goodnight.

By this time, I was going to the OA (Offene Arbeit) every Tuesday evening to have a couple of beers and chat with the other people after my class. My landlady, Elizabeth introduced me to the church social club.

The following week I called Helen and asked if she'd like to meet me there for a glass of wine and a chat. She said OK but she couldn't come before 21:30, because once again she had a lot of paperwork to finish before she went to work the next day. She arrived sometime between 21:30 and 22:00 and we drank wine, chatted and joked for about an hour when she said that once again she would like to go because of an early start.

I would have liked to have stayed but when she said that she could drop me off if I wanted to leave with her. However, I had the feeling that something was in the air so I left with her. When she stopped at the end of Johny Scher Strasse, she leant over and said,

"Will you be in Erfurt at the weekend?"

To which I replied, "Yes, why do you ask?"

"Florian is spending the weekend with his father and I thought it would be a good opportunity for us to get to know each other a bit better. Would you like to come to my place for dinner on Saturday evening?"

"There's nothing I'd like more. What time shall I come?"

"Let's say between 19:45 and 20:00. Is that OK with you?"
"That's fine. I'll bring a bottle of wine. What do you prefer, Italian or Spanish?"

"OK, it's a date. I don't mind as long as it's dry." As I turned to open the car door.

"Just a minute Alan."

As I turned back to her she took my face between her small sensitive hands and kissed me ardently on the mouth, her tongue just giving a hint of things to come on Saturday.

"I just wanted to thank you for a very pleasant evening. I'm looking forward to Saturday. Goodnight."

"Me too. Good night to you too, Little Witch!" as I returned her kiss and got out of the car.

Saturday 09.11.91 the rest of the week went by like a dream. A group of Abiturenten (High school students) came by yesterday and asked if I could give them some English tutorials and how much would it cost.

They left after we had agreed on the time and date, Friday afternoons from 16:30 till 18:00. This meant that my weekly total was verging on overload. I was teaching an average 16 hours for the training establishment and almost the same for our school plus running it and taking responsibility for the occasional translation contract that came in.

So I was very positively charged after I'd done my usual preparations before my rendezvous with Helen. I had already discovered that I could catch a bus at the end of J-S-Strasse that dropped me off at the end of Helen's street. So at a couple of minutes before 19:30 I crossed the road and a bus came within 3 minutes. At 19:45 I rang the bell next to Helen's nameplate. She released the door and I practically bounded up the stairs as if there was a fire and someone needed rescuing.

She welcomed me at the door and we hugged intensively and long, her petite hands lingering on my buttocks – a good signal. Cooking wasn't her thing and she had made something simple, mashed potatoes, frozen spinach and fried eggs – it was nevertheless very filling.

After we had eaten we took rest of the wine and a second bottle. We sat on her ancient sofa and chatted while she smoked a cheroot and I smoked a spliff. The mixture of food, wine, grass, the interplay of our pheromones and the general feeling of well-being that I was living made it only natural to lean over, take her small child-like face in my hands and kiss her firmly but gently on her lips which were red with the wine. She responded immediately and her tongue probed my tongue and lips. Pretty soon we were at V1 (the speed at which an aircraft can stop on the runway if there is a fault).

Her flat was warm so it wasn't long before we were exploring each other's bodies under our clothes when she broke off and said breathlessly,

"Would you like to go to the bedroom or shall we continue here?"

"To be honest, I would prefer the bed."

She got up and said, kissing me demandingly, "If you want to go to the toilet first I'll turn up the heating in the bedroom."

I stood up, went the bathroom, took of my trousers, had a pee and washed JT. Helen came out of the bedroom as I came out and as we passed she reached over and caressed JT through my underpants with a parting,

"I won't be long. Warm the bed please, I'm feeling cold." "OK." To her back as she disappeared into the bathroom.

She'd turned up the heating and lit a couple of candles; however, the room had a November chill so I slipped quickly under the winter weight duvet. She came in 5 minutes later dressed in a large T-shirt with nothing underneath, as I discovered a few minutes later. I was on the right side of the bed so she got in on the left and cuddled up to me immediately.

Before you could say Jack Robinson we were at V2 (this is the speed when an aircraft must take-off if a fault occurs).

Pulling my pants down she took JT in her small hands and said, "I want to feel him inside me. It's been a long time since I had a man. You don't have to worry about contraception, Florian was a caesarean birth and I was sterilised after the birth."

As I knelt between her slender legs and eased JT into her luscious quim she started squeezing him with her vaginal muscles.

Once he was fully embedded, or looking at it from another viewpoint, she was impaled, we soon found a mutual rhythm and within 20 minutes she came causing JT to release a barrage as her muscles massaged him to incredible spasms. I rolled over with JT still inside her and she lay on my chest until she felt him slipping out, upon which she grabbed him with her muscles and massaged him until he was hard again. Sitting up and moving her slender hips almost imperceptibly she said entreatingly,

"Can I ride you?"

"Sure, but don't expect another eruption like that!"

I said laughing as she increased her pace. I reached up and massaged her small, firm breasts pinching her nipples gently until she cried out as she came again and collapsed sobbing on my chest. After a few minutes she slipped off my chest and lay in my arm until we both dozed off. An hour or so later I woke up and found her fast asleep in the bed next to me. I went to the living room and smoked a last spliff and finished off the wine and thought that tomorrow was going to be a very pleasant day. After I'd finished the spliff I went back to the bed and fell into a deep sleep of contentment. As she was used to getting up early for work Helen made the coffee and brought two mugs of steaming freshly filtered coffee to the bed.

***

Late November 1991. It was around this time of year when my landlady Eliza decided that she needed to go on a self-realisation trip and left for an agricultural commune somewhere in the south of France. If I remember correctly it was a goat farm. This meant that Werner, the father of her two kids moved in and another chap, Ulli who was studying Theology at the university moved in as well. So it was a case of three men and two young kids in addition to Silke, a trainee kindergarten teacher in the flat.

We got on well together and we even held a dinner party; each one of us men were only allowed to invite women. I invited Kris, my business partner and Helen; Werner and Ulli each invited two of their lady friends. Kris only conceded to come if she could also bring her husband, Helmut because owing to their different work schedules they seldom saw each other.

From this moment, until I went to spend Xmas and the Yew Near with Linda and her family in the Taunus Mountains, Helen and I met once or twice a week - sometimes for the whole weekend when I wasn't at Linda's. We usually ended up at her flat and regardless of the time of day or night ended up by jumping on each other's bones - and other bodily parts together in the age-old tango of human encounter. Our relationship intensified and continued until July 1992. Things started to take up an unnatural rhythm.

It was one evening in November when I went to a performance and presentation of a book, the title of which was 'The Path of Least Resistance' a book in English in 'Rapunzel', a women's, artistic cooperative in Michaelisstrasse, which I mentioned in Chapter IV. The main reason of my visit was to promote our school; I therefore had an abundant supply of business cards in my pocket. Of course the ulterior motive for my visit was more that of a predatory Alpha male on the lookout for prospective sexual partners, although, theoretically and practically, I now had more than I could comfortably handle. Nevertheless, after the presentation was finished and the participants were asking questions I couldn't resist approaching the attractive, buxom young woman who had been taking notes of the proceedings, and saying to her as I offered my business card,

"If you need assistance in understanding the book. Just give me a call."

Indicating the complimentary copy, she was holding in her hand. She looked at me enquiringly as she took the offered card and said also in English,

"Thanks, but I think I'll be able to understand it. If I have any difficulties, I'll give you a call."

And with that she turned away, said goodbye to the hosts of the evening and departed. I ran into her the following week when I attended the inaugural meeting of the German – American Friendship Club in Le Cave, a bistro in the basement of the Gallery Am Fischmarkt opposite the town hall and run by Jacques Ives, a Franco-German from Saarland.

After the meeting was over she came over to where I was sitting and said that maybe she did need some help with the book. It was then that I discovered that she was a trainee journalist for the local rag and her name was Eike. Most of the other guests had already left but we sat there talking and drinking wine until almost midnight. She told me that she had to leave because of her baby sitter.

As it turned out we had the same way home as her flat was just this side of the flood ditch and Johny Scher Strasse is just a short distance over the bridge near Leipziger Platz. It was relatively warm evening and when we got to the end of her street she stopped and asked me as I went to give her a hug if I would like to come up to her flat for a coffee.

I hadn't expected the invitation and didn't think that anything was being offered other than the coffee so I demurred and went up to her flat. When we got there the baby sitter turned out to be her husband, from whom she was separated. After Eike had introduced us he left and she went to make the coffee.

When she'd put the kettle on she came out of the kitchen and went to the bedroom and checked on her two kids, Max and Moritz, who were four and six years respectively if memory serves me correctly but they were sleeping soundly. She then brought two mugs of steaming coffee, a la Turkish, i.e. boiling water poured on the coffee grounds. While we were waiting for it to settle she turned to me with that certain look in her grey eyes that told me she'd had more in mind when she'd invited me for a brew. I asked her if she would like to share a spliff with me, to which she said yes. By the time I'd skinned up and lit the spliff the coffee was ready to drink. We were sitting side by side on a somewhat dilapidated sofa and after she'd taken her first two draws on the spliff she put it in the ashtray and turned to me again with that look in her eyes, she took my face in her hands and kissed me gently, but determinedly on the lips. I returned it and put my arms round her. She pressed me back onto the sofa as her tongue started probing its way onto mine. We soon got to the preliminary stage of heavy petting and I noticed that she seemed to have rather a lot of small spots all over her back. When I commented on this she told me it was because of the mosquitoes that hatched in the stagnant pools on the banks of the aforementioned flood ditch and asked me if it bothered me.

When I said no she took off her top, skirt and underpants, knelt on the sofa and turned to me and said throatily,

"Take me from behind, Alan!"

"What about contraception?"

I asked as I slipped off my trousers and slid JT free of my pants and fed him into her soggy quim.

"It should be OK. My period finished two days ago." She said, gasping with pleasure as he sounded her depths. We soon found a satisfactory rhythm and within ten minutes she reached a small climax, crying out with a loud whimper.

Before I could also achieve fulfilment one of her kids started crying in the bedroom. She separated herself from JT and me and went to the bedroom. I was left sitting there with what seemed to be a still formidable erection. While she was gone I smoked the rest of the spliff. Eike came back after a few minutes and said that we should continue in her bedchamber, which was a small eight square metre cubicle just off the living room. She lay back on the bed and looked up at me and pulling me onto and into her said flabbergasted,

"Are you for real?"

"How do you mean?" I asked curiously.

"I mean, you didn't come and you're still hard." as she pulled me deeper and started to moan in satisfaction as JT probed her recesses.

I was almost ready to explode when the other kid started crying. She eased herself from under me and said quietly,

"Go to the toilet, I'll fetch them into my bed and you can wait in one of their beds and as soon as they are sleeping I'll come to you, OK?" It wouldn't be the first time I'd been robbed of my release so I quietly pulled on my trousers and disappeared into the bathroom and when JT had subsided a little I had a P and went into the bedroom where I climbed into the larger of the two beds. It didn't take long until I nodded off only to be woken some time later as Eike slid under the duvet, cuddled up to me and started massaging JT until he was ready for action. Without further ado she climbed on top of me and impaled herself on JT. As soon as he was fully embedded she started thrusting her hips, her large, full breasts swaying over my face so I paid tribute to them with my hands and mouth. This seemed to excite her even more and she thrust even harder and begged me to bite them.

I concurred and thrust back until I could no longer restrain JT and I groaned something to that effect. She was close to climax herself and simply said,

"Yes, come now I want to feel you explode inside me!"

Once again I left JT to his own devices as I cried out in pleasure, the spasms racking both our bodies as she collapsed gasping on my chest. After we had come down she extracted herself from me as JT slowly oozed his way out of her juicy grotto and said, "I hope you don't mind, but I think it would be better if you weren't here in the morning when the kids wake up. It's not so long since their father and I split up." I demurred and reluctantly got out of bed, got dressed, said goodbye and in five minutes I was in my loft bed in Johny Scherstrasse. Some weeks later at the beginning of December she called the school and told me that she wanted to write an article about some African asylum seekers and asked if I would accompany her as interpreter to the town's asylum seekers hostel just south of the main station because, although her English was fairly good. She thought she would have difficulty understanding some of the Africans. We fixed a time and it went without a hitch. After we'd finished she said that she would like to come and visit me for a return encounter.

As it happened this was perfect because I had the large flat to myself so I suggested that she could come round either on Saturday or Sunday evening. She said Saturday would be fine and she'd come round about 21:00.

She was on time and after the obligatory, preliminary glass of wine we made love on the carpet in front of the stove that I had fired up an hour previously so that the temperature in the living room was hovering around the 25C. After our first excursion into the realms of ecstasy we lay under the bed covers and emptied the wine bottle while we smoked a postprandial spliff until she got up and left saying that her baby-sitter couldn't stay too long. It was still early so I got dressed and went to the phone booth on the corner. I called Helen and asked if she would like to meet me in town for a drink. She said that she would love to but she still had some paperwork to do before Monday morning. But if I could pick up a bottle of wine at the Off license she said I could come and visit her as she would be finished in half an hour. I had a quick wash and managed to catch the 21:37 bus to Helen's.

When I got there she said she had almost finished her paperwork and asked me to open the wine and she would join me in a few minutes. I got the corkscrew from her kitchen, opened the wine and at her suggestion switched on the Hi-Fi. I thought at the time whether JT was capable of carrying out a late mission now that he had more or less recuperated somewhat from his recent encounter so I skinned up a spliff and listened to some radio station while I slowly drank my wine.

Helen switched off the light on her writing desk after about ten minutes and came through the open double door that separated it from the living room and said languidly as she dropped down next to me on the sofa, kissing me tenderly, "I hope you haven't drunk all the wine, I'm very thirsty and I haven't seen you for ten days." "Of course I haven't, I'm not a wino." I replied returning her kiss as I poured a glass of wine for her.

She lit up a cheroot and we chatted whilst we drank our wine and smoked. After twenty minutes or so we kissed, cuddled and petted until Helen said coming up for air,

"Do you want to spend the night here? Because I'm tired, it's been a very strenuous week and I'd like to go to bed soon."

"Of course I'd like to spend the night with you, but if you prefer I can walk home, it'll only take me ten minutes."

"No, you don't have to go. I'd like to spend the night with you. It's Sunday tomorrow and I don't have to get up early. Must Du gehen?" "Not if that's what you would like." I said kissing her tenderly on her lips.

"Ok, I'll go to see if Hannes is asleep while you use the bathroom.

He knows you're here. I told him when he asked who called, and as I told you, he has taken a liking to you ever since you started giving him tutorials with his two female classmates."

"Right I'll do that subito." as I stood kissing her once again, this time slightly more challenging. The rest you can imagine for yourselves.

WINTER SPRING, SUMMER & AUTUMN 1992

We had a very successful Xmas party in the school on the last Thursday before Xmas. Almost of the students arrived all bearing food and drinks. Kris and I had organised a cold buffet as well as beer and wine.

Werner, from my WG came with two actors from his troupe and performed a 'Monty Python' version of the Nativity. One of Kris' students, a chubby guy called Helmut recited Loriot's version of 'Advent! Advent! Ein Kerzlein brennt! (Advent! Advent! A candle's burning!). Satirical version of an old German Christmas poem about Prinz Ruprecht.

One of the highlights was when I persuaded one of my students, Marianne to perform an acted reading with me of 'Dinner for One' a well-known sketch staring Freddy Frinton as a butler who gets progressively drunk while serving dinner for Miss Sophie, his ancient employer.

At the end of the evening I managed to make it home to my WG with the help of Roland whom I mentioned in chapter II. I spent Xmas and the Yew Near at Linda's and met the rest of her family including her sister and brother.

**

When I got back to Erfurt on January 7th Chris asked me if I could take over her classes as she'd found a special offer for one week in Lagos, Portugal at the beginning of February and she would like to go for it because her and her husband had never been to a country in the so called free world. It wasn't a problem for me.

My commuting continued and as I mentioned in another chapter I acquired a contract with Deutsche Bank in Gotha for 8 hours a week, from Monday till Thursday for 10 weeks from the beginning of February for beginners. When I'd had the inquiry from the Deutsche Bank in Erfurt, where we were providing a Spanish course, I placed an ad in the TA for English teachers in Gotha. There were only a couple of candidates and one of them proved most suitable. Wolfgang was about my age and spoke excellent English that he told me he had acquired as a teenager in Munich during the American occupation after the Second World War. I cancelled my early class on the Monday, took the train to Gotha and introduced Wolfgang to the participants and distributed the course books that the bank was also paying for. This meant that after my commission of ten per cent and Wolfgang's fees I was able to split the difference with Chris. This, with the fees we earned at the training institute gave us both a relatively good deal of independence from the turnover of Studien-Treff, which in itself was doing fairly well.

We'd started two French courses, a course for Netherlands, i.e. Dutch, as well as a Spanish course for beginners, in which I participated, when my teaching and organisational and admin duties, as well as social obligations permitted. As agreed I spent Easter at Linda's.

At the time she was still working for Hoechst and was complaining of mobbing. At the end of April, I managed to persuade my Abitur students to perform my play, 'Confusions' an Evening of English humour and Drama, a series of sketches that I'd written myself and a couple of modified Monty Python and the Two Ronnie's.

I'd managed to get two days on the last weekend in May for our performance. Once again I had to play a couple of roles myself as well as being the Linkman/ director.

Sometime during a warm weekend in Erfurt after I'd once again spent the night at Helen's and after we'd been with her son to 'Le Cave' on Sunday morning for Brunch she lent me her car, as she once again had to catch up on some paperwork and she wouldn't need it until Monday morning.

I told her that I would bring it back early evening. I spent the afternoon driving around Erfurt and exploring the various extremities such as the airport.

Late afternoon I drove back to the centre and parked the car behind the Rathaus and went to the forecourt of the gallery opposite the Rathaus, where an enterprising French restaurateur had laid out tables and chairs for clientele. Gabi, one of the women I recognised from the Woman's Art house in Michaelisstrasse, whom I mentioned earlier, was sitting there alone recognised me too and smiled. So I asked her if I could join her. She agreed at once. We chatted until the waiter came and took my order. When I asked what she would like to drink she said that she'd have the same as me. So I ordered the house red. This turned out to be a very robust 'Vin Du Pay'. We sat and drank the wine and in the warm glow of the setting sun she told me a little about herself and her ambitions to be a successful textile designer because she'd studied design at university. In addition, she told me that she lived alone and had a 5-year-old daughter from her ex- partner. After almost an hour I told her that I had to return the car. As I stood up to leave she asked me what I was doing later that evening. I had no plans for the evening and I knew that Helen had to get up early the next morning so I said no, I didn't have any plans. She asked me to meet her on the steps behind the Krämerbrücke at around 20:30, which she told me is only a stone's throw from her flat in a semi-derelict house on Wenigermarkt. I said that that sounded interesting because I knew this was the place where I'd spent a very agreeable afternoon and evening as I mentioned in the chapter about the Krämerbrücke. I drove the car to Helen's and when I told her that I had a date she told me in no uncertain terms to go. As I walked out of the front door of her house she called down from her balcony and didn't say, 'Romeo, oh Romeo wherefore art thou'. Instead she threw down a plastic shopping bag, which contained my shaving kit and a change of underwear that had been left at her flat at some time during the previous months, with the retort that I shouldn't call her anymore.

I caught the tram back to town and just before 20:30 I sat down on the steps and rolled a spliff. Gabi came within ten minutes with a bottle of Krim sekt and a candle. We sat there in the setting sun on the steps and after Gabi had lit the candle we drank the wine, both of us sending out and receiving similar signals. Even though I had spent a very pleasant, satisfying evening with Helen, I somehow was a slave of my genetic and social programming because within ten minutes we were making tentative sorties exploring each other's needs and what we could. When the wine was finished she asked me if I would like to come to her place and have a coffee, because her five-year-old daughter was alone and she didn't want to leave her too long; and she said she would like to get to know me better. I took this as a green light, operation unknown.

DR. DOPE AND
PROFESSOR CANNABIS

As I mentioned in an earlier chapter I started dealing within six months of arriving in Erfurt. Initially it was very small scale, which was instigated by Linda, whose attitude was, if I was going to smoke it would make more economical sense to buy at a discount as well as buying the tobacco to make my Spliffs instead of destroying a relatively expensive product to make a new one.

So she financed me and I was able to buy fifty grams of fairly good Moroccan green, which was more than I used in a month.

However, one evening late in April 1992 I went to Le Cave, the French bistro on the Fischmarkt after finishing rehearsals with my students I discreetly rolled a spliff. It wasn't long before the waiter came over to the table where I was sitting with my students. I'd been frequenting the establishment ever since I'd attended the inaugural meeting if the German-American friendship society that I also mentioned in another chapter. After a moderately successful first half year and well received premiere in Haus Dacheroeden of my production of 'Confusions' I took a well-deserved holiday at Linda's for the whole of August.

When I came back to Erfurt I found that our two sponsors from Königstein in the Taunus had persuaded Chris to sell her share of Studien-Treff, which meant they were able to lever me out of control over the school. They even offered violence in the form of a friend who claimed that he had taken over the rental agreement and had changed the locks to the school. However, it took them almost six months, and I was able to retain my students, plus I still had several hours a week at the training institute that I had acquired for me and me. So I wasn't scraping the barrel because I started to spend most of the week at Linda's when I wasn't in Erfurt.

Sometime in January I'd acquired 8 hours of teaching English for the Deutsche Bank in Gotha. This meant that the income from this alone covered our rent and all the overheads for the school premises. In addition, I had located a local teacher who could fulfil the requirements. He came to Erfurt once a month and presented his invoice. At the time we still hadn't acquired a cheque book so we had to pay our staff with transfer forms for them to present to their banks. So it wasn't difficult to convince Kris that the income from this should not be paid into the school account. Especially as it wasn't part of our contract, the same as the income from my translation work.

I had already established an account in Frankfurt with the BfG Bank so it was simple to have the money paid into this account. After taking off the VAT and my commission of 15 % and the teacher's fee, I split the remaining net sum with Kris. This gave us both about DM 250 per month to pay for our costs. Sometime at the end of January Kris told me that she had seen an offer of a one-week package tour to Portugal and asked me to cover her classes for her. This was not really a problem for me.

The first major problem arose not long after she returned from this holiday. We were sitting in the office one afternoon before our afternoon/evening classes started when she asked me what it would take for me to give up the school. I jokingly replied that nothing less than million-dollar offers from Hollywood.

As it turned out the training establishment, where we were both teaching, had offered her a full time job with a fixed monthly salary and that would mean that she would see more of her husband as she wouldn't have to work in the evenings as she did for our school. However, it turned out to be a storm in a teacup. It was about this time when I persuaded my high school students and a couple of acquaintances and myself to perform an "Evening of English Humour and Drama", which was nothing more than few Monty Python sketches and some of the ones that I'd written myself on the lines of Becket and Pinter.

They were Martin, Grit, Tina, Thomas, Steffan and Falk – the students; Gundi, a young woman who had taken part in a weekend seminar that I had given, Gentle, a quiet spoken Nigerian refugee and Peter a young student who wanted to improve his spoken English.

Just before Easter I managed to organize a weekends trip to

London with my Saturday morning English breakfast group, Ellen the Little Witch and Penny an Austro-Canadian who had come to Erfurt to see her daughter dance in some ballet. It was a pretty successful, if an exhausting trip. It was the just after 19:30 on last Thursday in March when we left - our destination was Zeebrugge and the ferry we were booked on was sailing at 07:45. So we had more than enough time for the journey. Maik, the husband of one of the students took over the second leg of the journey when we stopped for a break west of Marburg. There were nine of us all together which meant that Ellen had to perch on the jump seat between the driver and passenger seat. We stopped once more and filled up the minibus and topped up our level of coffee just before crossing the border into Belgium. This avoided ending up with Belgian small change. The crossing time was only two hours and after eating a revolting breakfast in a 'Happy Eaters' restaurant just before getting onto the M2, we arrived at our hotel in Bayswater around lunchtime. After allocating the rooms I said that I was going to have a siesta and that I'd meet them in the Lobby at 15:00.

2B'z, OR NOT 2B'z!

It's not a question of, "Whether 'tis nobler in the mind to suffer the slings and arrows of outrageous fortune etc. It's simply a question of do I go to Double B's, a local pub I frequent and have a last pint on my way home from the OA (Offene Arbeit) a local church club, where I usually volunteer on Tuesday evenings, and where I occasionally cook, or do I go straight home to bed?

Before I moved to my current address in late spring 2000 I usually ended up dropping in because it was on my way home to a very pregnant Petra. Nowadays it's more often than not that I go straight home as it would mean a detour.

I first went to BB's shortly after it opened in 1993. I had brunch one Sunday with some friends, Helge, a freshly qualified architect, his girlfriend Anke, his sister Suse and her boyfriend Stefan, the main impulse behind a trio called Risse, from Eisenach that specialised in Sitar Rock before it became popular. I even helped him with a couple of song texts, for which he remunerated me with Moroccan Green. Some five years later I moved into a flat in Webergasse (Weaver's lane), the street parallel to the street where BB'Z is located. All I had to do if I fancied a beer was to cross an empty plot and I was in the beer garden of the pub in two minutes.

In 1998 there were still a lot of British building workers in Erfurt and they would congregate in BB's every Friday afternoon to wait for their paymasters. Some of them even lived there between jobs.

ROOM TO SWING A CAT

Saturday 24th April 1996. Just another usual Saturday morning. Rick has been spending most nights at my place in the Arnstädter Hohle since she started her cabinet-maker apprenticeship. Nevertheless, the coffee machine switched on at about 6:30 simultaneously with the lights in the garden under the bed. She turned to me and muttered, *"Kannst Du den Kaffe Heutmorgen holen, Bitte?"*

When I was properly awake I swung down from the bed, got two cups of coffee from the conservatory and took them back to bed. She dozed on so I got my book and made a Spliff, which I smoked and read until she finally surfaced an hour and a half later and took a swig from her lukewarm coffee.

I got us fresh coffee and after we'd drunk it she went to the kitchen to have a wash while I prepared our breakfast of Muesli, fresh fruit and natural yoghurt in the conservatory. After we'd had breakfast I went shopping while she did the necessary housework. The rest of the day passed without anything of note happening. In the evening we went to a party and dance in the OA.

We left just after midnight and walked to Tina's one room apartment next door to her mother's flat. Two gay guys we knew tagged along because it was on their way to a party in a squat in a derelict fish cannery in the north of town.

We drank a few more beers and listened to some music until the two guys said it was time to go. Tina said that she wanted to go too, but I said that I needed some sleep. By this time, it was well after 02:00. They left and shortly after one more beer I walked all the way to my flat in the old villa on the edge of the Steigerwald. It only took me 25 minutes and it was a relatively warm night. When I got home just before 03:00 one of the numerous church clocks in town struck three.

I was greeted by my two young cats, the heavily pregnant, Anna and her brother, Quinny.

I gave them both a few strokes, some fresh water and food, and climbed up into my loft bed and fell asleep immediately and started to dream.

About two hours later the sun rose, traversed the heavens and set, all in a space of maybe five minutes, just like in the world of the 'Little King' in St. Xupreys famous book.

This was the dream I was experiencing when suddenly in this utopia there came a cloudburst, and I came awake suddenly with a feeling of wetness between my legs; my first thoughts were,

'Had I wet the bed - something I hadn't done for over forty years, or had I had a spontaneous emission, a so-called wet dream. Something that also I hadn't experienced for more than half a century?'

With apprehension and curiosity, I lifted the quilt only to find Anna, who was just giving birth to her second kitten, staring at me, woebegone with her big brown eyes, as if to say, *'Don't be upset. It was the best place I could think of.'*

The first one was lying there and she was trying to lick it clean. As it turned out, it was the first of four. I quickly got down from the bed and fetched an old towel. Then I lifted her and the two new-born kittens onto the towel. Having made sure that she was all right I went to the conservatory and made a pot of fresh coffee and while it was brewing she gave birth to the third one. When the coffee was ready I took a mug back to bed and sat and stroked her, and talked to her; and watched her for the next half hour or so.

Finally, all four were lying there mewing as she licked them clean as they tried to find the way to her teats. When she was satisfied that everything was all right I got a cardboard box, put an old pullover and blanket in it, carefully lifted them with the towel and put them in the provisional bed. Anna didn't protest at this she simply settled herself in the box. She even gave me a look of gratitude, or so it appeared to me. After she had recovered from her exertions I fetched her bowl of milk and put it on the shelf at the side of the bed. Freeing herself from her litter she got out of the box, came and rubbed her head against my chest and drank thirstily until all the milk was gone.

About half an hour later, Quinny, her brother, turned up full of curiosity, but she wouldn't let me anywhere near the kittens. She even growled and spat at him when he climbed up onto the bed and tried to go near the kittens. I consoled him and got up and had breakfast. At about 11:00 I took the tram to the Anger and walked to Rick's place where she was just surfacing, because her mother had already woken her to ask what she would like for Sunday lunch, and if I would be eating with them.

SEPTEMBER 1997 REBIRTH?

04.09.1997. 00:30 It was my birthday yesterday. I'd been able to celebrate it in a shared flat in Allerheiligestrasse (All Saints Street). The other tenants were a couple about my age.

All my friends who I'd invited turned up and as they arrived I gave them all a twig with a blossom from my Indoor Garden, which was now in its second harvest. I'd mastered the task of cloning after I'd determined whether they were females or not – their male siblings ended up in the salad bowl.

Colm and his wife Ulrike arrived with a basket of fruit, Rick my still, occasional bed mate came with Bianca and her boyfriend, whom I nicknamed Abnorm because his academic approach to anything sexual can sometimes be too much. Diana, the lanky midwife who later told me about the empty flat in Schülstrasse, arrived and when most of the guests had turned up she gave a demonstration of Fire Eating in the street. Christian and Isabelle, a young couple I know from my teaching in Weimar turned up too with a friend of theirs, Petra, and Pablo, an Argentinean troubadour, with his guitar came after he had done the round of the bars in the town centre. He entertained us later with his South American version of Bob Dylan's well-known songs – he also astonished my co-habitants, Holgar and Dorothea when he tried to dry the blossom I'd given him in a frying pan on the gas stove, where the Tandoori chicken was roasting in the oven.

About 23:00 when they had eaten Rick, Bianca and Norm left, pleading tiredness or boredom. I never did find out.

By midnight there was only six if us still awake and enjoying the umpteenth spliff of the party. Apart from myself there was Chris and Easy, as she liked to be called, Pablo, who was putting the make on Chris, a friend of mine who I have often lusted after and Petra a girlfriend of Easy's. Chris and Easy left to go to 'The Engelsburg', the student's bar that I mentioned in Chapter VI and told Petra that they would come back for her in half an hour or so. Pablo came over to where I was sitting, winding down after a moderately successful party with a glass of water and asked me if I had any condoms because he thought his luck was in with Kris.

I had to disappoint him as I haven't had the need for them because Rick was on the Pill and had been since we started our on/off relationship.

Pretty soon Petra came over and sat on the arm of the sofa where I was sitting and started stroking my hair.

When I looked up at her she slid down next to me, put her arms round my neck and kissed me full on the mouth with her lips that opened like the oral orifice of an inflatable sex-doll.

We snuggled and snogged for a while until I suggested that it would be a slightly more private if we went into the adjacent bedroom where we lay on the bed and continued our explorations of each other's bodies. As it turned out Petra had the firm plump breasts of late puberty, so I gave them my undivided attention as she rummaged under my kilt, only to find that I was 'Commando' i.e. without any underwear. She found this both amusing and somewhat erotic because she soon slid to her knees at the side of the bed and started working with her scarlet lips with the practice of a connoisseur on JT. It didn't take him long to rise to the occasion.

In retrospect my first woman took seven years before she deigned to put her lips on JT; my first German woman took all of seven months ere she took him in her maw and now it had taken Petra less than seven minutes! However, an excursion into the nether regions of the female anatomy was just not to be. Just after midnight Chris and Easy came back to take Petra back to their flat as they had to get up early the next morning to go to college in Weimar.

At the time I was being kept on a long leash by Rick, because even though she no longer lived with me, she now and then condescended to let me sleep at her place when she/or I were in need of an exchange of bodily fluids. In addition to this the electricity in Arnstädter Hohle had been capped because the town authorities were hoping that the original owners of the property would take over the burden of maintaining the house.

Over the next few months Petra and I continued to meet clandestinely – in a small cafe near the station in Weimar when I was teaching and she was going to college there, occasionally on the train and sometimes at Easy's where we tried to consummate our desires. However, we were relatively unsuccessful, and as Petra was not on the Pill there was a need for condoms, which late on a Saturday night are not always easy to come by.

This led to the situation where I was vulnerable to approaches by young women. So when Petra came to visit me in the WG in Allerheiligestrasse one warm October afternoon it didn't take me long to succumb to her youthful charms.

We were about to finally consummate our encounter when the doorbell to the flat rang. I put a towel round me and cautiously peeped through a gap in the curtains in the bedroom and sure enough there was Rick. She had obviously finished early at the training workshop where she is doing an apprenticeship as a cabinetmaker. She disappeared from my line of sight and the doorbell rang again six times in a row. I turned to Petra on the bed and said with a note of urgency,

"It's Rick, we'd better get dressed."

If I let her in before Petra and I had made ourselves decent she would make a scene, which I didn't need. So I said to Petra after she had dressed,

"When I go to let her in wait until you hear me open the door to the flat and then jump out of the kitchen window into the courtyard. Give me a ring later."

I gave her a warm hug and kiss, opened the window and pressed the door opener for the main courtyard door. From there I went into the bathroom and wet my hair from the shower. Taking a towel, I wrapped it around me head and went in my underpants to the flat door to open it. I took my time and when Rick came in she hugged and kissed me somewhat coldly and said,

"Why did you take so long to answer the doorbell?"

"Can't you see I was in the bathtub?" I replied as nonchalantly as I could.

SPRING 1998
PRACTICE RAID

Thursday 23.05.96: 23:50. Spring had finally arrived and the seedlings were coming up great in the small conservatory adjoining my main room. I had two rooms in an old villa in the Steigerwald, the forest that starts at the southern edge of the town. The two rooms are separated by the main hallway of the villa, and one is unusable apart from being the kitchen area, which is partitioned off by a dividing, chipboard wall, and access to the bathroom and toilet. However, the bath is unusable because the bath water has to be heated by a coal stove, the flue of which is highly porous and the local council housing authority refuses to do anything about it because the house and surrounding wooded grounds have been allocated for return to the original owners. I'd survived the first winter in the converted villa by restricting himself to living in the one 40 square metre, 3.50 high room. In one corner, to the right of the double entry doors, was an ancient 2-metre high tiled stove, which, when it was fired up and throttled back, would burn for 2-3 days depending on what type of fuel one used.

I erected my inherited loft bed at the other side of the doors, which meant even when the stove was throttled down the temperature in bed was always a constant 20 0 C. Under the bed was my writing desk on which my antique computer sat, my wardrobe and sometime later my indoor gardens. The day started off as usual at 6:00 AM when the coffee machine in the conservatory switched on automatically; and when the coffee was ready the light on the writing desk went on under the bed before I was awoken by the smell of freshly brewed filter coffee. I swung down from the bed using the outrigger at the foot end, got two cups of coffee and put them on the shelf on the side of the bed. When I'd climbed back up I woke up my girlfriend, Rick by waving the cup of coffee under her nose. After we'd drunk our coffee she got up and got ready to go to the training workshop where she's doing an apprenticeship as a joiner and cabinetmaker.

I only had 2 hours of tuition at 9:30 in Weimar so I was able to spend the rest of the day collecting firewood from the adjacent forest and preparing dinner for us in the evening.

Four of my tuition group turned up at 18:30 and we shared our evening meal with the boys.

After we had eaten we worked until about 21:00 and I showed them a couple of English card games for about an hour. There is a dearth of card games in Germany. You can either play Skat, a very complicated and sort of three-handed Bridge using only 32 cards, Doppelkopf, a four handed version of Skat or Mau-Mau. Phil, one of the students and I caught the Nr. 4. 22:10 tram to town to see if we could locate some recreational substances. However, when we got to BB's my man told us that it would be another hour before his wholesaler arrived. I told Phil to go back to the villa and tell the others to wait for my return.

In the meantime, I went to the E-Burg, a student's club, and had a pint.

On returning to BB's my man told me that his deliveryman was stuck in a traffic jam and wouldn't be in Erfurt before 3 in the morning. I had another beer, and as I'd just missed the number 4 tram, I took the number 3 back to the Steiger. This meant that I had to walk through the park to get to my apartment. As the tram stopped at the turn-round tracks at the terminus I was surprised to see three police patrol cars blocking the road leading to the driveway of my villa. Within a minute another 2 cars arrived and then a policeman got out, obviously the Einsatzleiter (Raid Commander) and shouted, "Los Geht's!" (Let's go!). Upon which they all got back into their vehicles and one after the other they drove up the road and straight into the driveway of the villa.

I thought to myself, "Hello, hello, who's blown the whistle?"

The only thing to do was remain calm so I took the path through the woods leading to the villa and approached it from the side. As I emerged from the forest and made my way to the entrance of the house the last of the policemen, wearing combat fatigues and carrying machine pistols, were running up the steps leading to the main entrance of the house.

Ignoring them I walked into my living room to find not only Tina and my four students, but also 6 police officers plus a policewoman who were milling around in the large room. One identified himself as the Einsatzleiter (Raid commander) when I inquired what it was all about.

"Verstoß gegen BTMG (Infringement of the Drug Laws), he replied determinedly.

"Do you have the necessary search warrant?" I asked naively. To which he answered, "Nicht nötig (Not necessary). Gefahr im Verzuge (Risk of delay).

"Ok." I thought, "You're going to have to face the music, but with a bit of luck you won't be called on to dance!"

I said to Tina and the guys,

"O.K, I'll make a pot of tea while we wait for the next move."

As I opened the door to the conservatory one of the policeman followed me and watched while I took the kettle and went to the kitchen area to fill it. He followed me. While it was boiling I went to the toilet and he wanted to follow me, but he remained outside the door when I protested. After I'd made the tea I took it back to the living room and we drank it and ate some chocolate.

In the meantime, the Einsatzleiter had left the room. So I asked one of the officers where he had gone and he told me that he had gone down to his car. They allowed me to leave the room and go down to the car where the number one Honcho had just finished speaking on the radio. "What's happening now?" I asked, and as it was already well after midnight, "The parents of the boys will be getting worried by now. Why can't they leave?"

"I've just ordered a Sniffer dog." he replied. "OK, we'll give the kids a body search and then they can go home."

We went back up to the flat and one after the other the boys were searched in the other room. The policemen were a little taken aback when Tina told them that she was a woman. Because, at the time she was wearing her hair very short, namely less than 1cm. And she seldom wears make-up, however she is seldom to be seen without her beloved Doc Martins. However, there was a policewoman who subsequently searched her.

When the lads had said goodbye and left the officers were even more nonplussed when Tina said that she was staying the night. Strangely enough I wasn't searched at all!

It was 00:45 when the policeman with his dog arrived. It was a Riesenschnauzer. He first searched the living room, creating chaos on my already disorderly computer desk. The dog was then let loose in the other room where his super nose discovered some of my spice selection, i.e. an envelope with mustard seeds, a screw-top jar with cardamom and Datura Stramonium (Angels Trumpet) seeds wrapped in tin foil. Finally, they let him into the conservatory, where my cannabis seedlings box was not to be overlooked. All that remained was for me to accompany them to the main police station in Andreasstrasse along with the tray of seedlings and the spice find. When they got there I was given the full criminal registration, including fingerprints, mug shots and a provisional interrogation. By 02:45 they were finished and I was allowed to go home. They even offered me a lift home if I waited for a patrol car to return. I said, "No thanks, it's a warm night. I'll walk." At the time I came to the conclusion that the whole charade had been a training exercise because the Einsatzleiter and two of the officers spoke with a dialect that indicated that they were from Hessia, most likely from Frankfurt/Main.

KRAEMERBRUECKEN FEST
(THE TINKER'S BRIDGE FESTIVAL)

My first visit to the Krämerbrücke Fest was in the summer of 1991. I had recently arrived in Erfurt to help set up an educational training business, i.e., a private language school. At the time I was living in a WG, (commune) and one of the other co-habitants told me about the festival, which usually starts on the last, or the penultimate Friday in June, and continues until Sunday afternoon. She said it's easy to find the festival, even if you didn't know the town; head for the town centre and just follow the throng.

It was the first weekend I had spent in the city since moving here more or less permanently at the beginning of the month. I had nothing to do and as it was a beautiful warm, sunny day I put on my Bermuda's and my battered old Panama and took a stroll after lunch to take in the atmosphere of Erfurt, the state capital of Thüringia. The first festival was organised by the inhabitants of the medieval, timber-frame houses and businesses on the bridge in 1975, which is the oldest bridge over the river Gera, dating back to the 15th. Century and has no fewer than six stone arches. Back in 1975 the festival was mostly confined to the bridge itself. In 1991, however it had been extended to take in the island, which forms the foundations for the central arches, as well as the adjoining cobble-stoned square known as Wenige Markt (Lesser Market).

On the island a jousting tournament, archery contests, musical performances and other medieval activities were in full swing. Access to the island was either from the steps leading down from the new bridge, which runs parallel to the old one, or from a timber gangplank from the steps on the other side of the Krämerbrücke. To get on to the island and enjoy the show one had to pay 5 Taler,

i.e. 5 DM, this also gave access to the Wenige Markt. This was fenced off, and inside this stockade a medieval market place had been created. Straw was strewn over the cobblestones; dogs, cats, chickens and children ran underfoot. Stalls offering medieval wares and delicacies were set up all around the market place.

A blacksmith, with a real forge demonstrated his skills, and falconers showed of their proud birds. The multitudinous smells of mulled wine, beer, herbs, freshly baked bread, and burning meat filled the hot summer air. Right in the middle of the market place a side of beef was slowly turning over a huge charcoal fire.

The smell made my mouth water and I did not withstand the temptation. I strolled among the crowds soaking up the warm afternoon sun and absorbing the ambiance with a roast beef sandwich, the size of a baseball catcher's glove in one hand and a pint of the local beer in a plastic beaker in the other.

A muzzled, fully-grown brown bear on a chain was standing guard close at hand to the roasting beef. A medieval hot tub was located to the left of the main entrance.

This was half a two-metre wide barrel full to over-flowing with hot suds, in which 6 to 8 people could sit comfortably and drink beer or wine whilst enjoying a soothing warm bath. It also cost 5 Taler, but the wine or beer was included. I confess, I also succumbed to these delights! Outside this market, this little island of voluptuous, medieval indulgence, countless beer and wine stalls had been set up by the local breweries and taverns, and everywhere the omnipresent smell of Thüringia Bratwurst and Brätel grills! As the afternoon turned into evening I was so full of food, beer and impressions that I just sat down on the steps behind the bridge, smoked a Spliff and listened to one of the live bands performing until dozed off.

I woke up to the laser show on the island after the sun had set.

RAID II

Saturday 11.04.1998 21:40. It was already dark outside and Petra and I had just made love in our provisional cave-like bed in the smallest of my four rooms.

By this time, she was spending most Friday and Saturday nights at my flat in Schülstrasse, as well as at least one night during the week. In fact, it was the only room with a stove. The largest one had a 2Kw. electric radiator and at the time occupied by twenty-year-old Christian, a young friend of ours who was in the process of breaking up with his wife, Ishbel, sometimes known as Easy. Indirectly this marital breakdown was the trigger for this raid. But that's another story. At the time I was in the process of wallpapering the room. When the doorbell rang I got up and slipped on my old, but warm dressing gown. Through the frosted glass panes in the door I could make out several shadowy figures on the landing. Thinking that it might be some friends I opened the door ajar without putting the security chain on.

A burly man in jeans and leather jacket holding out my police ID forced the door open and shouted,

"Kripo, Verdacht auf Vertoß gegen BtmG!" (CID. Suspicion of violation of the Drug Laws)

Upon which he shoved the door fully open and pushed passed me into the hallway followed by about half a dozen or more uniformed and CID officers as well as a team from the Forensic Crime Squad. They spread out through the flat and one of the policewomen found Petra still in bed naked. Mr. Big found what anyone over 1.70 metres tall could see from the street if they stood on tiptoes - twenty-eight large plants, twenty-two small plants.

In addition, they confiscated the following: one silver-coloured tobacco tin with contents, belonging to Petra and one heating pad for a cat basket. In the bathroom they found several branches of Cannabis from the last harvest hanging up to ferment. The forensic squad then went into action in the kitchen. All my spices were examined and tested for toxic, hallucinogenic substances - to no avail.

They then started passing the numerous plants through the window and loading them into a six-pack, the local nickname for the police VW Transporter. It was about then that I cracked. Still just in dressing gown and slippers I went into the room where the plants were, grabbed two and said,

"Das ist Diebstahl! Es sind meine Pflanzen!" (That's theft. they're my plants!). And started to carry them away.

Upon which Mr. Big grabbed me round the throat from behind, the buckle on his jacket sleeve grazing my left cheekbone, and prevented me from moving further. Resistance was useless so I dropped the plants and he let go of me. This time there was no need for me to accompany them to the main police station in Andreasstrasse because they already had my particulars from Raid I. They finally left after about one hour and we went back to bed after stoking up the stove. They'd searched the cellars and a couple of outhouses, but they didn't search the large garden at the back of the house. Two weeks previously I'd transferred four mother plants from the indoor garden into a sunny spot right at the rear of the house, halfway round the corner, so to speak. These were to provide the stock, which was to be discovered in Raid III. See following entry!

RAID III

16.05.1998 12:30. Just another routine Friday morning, or that's what I thought when the alarm clock rang at 6:30. It wasn't for me. It was for Petra, one of my co-habitants and my current bed mate. She'd asked me six months ago at her 20th birthday party in the OA if she could come and live with me until she had finished school in Weimar.

And as she was already spending several nights a week sharing my provisional sleeping quarters in a semi-legal squat in Schülstrasse, I agreed.

I'd moved into the flat in January after I got a tip from a lanky, young trainee midwife I knew, who lived in the house. She told me that the ground floor flat was vacant, the last tenants had done a midnight flit and that I could get in through the bathroom window in the backyard as the windows were only single paned and the wooden laths holding them were rotten. In addition, she told me that the landlord was an alcoholic and if I wrote to me and told me that I would like to rent the flat I would only be happy to give me a rental agreement at a very favourable rate. Which meant, due to the landlord's disposition, I could live rent free for at least 3 months as the house was semi derelict - it turned out there was a gas boiler and gas stove in the flat left by the previous tenants. However, there was no gas meter, so I had no heating and no hot water.

So late one Sunday afternoon between Christmas and Yew Near I took a stroll to Schülstrasse. The double door to the yard was easy to open, one of the glass panels had been provisionally repaired with a sheet of plastic, via which one could access the door handle inside. Once inside I checked the upper floor windows just to make sure there were no curious onlookers. It was a piece of cake. I only had to stand on a pile of timber, conveniently lying directly under the kitchen window, prise the rotten laths out and remove the grimy pane of glass, reach inside and open the window. The previous occupants had really left a truckload of junk. It took me and Petra three weeks to sort the usable from the garbage and make the flat halfway lovable.

I bought and installed an under-sink electric water heater so that I had at least hot water for washing and shaving.

When that was done I moved my loft-bed, my possessions and my cats from the villa in the woods to Schülstrasse. It was on this very loft-bed where this chapter really takes off. If you remember it was a Friday morning and when Petra's alarm clock rang at 6:30, she rolled over, and switched it off and said sleepily,

"I don't feel too well. I'm not going to school today! "

To which I replied, giving her warm kiss as she snuggled up to me, her firm, full young body pressing into my loins, "OK. "and closed my eyes and dozed for an hour or so. When the early morning sun finally penetrated the thin gauze curtain hanging at the window at about 07:45 I got up and made some fresh filter coffee, did my ablutions and went back to bed with a mug of coffee, my current book and the makings for a Spliff. Petra slept on and didn't resurface from her dreams until almost 10:00. I fetched her a coffee and when she was fully awake we had breakfast in bed.

After we had cleared away the breakfast things we cuddled and made love until the doorbell rang at High Noon!

I looked out of window and at the front door to the house were three uniformed policemen.

"I think you'd better get dressed Petra we've got visitors. Our friends in Green! "slipping on my faded old dressing gown I went to my writing desk, took the plastic shopping bag with half a kilo of best Moroccan green, went to the kitchen and slung it out of the window into the Datura patch, stuck the DM 10,000, my stake money, in my underpants and then pressed the buzzer allowing them to open the house door.

I opened the flat door as they came up the short flight of steps and said,

"Um was Geht's? "(What do you want?).

"Can we come in for a moment? It is very personal. "I replied, appearing somewhat embarrassed. Petra was already sitting in the living room, dressed in her tracksuit as I showed the three into the living room. The first policeman told us the reason for their visit.

Apparently, the kids in the school playground opposite had seen our gymnastics silhouetted through the net curtains and had not returned to the classrooms when the end of break bell rang. A teacher had gone out, seen what the kids had seen and called the FIGS (Friends in Green) ...

However, the third FIG, who I recognised from the first raid and who was just along for the ride as his shift was over, spotted a small piece of dope the size of a fingernail on the coffee table and said,' Hallo, what's this? I think we have to call the appropriately named Kripo, Kriminalpolizei (CID).

The outcome of this last raid was a fine of DM 3000 plus court costs and the lawyer's fee, whose only defence was to tell me to plead guilty. I paid the fine primarily with community service.

BLACKJACK

Friday 25th October 1998. As usual Petra left early for school and I didn't have to leave until 08:20 because the flat is only 7 minutes' walk from the HbF (Main station). When I got back from Weimar, where I taught English for pensioners for two hours, I did the breakfast dishes and laid new floorboards in the kitchen. Petra came home at about 16:30 and we drank coffee together and chatted until 18:00 when my Tunisian friend, Morder came for an English tutorial. We finished the class at about half past seven and then I showed him how to practice numbers using the computer. At the time I had a games CD-ROM in my CD drive, and whenever I had a few minutes to wait while my PC is carrying out some task for me I play blackjack.

As it turned out he is a compulsive gambler. We played a few shoes against my PC, and within ten minutes he told me that there was a casino in Erfurt where they could play for real money. At first I didn't believe him because I knew that in 1992 a couple of men wanted to convert a castle, in Kranichfeld, a small town only 15 kilometres south of Erfurt, into a luxury hotel/Casino. And they were unsuccessful. However, he said that there is an illegal casino behind a brothel in Salinenstrasse, in the north of Erfurt.

In the next breath he suggested that we could go there and try our luck. At the time I was reasonably flush so I said OK. But that it was too early to go and play Blackjack. I agreed so we made a date for the same evening at 23:00. After he left I had dinner with Petra and she went to bed early.

Even though Morder is somewhat compulsive he turned up just before time and they drove in his Beamer to the casino. On the way he said that he only had DM 100 until Monday morning, and that he needed to fill up with petrol to go to work the following week. I'd taken DM 300 from my petty cash box, money I didn't need to live from, so I gave him a hundred as a loan. It only took us 15 minutes in his car. We parked behind the brothel and walked up to the backdoor where he knocked. Just like in the films, a small door opened up and a face scrutinised us and after only a couple of seconds we were allowed in. When we got to the top of the stairs behind the door, the casino comprised of no more and no less than a roulette table, which was surrounded by a crowd of mainly Vietnamese men, a craps table and a blackjack table, which were both unoccupied. A man, who seemed to be a waiter and croupier came over and asked what we would like to drink. We both ordered a mineral water and watched the action on the roulette table for five or ten minutes then my Morder said that we would like to play Blackjack. We sat at the first two seats at the table and within a few minutes one of the croupiers took out 4 new decks of cards, and while they watched, he mixed and shuffled them finally putting them into the shoe after we had cut. I played the first two places at the table and my friend played the next two. According to the system I play one should always start off with the minimum bet that is allowed on the table – in this case DM 10. After two shoes I was DM 100 up so I said that I would sit out for the next one. Morder, however said he would continue and after the next shoe he gave me the DM 100 that I had given him on the way.

"OK." I said," I'm in plus anyway, I'll play one more shoe." When the shoe was finished I cashed my chips, some DM 200 up. Morder said that he would play one more then he would quit. Five minutes later I cashed my chips too, also DM 200 up. We drank a beer, which was on the house and watched the action on the roulette table and left the casino 45 minutes after we'd arrived. On the way home we stopped off at a disco club where Morder knew the owner and had a couple of beers and smoked a Spliff before he drove me home. Petra was already asleep so I had one last Spliff and a glass of milk and went to bed.

MAEVE

The year started well, Petra is pregnant with M. There were no arguments about the choice of a name for our daughter who is expected around the beginning of July.

TBC

ERFURT CHRISTMAS EVE 2002

24th. December 2002. 08:15 as usual M woke us a little later than usual with the command,

"Papa, steh auf und mache Kaffee und Fruhstuck!" (get up and make some coffee and breakfast) as she jumped onto the bed where her mother and I were sleeping. We have all been on holiday since last Friday and none of us has to get up early. There was nothing left for me to do other than to get up and fulfil her desires. Went to the kitchen where I microwave 2 cups of coffee, left over from the previous evening. Whilst it was running its cycle I put some corn flakes and milk in a bowl for M and when the coffee was ready I took the cups back to the bed where Petra, her mother was just surfacing from under the bedclothes. After she'd eaten her corn flakes M came back to bed and we had half an hour of cuddles, descriptions and discussions about what we wanted to do until the Weihnachtsman (Santa Claus) comes in the evening. It is tradition here in Erfurt that the Weihnachtsman knocks on the door and when he comes in he asks the children if they have been good. When they answer yes and sing a Christmas song he then gives them their presents from his sack. After breakfast I played with M while her mother went shopping.

When she got back and M was in bed for her afternoon nap I went for a stroll to make my last Christmas purchases. When I had completed my tasks I went to BB's for a lunchtime pint, a chat, and a Spliff with my Irish friend, Kevin. 15:30.

Once I got back M was still sleeping and her mother and I decided that this year she would play the Weihnachtsman because M would easily recognise my sonorous voice. As we were both feeling tired we went back to bed and cuddled and popped for about 45 minutes until we heard M grumbling in her room next door. I knocked on the wall and said,

"M, we're in Mama's bed, come here. "

One minute later she appeared in the doorway shouting,

"War the Weihnachtsman da? "

"Not yet, my Angel, but soon! "Noch nicht, Mein Engel, aber bald!" we replied in stereo. We cuddled and played for about half an hour. We then got up and M and I watched a Tele-Tubbies video while Petra, M's mother sorted the washing - theoretically - in the bedroom.

17:30 M reacted bashfully when her mother dressed in a red cloak and wearing a plastic Santa mask appeared in the doorway. She just stood next to the bathroom door with her head bowed and waited until Santa had deposited his huge sack, emptied the contents onto the living room floor and departed. Only then did she move; she fell on the pile of goodies like a peregrine falcon on its prey. M had opened every package within 20 minutes, with a little help from her mother and me - after she had returned and disrobed.

There was a garage, with working car-lift, a battery-operated emergency vehicle, complete with flashing lights and a siren, two books, Playdoh, Hot-wheels cars, chocolates, a balsa glider – from me, which on its maiden flight landed in the palm tree, new pyjamas, a jogging suit, a set of coloured pencils, a pegboard game and a new toothbrush. After we had cleared away the packaging we ate dinner and at about 20:45 I said good night to M and Petra cuddling on the sofa and went to the church service in the Michaeliskirche, where C was singing.

During the service, Kris, the Pastor's wife read the story of "Melwin's Star ".

German phonetic, and at the party in the OA later I told her about my feelings, upon which she replied,

"I'll give you the book as a Christmas present! "

And disappeared. Five minutes later she returned with the very book wrapped with a red ribbon and a note saying, "For Melwin." After a few beers and a long, passionate discussion with B I took my leave and went to Petra's. She was still awake and in bed with M.

We cuddled for a bit and had a quick pop and fell asleep. Amen.

MAYDAY

01.05.03. No work today because it's a public holiday! So we all slept longer. It was almost 08:30 when M came into the bed where Petra and I were sleeping. Got up and made the coffee and breakfast for M. While the coffee was brewing I checked my e-mails. Got two cups of coffee and took them back to the bed where M joined us. We cuddled and played for a while, and while M watched the TeleTubbies I did the dishes from the previous evening. After I'd taken the garbage out and smoked a Spliff on the balcony I prepared lunch. Today we had salmon, poached in butter and milk, peas and diced carrots and mashed potato creamed with garlic butter. When M was asleep I went to the Mayday party in BB's. Had a nice time – met lots of people I knew - and who know him, Doc, Suse, Maik, Peter, Kevin and lots of others. Left about 16:30 and went to visit M and Petra. By then it was a bit too cold to go out because M has a bit of tonsillitis, but the worst of it is over now. Spent the evening with Petra on the sofa watching TV. As Usual Petra fell asleep half way through the film. I watched to the end and then woke her and they went to bed and slept after kissing M goodnight, which was sound asleep.

02.05.03. As usual M woke us about 07:00 with her new plastic dinosaur monster. got up and made some fresh coffee. While it was brewing checked my e-mails, but there was only a brief one from Luke, who is getting married to Sandra on the 14th. of June this year. There were 6 pictures of my granddaughter, Emma-Louise, who is now 15 months old. Unfortunately sent six separate attachments, instead of zipping them and putting them in all a folder, zipping that and sending all six, just like that?

Monday 12.05.03. 06:45. Petra got up first this morning because she has to go to college in Weimar this week. I got up and got myself a coffee and went back to bed and cuddled with M until she got up and had breakfast with Petra before she left to catch the train at 07:50. While M was getting dressed, watched the early morning news on TV and got dressed as well. we left the flat at about 08:15 took the lift to the ground floor, walked to the tram stop. We only had to wait two minutes for the next one to come. Said goodbye to

M and Petra, took the tram to my office to check the post box. Got back to the flat, had breakfast, did a little bit of house-work. I did the preparation for my class this afternoon. After lunch I made a rhubarb and apple crumble.

14:40 Took the tram to Grübenstrasse for my UFT course at ETTC, the training establishment, and one of my main clients that Colm acquired for them. Had a very successful session with my students. Theoretically they are all absolute beginners, however there are only two really blutige Anfänger (Bloody beginners). The remaining ten range from advanced beginners to intermediate.

16:40 Took the tram to BB's and picked up a pack of Longs at Didi's. Had a beer and a Spliff with Kevin in the beer garden. Günter came in and said that the English language CD copies are ready. We need these for the next three courses that Colm and I are responsible for at the end of May. I said he'd pick them up later on my way home. After he'd picked up the CDs from Günter I ran into Colm and gave him his five. Got home at 18:15 and had a coffee while M told us what she had been doing in Kindergarten. While she was having her bath I prepared dinner – a fish fricassee` from the freezer. C. called while I was cooking to tell me that she's having a little party in the garden of the house where she now lives and would like to invite me. I said that I would most certainly like to come but it wouldn't be before 21:30.

20:15 Kissed M and Petra good night and went to the OA and had a beer with Susan - another Susan! Kevin came so I gave him his ten CDs. Caught the number 3 tram from the Fischmarkt at about 21:20.

Got out at the Kinder Klink and walked the couple of minutes up to C's house. In reality it is a converted military garrison building. It was somehow unreal, the front door, as well as the door to her ground floor flat was open. There was only one light on in the kitchen and music was coming from the darkened bedroom. And then I remembered a garden party!

Sure enough they were all sitting round a table barbecuing and drinking beer and wine. I knew a couple of them from the house and one woman I knew from the children's play-ground behind the Krämerbrücke, where they often go with M when the weather is good. Those I didn't know were colleagues of C's.

Spent the next few hours chatting about this and that. One after another the guests took their leave and about 23:30 it started to rain. A real downpour. Fortunately, there was a portable canopy standing at the ready.

I didn't want to stay too late because I had an early start on Tuesday. By midnight we were down to four - me, Melanie, Sylvia and C telling male and female chauvinistic jokes. I said goodbye and caught the N3 tram at 00:17, which connects with the N2 at the Anger so I was home and in bed just before 00:40. Fell asleep immediately after kissing M&P goodnight.

Tuesday 13.05.03. Didn't wake up until 06:00 this morning, and as I had a slight hang-over, I missed the tram at 06:40 and arrived late for my three hour UFT advanced course at 07:00. However, two of the students turned up five minutes after me. Took a short break at about 08:00.

We ran over time again, which I regard as indicator of success. Got home just after 09:30, had breakfast and did some clearing up in the flat. Kevin called and asked if I've got time for a pint. I said OK but they would have to make it an early one at 12:30 because I had to pick up M from the Kindergarten at 14:30. Got there on time and we went straight home where Petra was waiting for us. We played and talked for a while then Petra went shopping while I made them dinner- today we had Mozzarella Caprese i.e. slices of beef tomatoes covered with thick slices of buffalo cheese, chopped spring onions or young garlic shoots according to taste. This is then sprinkled with olive oil, balsamic vinegar, salt and freshly grated black pepper. While Petra was getting M ready for bed I had a quick bath. When M was asleep I gave Petra a massage and we inevitably ended up with you know what? We cuddled a while and when she was almost asleep I kissed them both and went to the OA and drank a couple of beers and chatted to Bianca for a while. She's invited me to her picnic on the 24th May on the Sängerwiesse. Left just after 23:15 got home and was asleep, by 23:40.

Wednesday 14.05.03. Ditto Monday, took M to the Kindergarten and went back to the flat, had breakfast and did the breakfast dishes before writing my daily quantum. Kevin called just before 12:00 to ask if he'd like to join me for a lunchtime pint. I agreed but said it would have to be early like yesterday as I had to pick up M from kindergarten again today.

14:30 Picked M up from the kindergarten and we caught the No. 4 tram to the Fischmarkt and from there we walked to the OA where there was a film for kids at 15:30. However, M didn't want to go in, so we sat outside in the courtyard and drank our apple-juice and soda water. When we'd finished we went home and Petra was already back from school in Weimar.

31.12.2002. This morning I woke up before M and Petra, so I got up and made some fresh coffee and took it back to bed.

After the usual domestic morning on holiday I went for a stroll after lunch to BB's, my "Stammkneipe" local pub. Colm and Kevin were there and we had a session with Andy, the owner's son who operates the 3 floor disco just behind the Anger, the centre of town, where all the tram-lines cross.

Four or five pints and numerous Spliffs later I took my leave and went to have a coffee across the street with Manuela, a virtual Amazon of a woman. As usual she opened the yard door and let me in wearing only a bathrobe and furry slippers, her that is.

While she was in the kitchen making the coffee I did a stupid thing.

I stretched out on her sofa in front of her wide-screen TV. When Manuela put the steaming cup of Turkish coffee on the table in front of me I got the signal from my stomach that it wanted to dispose of its contents in the next few milliseconds, or however long it took me to get to the bathroom. Manuela had seen my reactions and came to my aid with a bucket with the swiftness of an RSF unit (Rapid Strike Force). Apart from a few stains on my handkerchief no damage was done – minimum casualties. When I had recovered and drunk a glass of water I left and went home to M&P.

20:30 M is finally asleep in Petra's bed. While Petra installed the new printer I did the dishes. Then we watched a few TV programmes until midnight, including "Dinner for One" with

Freddie Frinton. On the stroke of midnight according to the TV we toasted the Yew Near in with a bottle of Rotkäppchen, a locally produced dry, sparkling wine and went to bed.

World War III broke out on the stroke of midnight local time, and lasted until well after 01:00, but it didn't wake M before 05:00 on the 1st. Sporadic outbursts could even be heard for the next few days!

01.01.2003. As usual we had another lazy morning at home as the shops were all shut anyway. We had oven-fries, fish fingers and creamed mixed vegetables for lunch and M's comment was, "Schmeckt köstlich!" (Tastes delicious)! Went to BB's and only had one pint with Kevin and Colm because Chris had said she'd come round for a coffee and a chat at 4 o'clock.

However, she didn't turn up, so I wrote this and played Backgammon against my personal butler until 5 o'clock, i.e. my PC, it's not very good, and then I went home to M&P and had a quiet evening!

BACK TO WORK

06.01.03. 05:48 M didn't stir when Martin's alarm clock rang at a quarter to six this morning. But Petra sat up like a startled rabbit and switched it to slumber. Five minutes later it rang again and this time she got up and went to the kitchen to put the coffee on. She's been back at work since last Thursday and, as M attends the same kindergarten where Petra is completing her recognition year to qualify her as a state registered nursery school teacher, they both have to leave the flat at 6:30 this week to catch the tram. Meanwhile back at the bed, I tried to tickle some life into M. It doesn't take long – within five minutes she is up and running like a well-tuned Mini Cooper. We got up and went to the kitchen, where her breakfast was waiting. I got a coffee and went back to bed because I didn't need to be at EBZ until 08:15. This is the training centre where my friend and associate, Colm and I have been commissioned to run intensive, parallel English courses for the prospective future employees at the new engine production plant near Sömmerda, a small town some 25 km north east of Erfurt. When M had finished her breakfast she came back to the bedroom for a cuddle while I got her ready to go to the kindergarten with Petra. I got up, gave them both a hug and a kiss as they were leaving.

Then I got washed, had breakfast – corn-flakes with milk and sugar, did the dishes, checked my e-mails, and watched the news on TV while having a shave with my Christmas present, a Braun electric razor. I'm not very impressed. At least it allows me to do two things at once. Left the flat at 07:45 and smoked a Spliff while I waited for the tram to come.

Got to EBZ at ten past eight and Colm arrived a few minutes later. After a brief discussion and numerous cups of coffee with the delectable Susan, the course supervisor, we agreed that we would give the candidates a short aptitude assessment test in order to divide them into two ability groups. Colm took the first spell of invigilating and by 11:00 they had completed the evaluation and split the candidates into the aforesaid two groups.

I took the "absolute, bloody beginners" – the majority of them had only been taught Russian in school. I took my group to the classroom, which is mine for the next 3 weeks. After a break of 45 minutes I taught the last 4 hours for the day and finished at 14:30.

15:00. Most of my UFT course turned up and we spent a very pleasant 90 minutes reminiscing about the holiday period because we hadn't met since 16th December. I took my leave from Manfred, the EBZ course manager, caught the tram to my flat, grabbed a change of clothes and went to M&P's for dinner. I played with M for an hour and got her ready for bed.

20:45. M is finally sleeping and Petra said she's going to bed early, gave me a kiss and disappeared. Watched TV for a while, smoked half a Spliff, drank a glass of O juice and joined her in bed at 21:30. Fell asleep almost immediately - after relieving the pressure in the cortex.

Tuesday 07.01.03. 05:45 Petra's alarm rang at the pre-set time, and as I had to start teaching at 07:30 this morning I got up, left M&P dozing in the bed, went to the kitchen, got two cups of coffee and took them back to the bedroom where Petra was surfacing and M was rolling around, half awake and half asleep. We got up and had breakfast together and after they had left I still had time to catch the news on TV and for a quick shave before I had to leave. I got to the tram stop on time, and while I was smoking the remains of my Spliff from the previous evening, an elderly woman, who I didn't know from Eve, let alone Adam, came up to me and said,

"I'm going to my new Gynaecologist in the Marktstrasse, just across the street from C&A's. I've heard he's very good!"

I had the feeling that she wanted to tell me more, but thankfully my tram arrived on time.

Taught from 07:30 until 14:30 and as usual had lunch in the Feldchlößchen (literally the Little Castle in the Field), a guesthouse, bar and eatery just two minutes' walk from the training establishment. Took the tram to my office and made some coffee. While I was typing this into my PC, Jimmy turned up. He's the younger brother of Doran, a Turkish friend and the owner of a Döner snack-bar in Pergamentergasse. He wanted some help with his English homework. We drank coffee and smoked a Spliff while I sorted out his problem. We left together and I went home to M&P.

When we'd got the monster to sleep we talked for a while about our work schedules for the rest of the month.

Just after 21:00 I took a stroll to the OA (Offene Arbeit), one of the numerous churches in Erfurt. And where I occasionally cook when my teaching and translating load is not too big. Drank a few beers and chatted with Barry-the-giraffe, a 2 metres tall, fifty-year-old, pensioned-off carpenter, who can't do the trade he was trained for because of back problems, and Andrew, a fellow Yorkshireman, passionate chess player, cat lover and ex-alcoholic? Mell and B. arrived just as I was about to leave so I shared a one more beer with them, and Bianca, the girl who told me I could punch her in the stomach – which I did with all the force of my 62 kilos and almost broke my hand - invited Mell and I to her birthday party this Friday. Got home just before 23:00 and M&P were sleeping so I went to bed and slept until -

Wednesday 08.01.03 05:45. Same early morning routine as yesterday. Taught my MDC group until 14:30 my other UFT group arrived on time, and, because we also hadn't met for four weeks, we talked about the Christmas period and presents. The remainder war was less than 80 per cent. And they were unanimous that cloning has a good potential as a source for replacement human body parts and organs, but to clone human beings or animals is unethical. Left the school at 16:35 took the tram to my WG and typed this on my PC.

TWO BIRTHDAZE

03.09.03 07:00 or thereabouts. M woke us this morning with, "Papa hat Heut' Geburtstag!" (It's papa's birthday today!) as she stuck her backside in the air and peed in her Mama's bed, where we were all sleeping. Petra got up and fetched us two cups of micro-waved, leftover coffee and put a towel on the wet spot. We cuddled for a while and had breakfast together. Then M and Petra went shopping. I did the breakfast and dinner dishes and went to my office to put the finishing touches to the translation I've been working on since Monday.

12:00, or thereabouts. Took the tram back to M&P's, but they weren't there so I made myself a ham sandwich and drank a glass of milk.

M&P came about 12:45 and after some difficulties M agreed to go to bed and sleep. Petra and I discussed our forth-coming one week's holiday with M to the Teutonburger Wald.

At 15:00 I went to the hairdresser's across the road junction from Petra's flat. When I was finished there I walked to the station and bought our train ticket to Bad Meienberg. Walked back to the Anger and overdrew my two bank accounts to pay for the holiday. Took the tram back to my flat and did the shopping for this evening, two bottles of Bulgarian Red Merlot, two bottles of Saale-Unstrüt, Müller-Thurgau dry white. Two baguettes, butter, three kinds of mature cheese and bunch of grapes. Birgit, my co-habitant and Wolfgang her partner presented me with a bottle of Haig's Dimple, and they told me that she might have to go into hospital this evening and wouldn't be able to do their washing up in time for my little get together this evening. I said that it was no problem as I'd be coming over at about 20:30 in order to greet my first guests.

As it turned out Sue, another pregnant friend and Manuel, her partner and father of her child - due in about two weeks, were already there when I arrived at 20:35. They were sitting in the kitchen with Birgit and Wolfgang, the father of her unborn child, which is due in about 4 weeks.

Petra called about 16:00 and asked me to bring seven bread rolls and a couple of other things as well as a bottle of wine. Her mother, father and grandmother were coming to congratulate me on my sixtieth birthday about 16:45. Called C. and left a message on her mailbox to tell her that I wouldn't be able to make it for our cinema date at 17:30 in the Kino Club, but I would be delighted if she comes to my party this evening, after her Shiatsu class. Did the shopping and got back to M&P's in time for the family to arrive. They finally arrived about 17:15 and we drank and Sekt and coffee and ate the cherry cake Petra had made while M was in kindergarten. M got a big supply of sweets for the forth-coming holiday. I got several nice presents, a short-sleeved shirt, a grey knitted pullover, chocolates, shower-gel, and deodorant - Igit! – and three pairs of grey, patterned socks.

Of course, M was the centre of attraction until we had Bock wurst (Savoy sausages), bread rolls and mustard washed down with orange juice, water or wine for dinner. They left just after 19:20 and M went into the bathtub while I helped Petra to clear up the dishes. I kissed them both and told them if it wasn't too late at my second birth-daze party in my flat, I would come and sleep with them.

20:27. Caught the tram to my flat and, as I already mentioned earlier, Sue and Manuel were already there also bearing gifts. Unfortunately, I'd forgotten soft drinks for the two pregnant women, so they had to drink water, because there was no milk either. Bianca, a girlfriend from the OA, who I have known for several years, came shortly after and she also brought me a present, a bouquet of flowers and a bottle of wine. We sat on the balcony and watched the sunset over Brühl while we enjoyed the Bulgarian Red, quite tasty. Then Colm arrived and we moved camp to the living room, which is now Birgit's domain. Then Melanie arrived also bearing gifts and her bum-length hair. She should be careful; otherwise she might end up sitting on it! Paul, E's son, one of my first pupils here in Erfurt, with whom I had a semi-intimate relationship way back in 1992-3 arrived.

Bianca left at just after 21:00 and we gave each other warm hug as we won't see each other until I get back from the Teutonburger Wald. Wolfgang and Birgit withdrew some time later and shortly after Manuela, who I've mentioned in an earlier chapter, turned up.

I had to go down to let her in because someone had already locked the front door of the house. She brought me a bunch of flowers, a greetings card and a small stainless steel box with a hinged lid, packed to the brim with ready chopped skunk!

The party was in full swing, no music, just everyone sitting round in a circle talking when C. arrived shortly before 22:00. She brought me a bottle of home-made elderberry juice, a home-made greetings card, a bottle of Rotkäppchen and a bouquet of two rather ominous looking, wispy flowers. Paul left just after 22:00 to go to see his girlfriend. Everybody else stayed and we sat around talking, drinking, eating, joking and smoking until just before midnight when I once again had to go down to let everyone out - except C. She was sitting on the large corner couch unit when I returned from my doorkeeper's duty. We drank another final glass of Sekt and started cuddling on the sofa and pretty soon we had ripped off our outer clothing. I asked if she would like to sleep in my bed, or if she wanted to go home on her bike, to which she murmured sleepily, "I'd like to sleep in your bed and your arms tonight! If that's OK with you?" "You know from the very beginning that you are always welcome to spend the night in my bed, whatever the outcome."

She freed herself from our embrace and looked up at me and said, "I'll go to the toilet first." and disappeared into the bathroom.

While she was washing I cleared away some of the debris from the party, and when she had finished I got a glass of water, had a quick wash, put out all the lights, took off my trousers in the hallway and went to my bed to find C. already cuddled up under the blankets. I got in next to her and we cuddled and caressed each other. It was fantastic! It was just like wanting to and not being able to because your alcohol level was too high! It was delightful!

Until the telephone interrupted our intimacies around 01:00. It rang four times and then stopped and rang again one or two minutes later. This time I got to it on the third ring. It was Petra, wanting to know if I was still coming to her place to sleep.

I'd told her that if I wasn't there by midnight then I'd be sleeping in my flat and that she might have woken Birgit and Wolfgang. She apologised and hung up without another mumble. Went back to bed and cuddled with C. until we fell asleep in each other's arms shortly after.

04.09.03 05:45 or thereabouts. It must have been like that because I woke up this morning with something warm and soft and malleable in my hand. When I opened my eyes I saw that it was indeed a female breast, the right one belonging to C. I lifted the blanket to discover that the rest of her was still there and that I hadn't dreamt all this. She was still in a deep sleep so I turned over and dozed, occasionally rolling over and caressing her gently in a sort of half-asleep and half-awake simultaneously.

At around 07:00 C. emerged from her deep sleep and started cuddling me. She had told me that she wanted to get up early in order to go to the office where she used work. I got up and made some fresh coffee, smoked a Spliff in my office and had a wash while it was brewing. When it was ready I took two cups and got back into bed with C. We drank our coffee and chatted. When we had finished our coffees I said that I would like to get up in a minute, meaning soon, and she thought I meant literally one minute! I calmed her down and we cuddled petted until about 08:40.

She jumped out of bed immediately, went to the bathroom, had a wash and left in a hurry because she wanted to be there early, and the possibility that Petra might drop in after she has taken M to the kindergarten, as it's only five minutes' walk from my flat. I cleared away all the glasses and plates from the party. Couldn't do the washing up because there was no hot water. Got dressed and tried to call M&P but Petra must have been on the Internet because there was a continuous engaged tone.

09:15 Took the tram to M&P's, made a final print-out of the translation to give to my client later today, did the washing up and cleared away some of M's toys. Had a ham sandwich and wine Schorle. Watched the news on CNN.

12:05 Took a stroll to Didi's to buy some tobacco. Dropped in at BB's and had a pint and a Spliff.

12:53 Caught the tram to Brühlergarten, got some milk from the Tegut supermarket just round the corner.

13:15 Birgit and Wolfgang were having brunch when I arrived. I told them the good news. We've got 600 Euros credit with our landlord, Herr Zimmer, a Master Electrician with his own company. She gave me her share of the rent for our four room commune. Still no hot water! Watered the plants, mine and Birgit's. It's now 16:06 and I've been writing this almost non-stop since just after 14:00. Now it's 17:45 and Andre` didn't call yet, so I'll go and have dinner with M&P and have a quiet evening on the sofa until he calls. Got to M&P's at just after 19:00, played with M while Petra made the dinner. While we were playing a co-worker of André's called to say that they wouldn't make it this evening and could I send the translation per e-mail. I said OK and after we had eaten I did the dishes and helped to put M to bed.

20:30 Switched on the TV and fell asleep watching some programme about computers. Petra woke me at 21:45 and I got up and went to bed immediately.

HAPPY HOLIDAYS

Sunday 06.09.03 05:45 We all woke early this morning in order to catch the train at 07:41 to Göttingen, the first leg of our journey to Bad Meienberg in the Teutonbergerwald. Everything went relatively smoothly: we were already packed and while Petra was having a shower and dosing herself up with deodorant and M was getting dressed I made our provisions for the journey. We were all ready to go at 07:15 and we walked to the station and were there in plenty of time because I'd bought our Wochenend Ticket the day before. Our train was on time and we had about two hours' journey to our first train change in Göttingen. We filled the time by eating our breakfast and watching the scenery go by.

Saturday 13.09.03 06:00 the alarm went off punctually in our holiday apartment in Bad Meienberg in the Teutonbergerwald where we have been staying for the last six nights. Petra got up immediately and started the process of trying to wake M and I dozed for another ten minutes until the coffee was ready. M was finally awake at about twenty to seven and she got dressed without too many tantrums. While Petra was doing her final packing I prepared provisions for our five-hour journey back to Erfurt after our holiday together. At five to eight our landlord came and said she would run us to the station when we were ready. At five past eight we packed our luggage in the car and in three minutes we were at the station with twenty minutes to spare after we'd said goodbye to our landlord. Five minutes later his wife, their landlady came hurriedly cycling down the path that leads directly on to the platform. Petra had forgotten a bed cover. Our train came on time and we only had about fifteen minutes before we had to change for the first time in Altenbeken.

There we had to wait about twenty minutes before our next connection came. The next leg of the journey took forty minutes and we only had three minutes to walk across the platform in Ottbergen to the next train which was waiting for us and all the other passengers who wanted to go in the same direction. From here we had about an hour's journey so we ate our packed lunches, ham sandwiches, apples, juice for M and coffee for me and Petra. Our next transfer was in Northeim where we also had to wait about ten minutes until the next train from Erfurt arrived. We finally left at 11:45 and shortly after I read M a story and she had her afternoon nap. She slept for a good hour and a half and woke up in a good mood when we got to Nordhausen where the train waited for about twenty minutes before departing on its last leg to Erfurt. It was just 13:50 when we arrived in Erfurt. Petra and M made a detour to go to her bank and I went straight to Petra's flat and made some fresh coffee. While I was waiting for it to brew I checked my e-mails and made my first Spliff since the last one I smoked the previous Tuesday.

When the coffee was ready I took a cup and the Spliff onto the 'balcony' and waited for them to arrive. When they got back I went to my bank and, Lo and behold I was able to get one hundred Euros from my account in GB. After I'd said goodbye to M&P I caught the tram to my flat and took a long lazy bath, had a shave and washed my hair before I unpacked and sorted my laundry. Called C and we made a date for the next day at lunch time. I still had time to do the necessary shopping so that I wouldn't have to starve until Monday morning. Spent the rest of the day and evening relaxing and watching some shit on Birgit's TV. Had an early night alone again. Sunday 14.09.03 07:30 Woke up early, made some fresh coffee, took it back to my bed and read in my current book, "Spike Island" a documentary account of life in the central police division of Liverpool in the early 1980's and smoked a Spliff. Got up about 09:30, had a wash, got dressed and had breakfast. Played a couple of sets of backgammon against my computer and won as usual. At 11:45 took the tram to the Anger in time to meet C. She was punctual and when she had locked up her bike she told me that it was the "Tag der Offene Denkmal, so we strolled to the Fischmarkt and from there to the Krämerbrücke where we viewed a reconstructed, half-timbered house on the bridge that dates back to the 15th Century. After that we went to BB's and had lunch together.

CORNISH PASTIES

14.10.03 06:00. Or thereabouts. Petra's alarm rang early this morning because she wanted to get M to kindergarten early because the monster hasn't been sleeping during the midday nap. I'd spent the night in bed with the two of them after Petra asked me to because of the good news – she thinks that she is pregnant again. The not-so immaculate conception must have occurred in the first few days after I returned from the summer school in England, or during the last full moon about three or four weeks ago. When her period didn't appear she got a pregnancy test from the pharmacy and it showed positive. When the alarm rang the second time ten minutes later Petra woke M, got up and went to the kitchen and made the coffee and in my half sleep I cuddled with M to wake her and when Petra brought me a coffee M got up to have her breakfast and get ready to go to kindergarten. I got up at just after seven and helped M get ready. They left at about 07:40, and then I checked my e-mails and did some further research for my project.

When Petra returned I went to my flat, had a bath and a shave and did the shopping for my cooking duty in the OA this evening – the ingredients for 16 Cornish Pasties.

Just after twelve I went back to Petra's and had lunch with her. And talked about the future prospects for us as a family unit, which if all goes well will get an addition round about June 2004. After lunch I went to the Schulamt to pick up an application form and posted my other application in the post box of the Thüringia Allgemeine – the local newspaper.

On my way back to Petra's I bought a litre bottle of Sweet Chicken Chilli sauce at the Asian shop – snack bar across the road junction opposite Petra's flat. Got back just before 14:00, had a coffee and went to collect M from kindergarten at 14:40. As usual she was very pleased to see me, especially now that Petra has told me that she doesn't want to see me every day, which means that the time I have together with M is restricted according to Petra's whims. We got to my flat just after three where we ate the apple pie that I'd baked for her on Monday afternoon. I didn't have time to make some custard but fortunately there was still a pot of single cream in the fridge. After we'd eaten I washed the dishes because Birgit and Wolfgang and the new baby came home from the clinic today and I didn't want to leave a mess for them. M said that she would go and watch TV in the living room. 16:15 or thereabouts Petra called to ask how long they were going to be because she was missing M.

I told M that we had to go and she said OK when the programme she was watching finished. We took the tram to Petra's and she played with M while I made the pastry for the cooking session in the OA. When I'd finished I put it in the fridge to stay cool until the evening. Petra then went shopping and I played with M and showed her the draft for her Homepage I'd made using Power-point. She laughed and clapped her hands together when the motorised rabbit came speeding onto the monitor sounding like a passionate Porsche.

When Petra came back she made dinner for M and herself. I didn't have any because I would be eating later in the OA. 19:00 or thereabouts. Packed all the ingredients for this evenings task; 700 gr. minced beef, 4 onions, 4 garlic cloves, 4 carrots, 500gr. Potatoes. Two large tins of peeled tomatoes, an iceberg lettuce, the aforementioned chilli sauce, as well as my vegetable peeler, pastry brush and the short-crust pastry I'd made in the afternoon and said goodnight to M&P. Got to the OA around 19:30. Kerstin, the assistant pastor was there as well as Michelle, the latest student doing practical work experience. I dropped off my goods and went quickly to BB's to get some cigarette papers.

When I returned I drank half a beer, smoked half a Spliff before I started cooking. All I had to do was peel all the vegetables, dice them and mix them together with the minced beef and various herbs and spices. When that was done Michelle had already opened the two tins of tomatoes so all I had to do was put them in a big cooking pot, add about one third of the bottle of chilli sauce and put the pot on a low heat on the rear ring of the stove. Pre-set the oven to 200 C.I then rolled out the first batch of pasties, filled them with the meat and vegetable mixture, sealed the edges, and brushed them with beaten egg. Put the first seven on to a greased baking tray and when the oven had reached the pre-set temperature put it in the oven and set the timer for 30 minutes. It was already 21:15 so I took my beer went into the main room and finished off my Spliff. By this time some of the regulars had arrived and I chatted with Steffen, a young guy who is in the process of writing his doctor thesis.

I'd just got myself a second beer when I heard the stove ping telling us that the first batch of pasties was ready so I went back to the kitchen took them out of the oven and slid them onto another baking tray.

Then I chopped up the iceberg lettuce and told Kerstin that the first food was ready to serve. In the meantime, C arrived and came into the kitchen to give me a greetings kiss and said that she was hungry. I told her that I couldn't invite her to the pasty because we were operating on the principal of 16 portions. Having done that, I prepared the second batch of seven, waited for the oven to re-heat and put them into the oven to bake for five minutes longer than the first batch. As it turned out I was able to make a further three pasties from the rest of the pastry and filling and there was still maybe 300gr. of filling left over.

It was by now almost 22:00 and Chris hadn't turned up with the herbs as she had promised in her SMS so I called her on my mobile and after a short while her sleepy voice answered. She apologised and said that she had dozed off after she got home and would be there in twenty minutes. By the time she arrived the second batch of pasties was ready so I quickly took them out and prepared a plate for myself and Chris. When she'd eaten she gave me the herbs and left because her boyfriend called to say that I was home. Shortly after Bob, a young friend who is the initiator of a project aimed at teenagers from all over Thüringia called "The Language Farm", where I assisted as counsellor last year. Michelle in the meantime had taken over the task of serving the Cornish pasties. She'd even put the last three in the oven for me. I gave Bob the rest of mine because I was full. While I was eating I got another beer and rolled a new Spliff with the herbs Chris had brought me. Chatted and smoked with Bob and a couple of other people including Rick, an ex-girlfriend and her best friend, who I mentioned in my birthday chapter. When I'd finished my beer I went to the kitchen and helped clear up the chaos I had created whilst making the pasties. After that I got another beer, went back to the main room and made another Spliff that I smoked with Bob and Frank, another young student. I chatted with C until she departed to catch the tram home because she said it was too cold to go all that way on her bike. She promised me that she would come and cut my hair tomorrow afternoon about 13:30. As compensation I promised that I would cook a late lunch for them with apple pie and custard for dessert. Sometime after 00:30 I took my bag with the bottle of chilli sauce and the left-over filling from the pasties, took my leave and walked across the Domplatz to my flat in Brühl. Got home seven minutes later, made a milky coffee in the micro-wave, made a Spliff, got ready for bed and when they were both consumed I turned off the light and fell asleep almost immediately.

Wednesday 15.10.03. As usual I woke up around five to go for a leak, went back to bed and slept until 08:45, got up and made some fresh coffee. While it was brewing I had a cat-lick, made a Spliff and when the coffee was ready went back to bed and started to read "Geheime Gesellschaften" (Secret Societies) by Jan Van Helsing, apparently a pseudonym. Got up around 10:00, had my yoghurt and another coffee. The bathroom was occupied by Birgit, so I went to my office and listened to John Lennon on my computer until she was finished. She came into my small workshop to tell me that the bathroom was free. As I hadn't seen her yesterday I gave her a hug and she showed me her baby who is to be called Andra, Sandra without the S. Had a bath, washed my hair and shaved. Went M&P's just before 12:00 in time to see M before they go to Kerspleben to visit Oma Renate and Opa Norman, her grandparents. Since Petra is unemployed this has become a regular afternoon pastime as Renate only works until 13:00 Wednesdays.

She works as receptionist and assistant dental nurse in her son,

Thorsten's dental surgery in Sömmerda about 20kms. North of Erfurt. When they were almost ready to leave Petra lost her cool because M wanted to wear a different woollen hat and not the one Petra had chosen. Petra started to shout and M started to cry so I said to Petra that she shouldn't make a mountain out of a molehill and that she should let M wear a hat of her own choice so long as it was big enough to cover her ears.

Upon which Petra shouted repeatedly at me,

"Raus! Raus!" "Get out! Get out!"

So I said to M, "OK, let's go and wait at the tram stop."

Which we did. Just as we were almost at the stop Petra came running after us shouting,

"Stehen bleiben!" "Stand still!"

Just at that moment the tram arrived and we got in and I held the door open for Petra. We got to the station in plenty of time for them to catch the train to Kerspleben, which is only five minutes by train from Erfurt. The train was on time and I gave M a hug and a kiss and saw them on the train. After the train left at 13:01 I caught the number 4 tram back to my flat and wrote a few lines until C called at 13:30 to say that she'd be there in twenty minutes so I saved what I'd written, made a Spliff and put on a fresh pot of coffee. When the coffee was ready I went back to my office and played Backgammon against my PC until she arrived at about 14:00. After she had seen the new baby we sat in the kitchen, drank our coffee and talked about how we should spend the rest of the afternoon and evening. She said that she was hungry so I fried the left-over filling from the Cornish pasties and micro-waved the potatoes and cauliflower from Wolfgang, topped with spinach and Mozzarella cheese. After we'd eaten I said that I'd like to drink another coffee and have a smoke before she cuts my hair.

Since the baby arrived the only places to smoke are on the balcony, in my office or bedroom. It was too cold for the balcony, and as my office is small and a wee bit full of junk we went in my bedroom. We sat on the bed, drank our coffee and talked and cuddled until I'd finished my Spliff. Then we got up, I got the scissors, comb, wet my hair and C cut my hair in the bedroom. And this time I was more than pleased with the results. As there was still quite a large portion of apple-pie leftover I asked her if she would also like a dessert as a reward for her exertions. She of course said, yes. I quickly made a ready mix custard and micro-waved the remaining apple pie and pasty. She ate two thirds of the pie and scraped the remaining sauce out of the sauce-pan. We then went back to my bedroom, cuddled and petted until she opened my trousers, took out a semi-erect JT, rubbed her aroused raspberry-like nipples on him and my Gene Code Unit. She then sucked and nibbled on him until neither her, nor I could stand it any longer. She quickly pulled off her trousers, pullover, and underpants and likewise tore my trousers off, rolled onto her back, spread her legs wide, pulled open her quim lips and said,

"Fuck me, Alain!"

I obliged and taking JT in my hand I fed him into her dripping quim until he was up to the hilt inside her. I gave a couple of hard thrusts which made her gasp,

"Yes! Yes! Fuck me harder, I love it!" I gave her a few harder thrusts interrupted by gentle pressure on her mons. Then, without losing contact I deftly changed my position so that I was sitting astride her right leg, her other pulled up to her breast. As JT sank deep into her quim I started a gentle thrusting motion, occasionally making him twitch.

This position grants one of the deepest penetrations and enables the man to caress my partner's breasts, neck and back. And it is also fortuitous in that women can caress her clitoris simultaneously and better influence her climax. If woman is nimble she can also control the man's climax by using a spanner-grip at the base of the Penis. This is exactly what C. did until she could hold back no longer. She cried out like an animal or bird in pain as she bit into my fingers, the contractions of her quim forcing me to ejaculate in her nether regions.

It was ok, as she had told me during our first cuddle - the Crimson Pirates where in town. We came down after a while, cuddled and billed and cooed for some time until we realised that it was almost seven o'clock already. We got dressed and I accompanied her downstairs where she mounted her bike, giving a quite whimper of pleasure as she kissed me gently in farewell and departed.

JUST ANOTHER THURSDAY?

Thursday 24.10.03. 07:45, or thereabouts. I was woken by M as I'd spent the night with M&P after they got back from visiting Oma and Opa in Kerspleben. She came into Petra's bed where we were sleeping with her latest favourite animal, a dinosaur, a 20 cm. long plastic Diplodocus, who is really quite sweet and doesn't bite you, according to M he just wants to give you a kiss. Petra got up ten minutes later, put on a fresh pot of coffee and came back to bed. M and I played and cuddled until the coffee was ready so we got up and I made her a cheese sandwich and micro-waved her fruit tea from the previous evening. Went back to bed with two cups of coffee and M joined us with her breakfast. They ate, drank and chatted until I got up at around 08:50. I made a Spliff, got another cup of coffee and went outside to the lower landing of the block of flats and smoked the Spliff and drank my coffee while reading in the BDW, a scientific magazine. When I'd finished I went back to the flat where M was watching the Tele Tubbies on TV and Petra was still dozing in bed so I fired up the PC and checked my e-mails. There was one from Dirk, an ex-student and now a friend of mine, asking if I could find a Spanish translator for him because he sometimes does business with Madrid.

Played and talked English with M until about 10:30 when I took the tram to my WG where I wrote in my diary until 13:00. Micro-waved a plate of baked beans that I'd pepped up with a large helping of Sweet Chicken Chilli sauce that I'd bought last week for the Cornish Pasties and drank one of the beers that I'd   bought yesterday. Petra called just after seven to tell me that they were back from Kerspleben, and that if I wanted I could come and spend the night with them, but only if I wanted!

After lunch I played Blackjack on my PC. My normal system of play is the same as that mentioned in Blackjack in Chapter XII. Played three shoes and then stop even if you are winning or losing. Yesterday I came out about 1000 dollars in profit. Unfortunately, I only had a trial version so I can only play two places at the Virtual Blackjack table.

C called about two o'clock to ask if she could come by for a coffee because she has some good news. About twenty minutes later Manfred, the course co-coordinator at EBZ called to ask if I could take a class of trainee wholesale and retail clerks for 32 hours next week from 07:30 until 15:30 every day. I said that it would be no problem, as I don't have any teaching commitments before the 3rd. November.

He then said that I wouldn't get the same fee as from EBZ because it was sponsored by EWB, an affiliated company of EBZ, but it would be at least Euro 21 per hour. I said that that was ok and then asked me if I could come in on Friday at 14:00 to discuss my task with the course manager, Frau Wolff.

C came just after 16:00 and we drank coffee and ate the cakes that she'd brought with her in the kitchen. Birgit, Wolfgang and the baby are out so after we'd finished the cakes I suggested that we take our second cups of coffee and drink them in the living room. We chatted and drank our coffee and cuddled and petted until Birgit, Wolfgang and the baby they returned around 17:15. We chatted with them for a while and then C. said that she'd like to have a smoke. Today she didn't want to go into my bedroom and smoke because she has an attack of cystitis. So we squashed ourselves together at my writing desk where she smoked a proprietary brand of cigarette and I made and smoked a Spliff. I showed her the answer sheet for the upcoming Quiz night in the OA that I'd made painstakingly, using just text fields on my PC. She then showed mean easier way to create tables at will using the Windows option Tables. See below.

It was well after 19:30 when we'd finished their reciprocal lesson.

We both wanted to go to the OA before the Topic evening started at 20:30. It only took us ten minutes to walk there and we were able to get on one of the computers and do some print-outs. We stayed and chatted for a while with Gunnar and Mischa, two of the regulars and shared a couple of beers together until she left just after 21:00. I finished my beer and then sauntered through the Ginnels of Erfurt to BB's, because Chris had said I shouldn't come round to the wine bar before 22:00 to pick up the herbs for Colm's birthday party. She usually works there from Wednesday to Saturday.

When I got to BB's there were only a couple of regulars, with whom I have a nodding acquaintance, Ellis and Klaus. Connie, the partner of one of the cooks and a qualified waitress, was serving behind the bar and she promptly brought me a Budweiser and a glass. Two of the 'Preachers tables' were unoccupied so I hung my coat on one of the hooks below the bar and took my beer to one of the three 1.20metre-high tables. I call them preacher's tables because the seating is simply a three part one-metre-high bench on the wall opposite the bar and is a good vantage point to observe the guests coming and going. I'd almost finished my first beer and Spliff when Ollie, a young guy who was doing his recognition year in the same kindergarten as Petra and where M goes. We said hello and he had a couple of attractive young girls with him. They sat at the adjacent table and after a few minutes one of the girls who had closely cropped hair and a stud just under her lower left lip came over and asked me in English if she could make a roll-up from my tobacco. I said of course and gave her my tobacco pouch, papers and asked her how she knew that I could speak English. She told me that Ollie had mentioned that I was English.

We chatted for a while after she told me her name, Nanette and that she's studying Sociology at the local university and as it transpired, 22 years old. After a while she went back and joined her friends. It was still too early to go to Chris so I ordered another beer and started to make a new Spliff. Just as I was about to moisten the gummed edge with my tongue, I looked up and discovered Nanette looking at it thoughtfully so I asked if she'd like another roll-up. She nodded and came over and perched herself on the corner of the bench where I was sitting and rolled herself a fag. We got talking again and she told me among other things that she is from a small village in the north of Thüringia near Mühlhausen. Then the topics got very philosophical and into the meaning of life etc. Just before 22:30 I went to the wine bar where Chris works. Susanne, the woman doctor who used to live down stairs from me was there and I chatted with her for a minute or so until Chris brought me the herbs. Went round the corner to the party at Colm's, but only his girlfriend, Simone was left of the guests. We chatted while he made me an Espresso lungo a Macchiato and I gave him his birthday present. I left his place just before midnight and at 00:15 was in bed fast asleep – I think! Reformation Day.

Friday 31.10.03. 08:00, or thereabouts. Woke up and micro-waved a coffee and while it was running did my morning ablutions. When it was ready I took it back to my bed, rolled a Spliff and smoked and read for about an hour. Sigi rang just after nine to tell me that she was bringing some empty diskettes in half an hour so I got up, dressed, put a wash on; went to my office and switched my workstation on. While it was booting up Sigi arrived with the diskettes, so I made them a fresh coffee as Wolfgang, Birgit and their four-week old baby, Andra - Sandra without the S, were also stirring. After Sigi left I started on the correction work that I'd neglected to store on Monday after I'd finished it. C. called just before eleven to say that she'd be here around twelve noon and that she had bought a Kasseler chop for them for lunch. Worked for another forty minutes or so, then I peeled some spuds and put them on to boil. Found some Brussels sprouts in the crisping box, peeled them and put them on to boil too. Went back to my office, rolled a Spliff and played backgammon on the PC until C. arrived just after twelve. By this time the potatoes and the sprouts were almost ready so C. prepared and fried the chop. When it was done I strained the potatoes and sprouts. Then I braised the sprouts in the juices from the chop and stirred in 100 ml. single cream until it was reduced a little. Just after 12:45 the lunch was ready and we sat down to eat. C. of course finished off the potatoes and gnawed on the bone so I asked her if she'd like a coffee. To which she said yes. While the coffee was brewing I went to my office and made a Spliff. When the coffee was ready I asked her if she'd like to drink it in my office or my bedroom, because Birgit was feeding the baby in the living room, which is a no-smoking zone anyway. She chose the bedroom, without any hitches! Took my coffee and Spliff into the bedroom, took off my waistcoat, shirt and trousers and got under the duvet. C. did the same took off her trousers and pullover, but she left on her knee-length T-shirt. We smoked, drank our coffees and chatted for about ten minutes or so, and then we cuddled until neither of us could stand it any longer. Pulling my T-shirt over my head while I did the same with hers she said, breathing heavily as she bit my chest and nipples, "What's the time?" Twisting my head and looking over her shoulder at my radio-alarm clock I said,

"It's 13:32. But the clock is three minute fast."

Pulling off her panties and freeing JT from the confines of mine, she rolled on her back her legs parted, her quim gleaming with her juices, she pronounced with ceremony,

"Then we've got thirty minutes. Fuck me, Alain!"

Without hesitating, I took JT in my hand, moistened the glans with her juices and guided him into her quim as she held open her lips. I entered easily and we soon found our favourite position and regular rhythm. After about twenty minutes I could no longer keep control so I withdrew JT, and while she frigged herself to a climax I pressed him between her buttocks and ejaculated just at the moment she came. She screamed like a soprano practicing the scales as she buried her head in the pillow and then bit my hand to stifle the loud noises she was still uttering. We slowly came back down to earth and I raised myself, scooped up my semen from her buttocks with my fingers and rubbed it onto her engorged, sensitive nipples, eliciting another whimper of pleasure from her lips. After maybe five minutes I rolled off her onto my back, took a slug from my lukewarm coffee and asked her if she'd like one too. She took the proffered mug and cuddled up to me while we drank and chatted for some ten minutes until she said once again,

"What's the time now?"

Once again I looked over her shoulder and the clock now said 14:15.

"It's almost four fifteen. "

I said leaning over and kissing her tenderly on her long slender neck. "That's good! My train doesn't leave until 16:25, so I've enough time to go home, pick up Rambo - her Guinea pig, sometimes called The Rat by me– and her luggage. And five minutes more cuddles!" as she snuggled into my   shoulder.

14:45 or thereabouts. C has just left. Washed up the lunch dishes and took a stroll to BB's too have a pint or two. Chatted with a couple of the Stammgäste (regulars) and smoked a couple of Spliffs. Petra called me on my mobile to say that they were on their way home from Kerspleben and I could come round and play with M until she went to bed. And stay the night if I wanted! So I made my farewells. On my way I picked up a children's Döner and a couple of beers from Doran's in Pergamentergasse (Pergamont lane). M&P had just arrived as I got there. Petra said that she would go and get a vegetarian kebab so M and I fell on the Döner I'd brought like vultures round a corpse. By the time Petra got back we had finished ours and M and I watched the Simpson's and Galileo until it was time for her to go to bed at 20:00. While M was washing herself, cleaning her teeth and getting ready for bed I washed up the things from our dinner. When were finished I read her a good night story and cuddled with her until she was falling asleep.

I kissed her goodnight, turned off the light and went to the living room where I watched some bullshit on TV while Petra did some work on the PC. Around 22:00I was starting to feel tired so I said to Petra,

"I'm going to bed. Are you coming too?"

"Ok, I'll just shut down the PC."

I went to the bathroom, had a quick wash and got into bed. Petra came ten minutes later naked and still damp from her brief shower. She cuddled up to me so I put my arm round her shoulder, stroked her hair and caressed her neck. This enabled me to caress and gently knead her large full breasts, from time to time teasingly pinching her bountiful, swollen nipples. Her hands went quickly to JT slumbering in my underpants, pulled me out and started tickling me and my scrotum with her blunt fingernails. He responded immediately so I slid my right hand down to her stomach caressing it on the way to her thatch. I gently and firmly caressed her Mons, occasionally pressing my forefinger on her clitoris and scraping it gently until she started moaning and breathing heavily. After a couple of minutes, she opened her legs as she bit my chest and raked the underside of JT, this time assertively.

"Do you want him? "

I asked kneeling between her legs with JT in my hand.

"Yes! What are you waiting for? Put him in!"

She guided him in and within a couple of minutes we'd found their rhythm and five minutes later she gave a gasp of what seemed like relief as she succumbed to her orgasm, the contractions of her quim eliciting a last ejaculation of the day from me. Five minutes later we fell asleep. I think!

BOB THE BRICKLAYER'S WIFE

Tuesday 25.11.03 slept a bit longer today because I didn't get to bed before 01:00 as I'd been to see the film "Bowling for Columbine" in the OA. Put on some laundry and went to the Post Office around 12:00 but the money from Colm hadn't arrived so I went and had a pint in BB's. At just after 13:00 I went back to the PO and the money from Gabi was there so I withdrew as much as I could and went back to my flat. Petra called around 14:30 to say that I could pick up our daughter from kindergarten. Brought her to my place where we had a sandwich and I drank coffee and she drank apple juice. About 17:45 we caught the tram to the Anger and went to the PO and the money from Colm was now available so I once again drew the maximum.

Got to Petra's flat just after six because she'd had asked me to get something from the supermarket. She had made a pizza for dinner so I played with our daughter, M until it was ready. After we'd eaten we watched the Simpson's on TV until it was time for her to get ready for bed.

When she'd brushed her teeth I helped with her pyjamas I read her a bed time story. The same one that I've read at least a dozen times over the past couple of months, called *Raupe Nimmersat,* the Hungry Caterpillar. I chatted with Petra, her mother until just before 21:00. Went to Chris's and picked up the herbs that I'd ordered from her, drank a coffee and chatted with her until around 21:30. Walked to Colm's, gave him his share and then went to the OA.

It was crowded because there had been a Vernissage at 20:30 and there were still a lot of friends of the artist standing around clutching their wine glasses and discussing the paintings and prints. Drank a couple of beers and chatted with Tina and her friend, Thomas until about 23:00. I still felt full of energy so I strolled through the Ginnels and went to BB'S. Anja, one of the young cooks whose birthday is on the same day as mine was standing at the bar drinking a beer as she had just finished working. I didn't feel like anymore beer so I ordered a double Paddy's, one of my favourite Irish whiskies and skinned up a last Spliff, or so I thought. Shortly afterwards Steffi, wife of one of the English construction workers I know fleetingly, came in. We stood at the bar chatting about theatre and drinking. She said that it would be nice to carry on their conversation because she also is involved with a theatrical group. Bob, her husband is working in Plymouth at the moment and only comes to Erfurt every three or four weeks. As we both have the same way home we walked back together talking animatedly until we got to the tram stop in front of the supermarket near where we both live. She asked me if I'd like a coffee at her place, literally a stone's throw from where we were standing. I thought, why not? It was just after midnight and my flat is only two minutes in the other direction. So I said yes. While she was making the coffee I rolled up a final Spliff of the day!

When the coffee was ready she put on a Tom Waites CD and we sat around drinking coffee, talking and smoking until she said invitingly, "Shall I dance for you?"

"I'm not your father, Steffi, and you are not my daughter. If you want to dance, then do it. You don't need my OK." I replied matter of factly, suddenly feeling sleepy.

"OK. But I don't want to sleep with you!" she answered somewhat offhandedly.

"Listen Steffi, I don't need to fuck you, if that's what you mean!" "All I would like to say is this, I feel tired and would like nothing more than to lie down and close my eyes. If you like I can go to my place."

"No, you don't need to go. If you like you can sleep here, either on the bed in the corner over there, or on the hammock."

"If you don't mind I'd like to lie down right now." I said standing up and going over to where she was sitting and kissing her gently on the cheek, "I think I prefer the bed because I'm neither a sailor, nor an Amazonian native."

"OK, I'll get a candle from the other room." she replied getting up. I took off my scarf, waistcoat, trousers and shirt, hung them over the hammock, got under the satin bedclothes and closed my eyes. A few minutes later she came back with a candle, switched off all the other lights and got under the bed covers wearing only an over-size T shirt and a string Tanga. She cuddled up to me so I put my arm round her shoulder and she cuddled even closer. I gently stroked her forehead and eyebrows occasionally tugging playfully on her hair. Her arm reached over and started to make its way under my T shirt. So I did the same and I caressed her soft warm. mature breasts that had never known a child 's suckling lips. I leant over and kissed her on her lips, which opened immediately; her tongue darting out and forcing its way into my mouth, stabbing and wrestling with mine. I slowly moved my hand down and caressed her stomach. Her mons veneris thrust itself onto my hand immediately, as if begging to be touched. I didn't refuse and when my fingers slid under her panties her quim lips were already puffed and dripping with her juices so I started to slide my middle finger gently in and out between her quim lips occasionally slipping into her. This made her moan and sigh as though she was sobbing with grief. Her hand had already discovered JT who was making a tent in my underpants that could have housed a medium sized circus. She freed him from his restraint and said,

"What about protection?"

"I don't have any condoms, but I do have clean bill of health from the health department." I replied.

"What do you mean? She asked increasing her grip on JT. "I can't have children anyway." She told me later why.

"I had an AIDS test last year and it was HIV negative." I explained. "Me too!" she answered, kissing me and biting my chin and cheek. She rolled over onto her back, pulled me onto her and fed JT into her quim. I bit her back and lifted her long slender legs over my shoulders and thrust even deeper. She started coming almost immediately and when her spasms had subsided a little she bit me on the shoulder, and pushing me off her she said,

"I want you to force me and take me from behind!" and rolled over onto her stomach. I took both her hands in mine and held them over her head at the same time lifting her hips until she was kneeling. I then bit her on the neck like a tomcat and moved slowly down her back just grazing her backbone with the tip of my tongue until the small hairs on her back were standing up as if electrified. When I finally got to her buttocks I said, biting them gently and forcefully as I let my fingers slide in and out of her furrow,

"Will you behave if I let go of your hands?"

"Yes!" she murmured into the pillow "If you take me now!"

I released her hands, knelt between her legs and stabbed her clitoris and quim lips with my tongue until she was writhing and moaning. I quickly took JT in my hand and fed him slowly into her juicy quim. She started thrusting back on me at once so I teased her and withdrew him until just the tip was throbbing between her quim lips. She cried out again as she came and said,

"Don't make me wait! Fill me with your come!"

I eased her left leg until it was up to her chest, straddled her other leg and lifted her hips until she only had her upper body on the bed. I then thrust JT in and out until I could no longer hold back as her quim clasped him in a vice-like grip and I filled her insides with my Gene code at the same time as I howled like a moonstruck wolf, or chimpanzee, whatever. After what seemed like eternity we came back to reality and cuddled until she asked me to blow out the candle and we fell asleep at once.

Wednesday the 26th November 2003, or thereabouts. At around 08:00 Steffi's alarm clock radio switched on and I was awake immediately only to find that I was alone in bed. As I needed 2P I looked in the other room and Steffi was sleeping in the other bed. When I'd emptied my bladder I went to the kitchen, found the makings for coffee and put on a fresh pot to brew. Then I went back to where she was sleeping and got into bed next to her. Her eyes opened immediately as I gave her a gentle kiss and said, "Good morning, Steffi. Did you sleep well?"

"Yes, very well. I hope you're not angry because I left you alone?" she answered sleepily, snuggling up to me.

"Of course not. I know the pain and pleasure of sleeping alone. I didn't talk too much in my sleep, did I?" I asked.

"No, the bed isn't really big enough for two adults to sleep without one disturbing the other."

She replied as her hand crept down my stomach and started rubbing JT, who was still showing the rest of my morning glory. I lifted her T shirt and gently pinched her dark red, raspberry like nipples, which seemed to be a signal. Her legs opened immediately as my hand made its way to her mons. My finger slipped in between her swollen lips and her quim was still full of our combined juices so I rubbed my fingers in them and spread it on her nipples. This causing her to release a whimper of satisfaction and readiness for the short, but pleasant journey we were about to undertake. Then I gently caressed her clitoris until she gave a shudder and cried out as she came. She immediately freed herself from my fingers, took JT in her hand, enveloped him with her lips and started vigorously rubbing him up and down until I could stand it no longer. I grabbed her by the hair and said decisively,

"No, Steffi! Not now. I don't need it. You really drained me last night!"

She stopped at once and let her lips trail up my stomach and bit my chest as she snuggled into my arm once again.

"OK! Would you like a coffee?" she said kissing and nibbling on my ear.

"Yes. It should be ready by now! "I replied getting out of bed and pulling up my underpants to cover a semi-rampant JT.

"You've already made it? That's fantastic!"

I kissed her and said,

"How do you like it?"

"Just milk, bitte."

Went to the kitchen, got two cups of coffee and went back to the bed. We sat drinking our coffee, chatting and cuddling until around 09:00 when she said that she had some people coming at 10:00 for a rehearsal as they are performing on Friday in Rudolstadt.

We got up and dressed. I gave her a hug and kiss, said farewell and wished her "Break a leg!" for her performance on Friday.

Went to my flat at 09:10 and went to bed! Read for an hour or so, got up, did my ablutions, took down the laundry I'd done yesterday and went to BB's for a pint around 13:30.

Thursday 11.12.03 23:00 or thereabouts. We had ice-rain tonight.

167

Sleet that freezes as soon as it hits the ground turning it into a skating rink making walking a hazardous occupation, especially on cobblestones. So on my way home from the OA I took the short cut through the park to the tram stop that Steffi had shown me as we walked home together last week. Sure enough there was a light in her window, but I decided against ringing her bell like I'd done the previous Saturday at 02:00 in the morning, and went to my flat instead. However, my resistance was low so I called her. She said that she'd just got out of the bath and was going to eat something. She also said she would be more than pleased to receive me for a literary salon. I said that I too was feeling hungry and that I would be there in about twenty minutes.

About 23:30 I walked and or skated the 200 odd metres to her flat and she answered the doorbell immediately smelling of bath oils dressed in leggings and a long loose top. We hugged and kissed in the doorway of her flat and she led me into the room where the grate of the tiled stove that heats both rooms is located. She sat on the cosy inbuilt seat and I sat on the armchair opposite. We chatted about our literary ambitions, drank wine and smoked for about an hour or so until she said that she wanted to dance and if I liked I could watch her from the comfort of the bed. I thought this was a good idea so I went 2 have a P, undressed and got into the large bed.

Steffi is a tall, slender woman maybe 4 or 5 cm taller than me, and she moves with the grace of a willow sapling, swaying and bending with the wind. She put on a Brian Ferry CD and started to dance as though she was in a disco trying to attract the attention of the spectators standing around the dance floor.

I watched her through half-closed eyes and by the time she had finished dancing I could hardly keep my eyes open. In fact, I was almost asleep when she got into bed wearing only a thong and a cut off, long-sleeved T shirt.

Almost automatically I put my arm round her, kissed her tenderly on her naked neck and said sleepily,

"Good night, Steffi, sleep well."

She sighed and possessively pushed her calloused, muscular buttocks into my lap and replied,

"Good night, Alan. I'd like to sleep with you tonight, but I can't because I've got the crimson pirates."

As she proceeded to massage JT with her dexterous bum until he reacted and threatened to burst out of my underpants. I caressed her breasts and pinched her nipples until she slipped out of her thong, took JT and rubbed him along her furrow and said throatily,

"Have you ever tried 'A Tergo?"

"What's that?" I asked, half suspecting what she meant.

"Actually, it just means from behind. What I meant was anal sex!"

Thinking back, I replied cautiously,

"It must be fifteen or twenty years since I took the Milky Bar Road, and I can't even remember if I enjoyed it or not! Why do you ask?" already suspecting the answer.

"I only did it once before and I enjoyed it, I think. I'm still pretty oily from my bath. Shall we try it?"

"I'm game if you are."

I answered as she took a firm grip on JT with her right hand and reached over with her left to the bedside table where an open jar of body lotion was sitting. She took a large dollop of cream and spread it over JT, her rear entrance and pressed me against her sphincter until my glans burst through and the rest of him followed like a ferret's tail down a rabbit-hole.

"Play with your clitoris!" I said firmly. She let go of JT and started to thrust back and massage him with her sphincter at the same time caressing her clitoris. I reached up with my free hand and stroked and squeezed her breasts and nipples gently. JT was soon tickling the tampon through the thin tissues that separated him from the blood soaked, cotton candle until she cried out as her orgasm washed over her, triggering a violent spasm in both her vagina and rectum which forced JT to release my Gene code. This time into regions where this man has previously seldom set foot, hand or any other appendage.

Once again I roared like a Gibbon. After what seemed like an eternity we both came back down to earth and cuddled until JT slipped out of his temporary refuge as Steffi turned to me, kissed me longingly on the lips and whispered tenderly,

"Good night, Sweet Prince. Sleep well my Svengali!" "Good night, Shepherdess. May light illuminate your dreams." We fell asleep immediately.

12.12.03 Woke up at some time before noon needing 2 P, I think, and found Steffi lying cuddled up beside me still fast asleep. I got out of bed carefully and went to the kitchen, put the kettle on to boil, set up the coffee pot with filter and ground coffee and went to the bathroom, where I emptied my bladder and washed in cold water. By the time he'd finished my ablutions the kettle had boiled so I poured it on the coffee and made a Spliff, which I smoked while I drank my first coffee of the day. When I'd finished I took the coffee with milk and sugar and two cups on a tray into the bedroom where Steffi was stirring. Poured out two cups and got back into bed with mine and kissed her gently on the ear and said,

"Good morning, sweet Steffi."

She turned over at once and kissed me on the mouth, her tongue still sleepy probed my lips until it found mine and she said,

"Good morning, you Pagan. You've already had a coffee and a smoke!"

"Yours is in the pot next to you." I replied reaching over and gently caressed her breasts.

"Let me have a coffee and a cigarette first before we start any early morning gymnastics!" she said laughing and reached down to where JT was slumbering and squeezing me firmly but gently.

"OK, would you like me to pour it for you?"

"Yes please! But I need to go to the toilet so could you roll me a cigarette too?" she responded, as she kissed me and gracefully got out of bed. While she was gone I skinned up another Spliff, a normal roll-up and poured two cups of coffee. When she returned we sat in bed drinking coffee, talking, petting and smoking until the coffee pot was empty. She then showed me her book on Tantric Sex techniques. I don't know if it was the pictures in the book that turned us both on simultaneously. She gave me the book to put on the bedside table and as I did this she took JT in her left hand, pulled the foreskin back, bit me once on the chest and engulfed him her lips. He came awake immediately and rapidly reached his full fighting size. I caressed her hair and stroked and pinched her slender back and buttocks until I could no longer stand it and said somewhat breathlessly,

"Steffi, I don't want to come in your mouth! If you take the tampon out; you can ride me if you like."

She stopped her administrations, extracted the offending object, deposited it in one of the empty coffee cups and quickly straddled me impaling herself on JT.

When he was in as deep as he could go she sat upright and started thrusting with her pelvis, while I squeezed and stroked her breasts and nipples until she collapsed on my chest as a small orgasm shook her slender frame. Ten seconds later the telephone rang and broke the magic. The answering machine switched on before she could extract herself and get out of bed. The caller hung up without leaving a message, so she came back to bed and when she saw the bed sheet full of bloodstains, and my thighs, underpants and groin also displaying the badges of their suspended skirmish, she laughed loudly and said.

"You look as though you've been castrated or performed a do-it yourself circumcision!"

"In a way you're right." I replied, "You absolutely delighted me with all three orifices during the last twelve hours and I enjoyed it immensely. What about you?"

"It was great. It's just a pity that the Scheiss phone rang!"

We cuddled for another ten minutes or so and then we got up and dressed, said their farewells and promised to try to see each other before the festive season gets under way. On the way to my flat I looked at the church clock and the hands were at 14:15!

We had one or two more encounters over the next few weeks, once at her place and once at mine.

Betreff: nasowas

Von: Babuschka@web.de>

An: schnell

Datum: 16.07.08 09:28:16

Anlagen: pic07685.jpg, pic03958.jpg, pic13110.jpg, pic25452.jpg, pic06656.jpg, pic00319.jpg, pic29124.jpg, pic12784.jpg, pic19436.jpg, pic03289.jpg

Hallo an alle da auf der anderen Seite, jetzt hat mir irgendwas den ganzen Text verschluckt und das schoene Briefpapier ist blank wie zuvor. Das macht Spass!

Gruesse kommen aus Suratthani, wo ich seit Anfang Mai wohne. Ich unterrichte hier an der "Prince of Songkla University" Englisch. Die Studenten sind herzig und erstaunt stelle ich fest, dass es mir Spass macht. Jedenfalls voruebergehend. Auf lange Sicht bin ich weiterhin und nurmehr bestaerkt mit Ausbruchsgedanken beschaeftigt. Weil das Gehalt hier nicht so ueberragend ist, unterrichte ich vier Abende die Woche von 6 - 8.30 am AUA Language Center (American University Alumni). Der Manager dieser Sprachschule hatte mir die letzten zwei Monate ein Dach ueberm Kopf gegeben. Und weil ich ja doch Glueck habe, ist es auch die Person, dessen Gesellschaft mir hier am angenehmsten ist. In Suratthani gibt es eine recht grosse Clique von Englischlehrern, ca. 60. Die sind alle nett, aber eben groesstenteils nicht meine Wellenlaenge. Suratthani ist soweit ganz nett. Eine kleine Stadt am Golf von Thailand. Bin wieder auf der ruhigeren Seite des Istmus gelandet. Die Andamanensee ist waehrend des Monsuns eine ueberaus nasse Angelegenheit. Trotzdem vermisse ich Koh Payam und ich schlage mich grad mit dem Gedanken an einen Wochenendtrip dahin. Letzten Freitag bin ich dank der Hilfe eines Studenten in ein schoenes traditionelles Holzhaus gezogen. Traditionell heißt, eine grosse Eingangshalle dominiert das ganze Haus und es gibt, soweit ich das überblick, nur ein Schlafzimmer. [Einige Türen sind mir verschlossen.] Habe also nach 8 Monaten aus dem Koffer mal wieder meine Sachen in einem Schrank. Wow!

Und eine Waschmaschine gibt es auch. Was für ein Luxus das ist, könnt ihr euch wohl kaum vorstellen...Ich muss jetzt mal los. Anbei ein paar Fotos, die mir eine Studentin geschickt hat. Ganz liebe Gruesse aus der steten und nun auch himmelwasserreichen Tropenhitze.

Ciao, Babuschka

BRAINWASHED BRITAIN

Having recently returned to the UK, after spending the last 35 years living and working in other parts of the world, I have arrived at the conclusion that Britain has been contaminated with a toxic infection, very much worse than Avian or Swine 'flu.

The name of this virus is CAI - no I haven't misspelled the acronym - it stands for Creeping American Imperialism. I believe that the majority of ills that beset Britain have their origins in the USA. Whether it be obesity, or the incidence of violent crime, the nauseous obsession with so-called celebrities and their clothes, the slavish imitation of US vernacular, even at Auntie Beeb; the fact we throw away 30 % of our food, and the absurd belief that we live in a democracy.

Who is to blame for the uncontrolled spread of this malady? None other than the media, whose sole objective is to increase circulation, or advertising revenue and the advertising agencies, whose sole aim is to awaken superfluous desires, at the same time keeping the general public anesthetized with irrelevancies, just as all previous totalitarian Empires have done in the past.

How can we break away from this state of affairs? First of all, we must abandon this misguided concept that 'Economic Growth' is the answer to all that ails Britain. In addition, we must accept the fact that 'Sustainable Growth' is in itself an oxymoron. We must first strive to attain a 'Steady State Economy' as proposed by Herman Daly, Dr King M Hubbert and even Adam Smith.

How can we achieve this? First of all, accept the premise that GDP is a false measure of prosperity. A more reliable yardstick for affluence is per capita income. As most informed people know Britain, as well as the other EU states, has a negative population growth rate, which means that we have to appeal to people to emigrate to this country.

The only reason why any government tolerates immigration, limited or not, is not only to perform the tasks that we are no longer willing to do, but also to be consumers of the increased production. What happens when this enlarged capacity cannot be sold? If you would like an answer to this question take a trip down the M5 past Avonmouth and you will see thousands of vehicles waiting patiently for prospective buyers. A couple of years ago there were more than 2 million cars produced and left unsold in Europe. This situation applies to almost all articles produced today. That's why we have the BOGOF offers we see in the shops. If you would like more information about this read the theories of Herman Daly, Dr King M Hubbert and even Adam Smith.

THE MAN WHO LIVED IN A HILL

Imagine if you can a southern slope of the Yorkshire Wolds just north west of Market Weighton, crested by and flanked by dense, deciduous woods.

It is shortly before dawn, the pale moon and starlight reflected on the glassy stripes in the shape of the chevrons on an NCOs' sleeve, crested by a single phrase; 'Per Ardua ad Astra' in neon on the roof of the complex.

As the first sun's rays sliced the crest of the western incline of KP Hill, the lights went out immediately in the uppermost sliver of the chevron below it and on the slope opposite - a total of 200 metres of high power blue and white LEDs. Fifteen minutes later the second stripe, five metres lower illuminated with an equal array of lamps, this time with a combination of red and white LEDs went off. The shutters below the lowest of the arrays wouldn't open for another two hours and automatically close twelve hours later, because this the cloning department.

This comprises 200 incubator beds, each holding 100 cuttings. Every hour they are treated to an increase of 5 % in the CO_2 level. They receive 20 hours of sun/artificial light a day and are kept at a constant 24o C. In addition, they are drip-fed with an organic nutrient solution. They remain here for about two weeks until they have taken root, they are then transferred to the topmost terrace where they stay under 18 hours of day/artificial light until they have four inter nodes. The growing tips are then pinched out in order to encourage side shoots to grow. When they have reached a metre in height they are then relocated one terrace lower to the flowering zone, where they will only receive 12 hours of daylight to initiate the blossoming. On the ridge above the complex the *Himawari* 'Sunflowers', as well, are already harvesting the sun's early morning rays, their parabolic mirrored surfaces are automatically corrected to follow the energy giver as it makes its way across the spring sky; the same as the numerous photo-voltaic arrays on the slopes between the terraces. The area between the upper terraces and the staff quarters below the summit is a fruit and vegetable garden, where the lazy chickens are just coming out of their coops and the goats are already grazing. The light from the 'Sunflowers' is piped through fibre-optics to the working and living areas of the KP Hill. One after another lights go on in the staff premises; the first being the director, Alain Percy. He's seventy, but looks 15 years younger, his boyish good looks embellished by his piercing pale blue eyes.

Before the wake-up call resounded he reached out and killed it. He got up immediately, washed and put on a clean overall from the upright locker next to his Spartan futon bed and made his way to the control room. He wasn't the first. Jenny, a young agrobiologist from Australia was already sitting at the main terminal drinking coffee. She turned as Alain entered.

"Morning, Boss, every thing's normal. I made fresh coffee, hope you like it."

"I 'm sure I will," he replied taking a mug and filling it with the freshly brewed coffee. Taking a sip, he said, "Not bad! What is the prognosis on sectors 15 and 16?"

Jenny punched a couple of keys on the keyboard and the disembodied voice of the control programme spoke the following,

'ALL CUTTINGS IN SECTORS 15 AND 16, BEDDED 12 DAYS,

MANY ALREADY ROOTED.'

"I'll get the team on to it after breakfast Boss."

"Good," he replied as other members of the crew drifted in taking coffee or making tea and taking their seats at the conference table, which had been found at a Car Boot Sale. When they were all seated Alain said,

"Good morning everyone. Did you all sleep well?"

There were muttered replies. However, there was an air of contentment on all their faces.

"OK," he continued, "What's the status quo? Tim, you're at the sharp end, what's your estimate for confirmed delivery this week." Tim and his crew were responsible for the fermentation and delivery of the end product. He was a lanky young man who used to be a roofer, but he had to give up his trade due to back problems. However, he had no trouble handling the 10 kg sacks of their goods, because he was a government authorized trader.

He replied, sipping his coffee, "With a bit of luck and tweaking the temperature in the fermenting bays (in the bowels of the complex) we should be able to ship 25 sacks by Friday, and I think we should be hitting 30 by the end of the month."

"That's good news, Tim. It means that there'll be a bonus for everybody again." Alain said making a quick mental calculation: 250 kg/ @ £ 100/kg.

Turning to the couple on his right,

"OK. Steve and Gerlinde, any problems in the grow zone?

"No Boss," they answered in stereo as they cuddled closer together. "Great. Because there's a new coffee house in Newbald that wants to do all its own flowering and fermenting and mix with herbs. Tim when you deliver, its cost plus 10 % delivery charge." "Got it, Boss," he replied making a note in his PDA.

"OK. Jenny's crew has got a lot of rooted cuttings, let her know where you have space and pass it down the hill. Any questions before we finish with Roland and his team in the flowering zone?"

No one responded and Roland promptly replied, "All the standard crosses are doing well and I'm very impressed with the 'Jack Herer' Northern Lights hybrids. The buds are the size of small broccoli heads. So I suggest we have a preliminary sampling on Sunday if everyone is in agreement?"

There was a round of cheers at the table to which Alain joined in. When the cheering had subsided he stood up and said, "OK, let's get to work!"

A DIFFERENT POINT OF VIEW

We all know the real motive for the invasion of Iraq. Under the pretence that Saddam Hussein had WMD it was to secure the US, the Far East and Europe 's thirst for oil. Therefore, it does not require a great stretch of the imagination to realise that this was also the primary reason for the assault on Afghanistan, with the secondary aim of making the streets of Europe and the US safe from terrorist attacks. In addition, of course remove the source of finance for the Taliban, namely the destruction of opium poppy cultivation.

What most people don 't know is that the purpose of this was to maintain the market price of heroin for the legal British and Turkish producers, who supply the drug for medicinal needs.

This leads me to my second point of view. Who is really accountable for the death of the sex-workers in Bradford? In my enlightened intellect the British government is responsible for their deaths. These three unfortunate women would not have needed to prostitute themselves if our government took an unbiased approach to so-called 'drugs' and distanced itself from the so-called 'special relationship' with the US.

The same applies to the Vietnamese cannabis factory that was recently found in Hull. Supply and demand.

There were approximately 2.75 million regular consumers of cannabis products in 1994. If we assume a growth in use comparative with a rate of inflation of 2% this translates to an estimated minimum of more than 6 million regular consumers today. When asked the majority of these otherwise responsible members of society would say that all they want is a clean reliable product the same as clients in public houses and off-licenses.

If these citizens were allowed to grow their own cannabis, which would ensure an unadulterated product, without being harassed by the ill-advised authorities - then there would be no place in society for those among us who are only interested in making a quick profit. Finally, I heard on the news yesterday that the two young men who died from an apparent overdose of Mephedrone, or M Cat. And it transpires that there was no evidence of the plant growth substance found in the post-mortems. So much for the knee-jerk reaction from the current cabinet and the already ridiculed Hull MP and ex Home Secretary, when the mood is for radical change in the misuse of substances laws.

Von: claudia <ckue@web.de>

An: Alainwalker <walker@yahoo.de>

Gesendet: Dienstag, den 2. April 2002, 11:52:42 Uhr

Betreff: Re: Re: Re: Re: <no subject>

Hi, Alain,

Did you get my last e-mail to Eastern? I'm sorry I was so unconcentrated this morning. Still I felt tired and then at the same time the house caretaker came and asked me to choose a coloured Easter egg. I could not tell him that I'm busy, because he speaks only Czech. So I chose an egg while I was talking to you.

The theatre festival started with mixed experiences. Roland and Boris, the organisers, are a little bit angry about a few things.

Me by myself, I am happy, I had a good day and after the Bergjugendabend Steffen and Bjorn, the two German lecturers from Hungary visited me and we had a long interesting talk till 3 in the morning.

The festival goes till Friday night and I think I will be very tired after that. The week after it seems, I'm free and I would love to see you. I still cannot decide when to go to Germany, because preparing my lessons takes still too much time, so I can hardly leave for 4 days. And to go for less time would be murdering. So you think you could come then?

Ja! The weather is fantastic. In a few hours a do my first workshop. Love to you!

Claudia

GROWING OLD INELEGANTLY

Unlike the recommendation in the Dubliner's song to 'Maids when they're young not to marry an old man ', I have not lost my Fellorum or my Dingdorum: In reality, my fellorum is still functioning superbly and my Dingdorum is, to quote the 'Talking Heads'; "The same as it ever was", albeit, not to the same degree when I was a few years younger.

My last active service versus the adversary was before I left for Thailand.

***

E-mail to cosmo@web.de

From: schnellAlain@web.de

Date: 03.04.2010-07-05

Time: 18:30 GMT

Dearest B,

The contract in Erlangen is now reality. I don't know if I told you; two weeks ago I was logged onto tefl.com and saw this job offer in Germany. The possibility of a full-time contract, however they were looking for teachers in the Erlangen-Nuremberg area. Nevertheless, it had a Skype phone number, so I plugged in my headset, dialled the number and was put through to the owner, an English woman called Rosie Norman. We chatted for almost 30 minutes and she seemed very much taken with me, so I said I would send my CV per e-mail. The next morning, I had a mail from her saying that she thought I would fit into her team very well. She also asked how soon I could be there, as the 13-week course was due to start on the 28th of April and how long would I stay in Germany. I wrote back immediately and asked if she knew the film 'Last Man Standing.' And, as I'd already bought my ticket I told her that I would take the Air Berlin flight to Nuremberg on the Thursday the 24th. She mailed back at once and said she'd pick me up at the airport. Which she did in her Mini Cabriole – it's enough to say she "*Faehrt wie ein Wildsau*"! (She drives like a crazy wild pig). After she'd shown me the school and we'd discussed the upcoming contract she checked me into a B&B Pension.

We had a meeting in Nuremberg at 10:00 on Friday with the Veranstalter, Juris Prudentia, which I think is something like a Law Association. It turned out that I have an apartment 2 floors above the classrooms. It's fully furnished bed, writing desk and wardrobe etc., right in the middle of the Altstadt. There is even a TV and the possibility to get a land-line connection, sprich Internet, which means that when I get up in the morning, all I need to do is go down two floors and get a freshly brewed coffee! The Hausverwaltung is in the same building and everybody is bending over backwards to help me, e.g. the Hausmeisterin told me yesterday that as tomorrow is 1st Mai, she's going away and won't be back until Friday morning, she'd give me an electric kettle, so all I needed to do was buy the makings for instant coffee. The course build-up is 5 weeks Refresher, 4 weeks Business and 4 weeks Technical English finishing on the 27th July - 13 weeks @ 37 hrs. @ 20 Euro. When the refresher course finishes at the end of May I'm hoping to go to the UK for a couple of days to finalise my Pension appeal. If that is resolved in my favour then I should get 1 years back pension credit, about £ 7500. In September I will be entitled to a State Pension, and I can study for one year at York College and with luck I'll get a Bursary. However, if this course in Nuremberg gets good feed-back then I'll most probably come back here if there is nothing in Thailand to convince me to stay there!

In addition, via mitfahrzentrale.de I have a regular opportunity to go to Erfurt for the weekend. There's a young woman from Eisenach who works for Siemens here in Nuremberg and drives home whenever her shifts allow it. As a matter of fact, I was there last weekend and stayed at Manuela's and I was able to see my kids for 6 hours.

On Sunday the course organiser had arranged for me to stay in a hotel just 5 minutes' walk from the school building. So you see I'm planning long-term. I've got to stop here as my lighter hat gerade den Geist aufgegeben.

Write soon and

LOL Alain XXXXXXXXXXXX

***

The following pages are a transcript of text on a page torn out of a school notebook given to me by a homeless man who was giving away all his belongings, including clothes and music cassettes in numerous plastic shopping bags; you figure it out!

BERLIN

Gegen die verblendete Masse muss man überparteilich gelenkt, trotz aller ehemaliger Verschiedenheiten, zukunfts Gewinn bringend zusammenarbeiten.

Ob Rot oder Braun, Bonze bleibt Bonze. Eine deutsche Kuehe haut die andere neudeutsche Pleitekraehe nicht die wohlvertrauten Bürokraten schnauze ein. Es ist zum Erbrechen, mir ist jedenfalls kotzübel beim Lesen von diesem Ibrahim Bohme Scheiss. Schlimm daran ist, dieser aersche meinen das so und machen Gesetze mit aehnlichem Inhalt daraus. Mir fallt momentan Tucholskys Definition über Demokratie ein. Demokratie: hi-hi-hi.............

BEDURFTIGKEIT

Sie waren Beide mal vor Neudeutschland in einer 2 Zimmerwohnung glücklich, Marina und Dieter. Dann kam unblutige Revolution.

Neuefriedlichen-kapitalistische-Wohnungs Freundlichkeit breitete sich aus. Das hatte für die Paar einigen kleineren Folgen. Sie verliessen mit Hilfe von Treuhand-vermittlung ihre einigermassen bewohnbare Zweiraum wohnung. Stadtrat und Asylwohnraumarsche besorgten dunkle, mit Schwamm, ausgestattete Einraumwohnung. Einige Zeit spaeter wurde Ihres Haus verkauft. Aus dieser miesen Einraumwohnung müssen sie ganz schnell raus. Der neue Besitzer modifiziert und renoviert. Auf Grund der miesen wohnlichen Situation sowie der Ausweglosigkeit, brockelts in der EHE. Er fängt an zu saufen, kurze Zeit spaeter steht er ohne Job da. Sie benutzt den noch intakten Gasherd ohne das Gas zu zünden mit tödlichem Erfolg. Sie waren Beide mal in einer Zweizimmerwohnung Glücklich...

Berlin Prenzlauer Berg 8.92.

BERLINER U-BAHN

Gegen 22 zig Uhr stiegen etwa lust Walkerige, angeheiterte-slawisch sprechende Typen in die gerade eingefahrene U-Bahn Richtung Westberlin.

Alle hatten mausgraue Scheuerlappen und die Schuhe gebunden im August, ausserhalb der Faschingszeit. Die Gruppe wollte nach erfolgreicher Wohnungsinhaltsumlagerung auf einen Lastkraftwagen nicht unnötig auffallen. Drei oder vier Stationen spaeter sammelte, die Polizei bei einer Routinesicherheitskontrolle Scheuerlappen mit oben Menschen dann, ein.

Die Moral von der Geschichte nach illegaler Wohnungs Beräumung, Scheuer Lappen nicht vergessen. August 92 Berlin.

ARABIAN NIGHTS AND DAZE

As I mentioned in Lin-Fout I went to Saudi Arabia in January 1976 For the British Aerospace Corporation as a technical trainer with the intention of paying off our mortgage. We had the idea to buy a derelict cottage in the country and renovate it to our taste. As it turned out Allah had something different in mind when I arrived in the country.

Several years later when I was working for Glass-Mate GmbH in Offenbach I was often called on to solve technical problems with the equipment in the Emirates, Oman, Bahrain, Kuwait and Saudi Arabia on numerous occasions. In addition, I also had to trips to Baghdad/Ramadi and one to Basra during the war with Iran.

This was also a time of regrouping. My relationship with Angelika had gone belly-up. I was a single parent solely responsible for the welfare of my two sons and had to hold down a responsible job. Except for one occasion when I was discussing the joint project with one of our Saudi partners, Sheik Turki Banda and his German site manager, Horst Bender in his sumptuously appointed air-conditioned office in Jeddah. When the phone rang the Sheik picked it up and said, *'Aiwa, Herr Nossem, Wie geht es Ihnen?* I'm fine thank you. Ja, Mr Jackson is here, moment mal.' and passed me the phone. It was my boss in Germany begging me to change my return flight plans and come back via Abu Dhabi, because one of our clients there was having problems with the equipment. He said that he was deeply sorry that I wouldn't be home for my birthday, but asked me to fly back when the fault was resolved. He needn't have been.

I was scheduled to fly back the following day and I wasn't complaining, it meant another DM 99 daily expense allowance that I could claim tax free for two more days. After I'd reassured my boss that I would take care of the situation I got Sheik Banda's driver to drive me to the travel agents in down town Jeddah, where I was able to change my return ticket to FfM via Abu Dhabi at no extra charge. This took a little longer because we when arrived at the travel agents it was time for evening prayer so we had to change the ticket in the back office.

I caught the 23:00 Saudi Air flight to Abu Dhabi. A driver from our client was waiting with my name scrawled on a piece of cardboard. He drove me to a hotel and picked me up at 08:30 the next morning and drove me to the client's premises. Subsequent to drinking the obligatory two cups of heavily sweetened mint tea I was able to clear the problem within an hour. The Lebanese owners were delighted and before we went to lunch he took me to his brother's shop in the gold Souk. He said that I could select something as my birthday present. Not being a great aficionado of gold, I prefer silver, I chose a discreet silver medallion impregnated with the mnemonic for Virgo and a small, thin chain. Not satisfied, he then asked me if I had a wife or fiancée in Germany. At the time Heidi was living with me and my two sons, so I chose a pair of gold ear-rings with small teardrop pendants. When we had finished lunch he drove me to the hotel and said that he would send a driver to take me to the airport in time for my night flight to FfM. I spent the rest of the day at the pool, relaxing, swimming, sketching and chatting to the Lufthansa crew, whose flight I'd be on that evening.

HAWKS, DOVES & HOODIES

Rasham was neither Hawk, nor Dove. To me she was the original hoodie. In reality she was a young, untrained Barbary Falcon. How she came into my household and my life, and how I fell in love is portrayed below.

I was sitting in the tutor's common room one afternoon, when Nadeem, one of my RSAF students came in. At the time I was tutoring apprentices in technical English for BAC, British Aircraft Corporation, in Riyadh, the capital of Saudi Arabia and greeted me, *'Marhaaba, Imam Mel, sabaahul khayr* (Good Morning, Sayeed Mel.).

'Masaa'ul khayr! Nadeem!' (Good evening), I replied, with a touch of irony.

After further niceties he got down to the nitty-gritty: His cousin, Prince Usaama had just come back from holiday in Zurich; he'd bought two radio-controlled model aeroplane kits, and could I help him, the Prince, build them. Furthermore, the Prince would, could be very grateful for any assistance, and Nadeem's esteem in the clan pecking order would be improved. A quick think and I said yes, I could help him.

'The Moving Finger of Time had writ and moved on.'(Omar Khayyam).

The following evening, I was picked up by Nadeem and driven to the Prince's palace, not a large edifice, but non-the-less impressive structure with three-metre-high walls and an ageing Sikh guard with an ancient Kalashnikov. We didn't have to wait long and were ushered into a large, 60 square metre reception area to the left of the entrance. The room was lined with plush armchairs and heavy carpet-like curtains. The Prince sat in the middle at the end of the room, flanked by his adviser's, family, etc.

Nadeem had told me that the Prince was 18 or 19, he wasn't sure. He was so skinny that he had difficulty lifting his left hand because of the solid gold Rolex he wore. After the obligatory cups of very sweet mint tea, the aforesaid model aeroplane kits were produced. I examined them both and told the Prince that I could build one

189

because the instructions were in English, whereas the other, the simpler, one was only in German.

The Prince was overjoyed and said he would send his driver for me the following day. I could have lived at the palace until it was ready for its maiden flight. However, via Nadeem, I managed to agree with the Prince that I would take the kit with me, and Nadeem would keep the Prince up-to-speed.

After the deal was sealed we adjourned to an equally large dining room, where our hands were washed and dried by two Egyptian servants before we ate, not on the floor as you may imagine, but European style with tables and chairs. Of course, Nadeem badgered me every day for the next three weeks until it was finally ready. It would have taken longer if my two sons hadn't helped me. He was elated and asked me what I would like as a reward for helping the Prince. I could have said, a solid gold Rolex, a new Cadillac, etc. Ever since I visited a Falconry Centre near Gloucester, I've often had dreams of self-sufficiency and Falcons were part of this. So, half-jokingly I said, 'A Falcon.'

One evening the following week there was a knock at the door, and there large as life was Nadeem with a hooded falcon on his left wrist. I asked him in and he dropped the bomb! The falcon was mine. He'd even brought a hunting perch until I obtained a permanent perch. To cut a long story short he told me that the bird was untrained. At first I was a little concerned. However, I remembered the falconry centre near Gloucester that we had visited on one of our holidays in the UK. So I wrote to the owner and as luck would have it he had recently published a beginner's guide to falconry, a copy of which he posted to me by return mail. He also asked me to send a photo of the bird so that he could identify it. This I duly did and he wrote back and told me that it was most likely a female Barbary falcon, and that if I brought her back to the UK we could breed her with one of his Peregrines for which I would receive half of the resulting eggs: not a bad deal considering that in Saudi Arabia such an egg could be worth as much as £ 1000.

By the time I got the book Rasham was already accustomed to me as I had made her a perch which sat next to my bed – much to the annoyance of my wife, Alexis. Whenever I came home from work and she heard my footsteps she screeched a falcon greeting. As soon as I received the book I started training her immediately. Starting with a fine fishing line tied to her jesses, the leather thongs on her legs, and gradually increasing the distance to 50 metres from my gloved hand in which I held a piece of meat, she was soon ready for free flying and kill training. So one Sabbath – Friday I went to the local souk and bought two 6 week old chickens. I let these run around in our garden and released Rasham some 20 metres distance. She promptly flew and hit one. However, failed to kill it with the impact. Alexis blew a fuse because the chicken was squawking, so I had to kill it myself along with the other one.

During the early stages of training I took her into town one day and bought the hunting perch and a new decorative hood. I immediately got into an Anglo-Arabic conversation with one of the shop keepers who told me that she was worth about 20,000 Riyals, at the time around £ 3000.

I was also invited to go on a hunting trip by a couple of Bedouin who were camped close to our compound. I had to turn this down because the Bedouin concept of the day after tomorrow – *Bahd bukra* is not as urgent as the Spanish Mañana.

I did not bring her to the UK when I returned: I gave her, her freedom instead. One evening just before sunset I took her on my off-road bike into the desert and released her I returned to the same location on three subsequent evening. The theory being if she couldn't find food she would return and if she didn't then she had managed to feed or had died. It was the end of an extraordinary symbiotic relationship that I will never forget.

DEMONS IN THE DRAINS

This all started one Friday in early January 1977 shortly after the rainy season when we discovered that the underground water cistern for our modest three bed room 'villa' was almost dry. The house was in a 60 square meter plot surrounded by three-metre-high walls. This meant no water for washing, or drinking after it had been filtered. I called company HQ and asked them to send a water bowser. This turned up 20 minutes later only to discover that the tanker was too wide to get down the narrow alley created by the walls of the adjacent villas. It was also unable to get close enough to the wall from the free standing side because the rains had churned the litter covered desert into a quagmire. Luckily I was able to contact Hussein, one of my students and asked him if he could send a smaller bowser. Thirty minutes later he arrived shortly before the aforementioned tanker. Within ten minutes the cistern was full. Hussein insisted in paying the driver who was a cousin of some sorts. A few weeks later we moved into a company bungalow in the family's compound which had swimming pool, tennis and squash courts, an outdoor cinema for the hot months, social club, etc. So I invited Hussein and his wife, Jasmin to dinner one evening. They arrived punctually, his wife wore the *Hijab,* the traditional Saudi veil until she was in the house. Lexi, my wife had made a ham-free quiche. They both enjoyed it so much that Lexi said she could show Jasmin how to make it. We agreed on a date the following week. When we arrived at their house, which was the family home, a modest villa, Lexi was ushered off to the kitchen with the women of the family. I was directed to a small lounge with the men, Hussein, his father, younger brother as well as a couple of cousins where we drank sweet mint tea and smoked. After a while there were loud screams from the kitchen. It turned out that, because my wife had the habit of scalding the chopped onions before putting them in the pastry case, and she had poured the hot water into the open drain which caused the women to scream. According to local superstition the drains were occupied by demons who were responsible for the unpleasant smells that emanated from the drains.

SPANISH SIESTAS I

My first visit to Spain was in June 1964 on my honeymoon; two weeks on the Costa Brava at a small resort called Estartit. It turned out to be other than enjoyable because my wife Alexis acquired bad sunburn on her shoulders and the tops of her breasts on our first evening. Due to a strike, or go-slow by the French air traffic controllers we had to land at Barcelona airport instead of Perpignan and were bussed through the early morning suburbs of Barcelona. On the return journey we spent 12 hours at the airport in Perpignan because the French ATC was still on strike.

Hi BB,

I'm fine, thought I'd try a new font for a change; maybe this will give you some idea of my mental state. The garden is on hold because of the incessant rain. Thanks for the laughs, I don't want to seem ueberheblich, however, I am familiar with the 'lost in translation' gaffs, I used them several years ago to liven up my afternoon sessions and I bought a book called 'Lost in Translation' in Nuremberg and gave it to MW2 before I left for Thailand.

Otherwise I'm fine. I've cut my tobacco consumption to six roll-ups/ day, primarily because I don't have anything to spice it up! As a result, I've put on a couple of kilos and now look 5 months schwanger!

Nevertheless, I have 7 seedlings, seeds from last year's harvest. If I was a cat, I have a suspicion I'd soon look like this. See attachment. Finally, I tried to call you today to no avail, Maalish, that's Arabic for Egal. Take care,

LOL Top Cat

Hey Mental Alain,

I like the different font... How do you like this one? I know that you know. I just wanted to share some laughs.

Btw: a little overweight is quite (!) cute when you have fur... ;-) I reckon by now the sun will allow you to work it off in the garden. We have a heat wave with over 40 degrees. I have a heat rash covering my face and my shaved head. Delicate, delicate!! Two more days and I'm off to the island again. We have a two-week break and I really need it. Happy Songkran on 13th April - wish me good luck! I'll throw some water in for you, too. Bye for now, Pimply B

Von:web.de" 4:36:45

Schulze<cosmo@web.de

Re: funFrom: Schulze Süße Weihnachtsgrüße an Dich

SPANISH SIESTAS II

The second time I ventured onto the Iberian Peninsula was in the summer of 1987 after I had finished my first personal theatrical adventure. It was when Heidi, my yuppie girlfriend said that her school friend, Marlene had decided to stay in Spain because she was co-habiting with a Swiss teacher, Helmut, by whom she was pregnant. I could stay there if I earned my keep. More later. Marlene had fled Bavaria two weeks after *Chernobyl* with the intention of going to the Canary Islands with her daughter, Malene and her dog. As I had once played squash, with, and got two kittens from Marlene, I decided to go there and wind down and write some new sketches. Unfortunately, I got a couple of small translation contracts just before I left. They didn't present a major inroad on my free time as I had ten days to deliver.

I travelled there using the Mitfahrzentrale (Lift agency) in Frankfurt/Main. My girlfriend, Heidi (See Whirlwind) drove me to the pick-up point in Wiesbaden where I got a ride to Paris for DM 20. I stayed with my friends Bogdan and Claudine (See Summer '78) for a few days until I found a ride to Conil de la Frontera, a small town on the Costa de la Luce, where Marlene was holed up. It worked out pretty well as I got a ride with two chubby French waitresses, Danielle and Claudine with their Algerian boyfriends who were driving to the ferry in Cuerta. My friends drove me the apartment of the two Parisian Mademoiselles late one night because they were planning an early start. The next morning, we set off at 05:30. After two hours driving and well clear of the Parisian sprawl we stopped for breakfast at a Motorway services and Danielle had a twenty-minute power-nap.

Although the two women knew less English than I knew French we managed to communicate in a patois of both languages and Arabic.

Somewhere along the trip we stopped for lunch just over the Spanish border at a real restaurant, as the ladies told me, (A Truck-stop). As we were travelling in a convoy of two cars I alternated between the two. This meant that I had a change of travelling companions every couple of hours.

The sun was setting as we pulled into the courtyard of the Pension hotel in the industrial area of Burgos. The ladies generously said I could have one of the rooms for no extra charge as they'd booked three. However, I insisted in paying for my own dinner and a round of drinks.

There was no breakfast the next morning at 05:00, just thick black coffee in the dark kitchen just before daybreak. Once again after a couple of hours driving we stopped for food, this time at a Truck stop on the outskirts of Valladolid in the Estremadura, taking a good hour over it. This time Claudine, whose car I had occupied from Burgos, said she didn't need a nap so we set off once more fully fortified. I managed to understand that by taking this western route we avoided the traffic around Madrid or the coastal road south. About four hours later we stopped for lunch just north of Seville at a small town called San Jose de la Riconada. We arrived in my final destination, Conil de la Frontera a small holiday resort some 26 kilometres east of Cadiz some two hours later.

It was only about 500 metres from the main Cadiz/Gibraltar road. After we'd drunk a farewell coffee they went on their way with the intention of catching the next possible ferry to Cuerta on the North African coast. The address my girlfriend's friend, Marlene had sent me was about seven kilometres away. 'Barrio Nuevo', down a two kilometre road, not much better than a cart track at the restaurant in El Colorado, also on the Cadiz-Gibraltar artery.

I found a taxi driver and negotiated a price. However, he refused to go the last 200 metres, because, as I understood him, it would kill the suspension.

Martine, her Swiss partner, Helmut and her 6-year-old daughter Malene, whom I later taught to swim along with Jonas the six-year-old son of Berndt and Julianne greeted me as I staggered up the rutted track to their small-holding, complete with newly built house with a 5x3 metre swimming pool. Berndt and Julianne were a young German couple who were trying to make a living selling their artefacts to the tourists at the market in Conil. Berndt's specialty was framed miniature water-colours on plain silk and tee shirts with similar motifs. Julianne made costume jewellery.

After a week or two I settled into the rhythm of life on the Finca. Helmut was trying to grow organic tomatoes and other vegetables, so part of my board was earned by helping him with the daily harvest and taking it to the local restaurants and bars in Conil. In addition to this project he was also offering excursions to the Parc Nationale. This meant that he was occasionally away for three days at a time. While he was away it one of my tasks was to ensure that all the irrigation sprayers were functioning correctly, mow the beans and feed them to the sheep.

I got into the habit of going with Berndt and Julianne and Jonas when they drove into Conil to sell their wares. They did this 3-4 times a week and I gladly took on the role as 'Uncle' Alain for Jonas. I spent a very pleasant, relaxing four weeks. On the Friday before my departure I went to town with them and we had a small farewell party in a local restaurant after the market closed down for the night. We then played table football for a while and then I got separated from them while we were strolling through the town because I had stayed too long in a shop flirting with the Austrian salesgirl.

What happened next was caused by 'El Levante', a hot wind that comes across the Straits and doesn't have time to absorb moisture so it's like constantly breathing in the hot air from a pizza oven. It cooks your brain!

I aimlessly wandered the streets and narrow alley-ways in a daze for an unknown time until I found myself at the café where the two Parisians avec their Arabian 'fiancées made their Au Revoires.

By then it was almost midnight and Berndt and Julianne would be long gone, so in my stupor I asked an Anglo-Spanish couple sitting on the terrace where I could find a taxi. They told me that that taxis could be found in the town centre. I had a quick espresso and made my wavering way down the hill to the town centre. Indeed, when I finally arrived, there were not only a couple of taxis waiting for fairs, but a traffic policeman directing the numerous cars cruising around the monument in the centre of the Plaza at midnight! I soon agreed a fare to Barrio Nuevo and got to bed by 01:15 and slept like a log for nine hours.

The following trip was the Saturday evening. As usual I took

Jonas under my wing and we strolled around the market place next to the beach, where a summer Fair was happening. I treated Jonas and myself to a couple of rides in the 'Dodgems'. This made us hungry so we went and ate *'Sardinas con Patatas Fritas* with the house ketchup.

It was Saturday night in Andalucía, the home of Flamenco. In the school playground next to the market a junior Flamenco dance tournament was underlay; Medals were to be won in various age categories, i.e. under 10s, 10-12, 13-15, etc. It was incredible all these young dancers giving their all dressed in miniature versions of the typical Flamenco dress. Jonas was fascinated and so was I. But my attention was not on the young dancers, rather more on the tall, willowy, red-haired beauty, who reminded me of a young Kathryn Hepburn. She was a head taller than all the people around her. I assumed that she was standing on the steps down to the playground. I discovered that she had a face full of freckles that broke into a broad smile when I approached her and told her whom she reminded me of. To my surprise she wasn't standing on the steps: she was a whole head taller than me. Nonetheless, I took the bull by the horns and pretty soon we were communicating. She told me that she was Swedish and her name was Agnetha. She had arrived two days ago with friends on a package deal. They'd gone off somewhere else for a couple of days. We had a glass of wine at the bar near the market and made a date for the following evening.

We rendezvoused at the same bar at 22:00 and went for a meal in one of the numerous restaurants. After dinner we visited a new acquaintance of hers, Magda, a young German woman who was trying to make a living running a German Pub halfway to the *'La Hola* 'an open-sided bar at the end of the beach. Well lubricated we left Magda's and made our way there where we drank and danced until the sun came up over Capo de Trafalgar at around 05:30.

Agnetha took me by the hand and led me to the beach house that she'd rented with her friends. She told me I could sleep in any bed so I stripped down to my *'Cache du Sex'* and slid under the sheet. By the time she got into bed beside me I was on my way to the stars. Sometime hours later I woke and found a warm, naked body next to me. The outcome you can figure out!

The next day we said goodbye and promised that we would write.

That evening Berndt, Julianne and Jonas drove me to the station in San Fernando, an outlying suburb of Cadiz, where I could catch the night sleeper to Madrid. Jonas was very sad when we parted, but I promised I would write and come again. Which I did (See next episode). The train was on time and I soon found my allotted berth. I made my way to the restaurant car where I had a couple of nightcaps with a charming young woman from the USA until we'd left Seville, when I climbed in to the uppermost bunk.

I was awoken as the train stopped at Madrid main station, Atocha, as I found out from the pretty Spanish girl whose eyes sparkled as she answered my mumbled, '*Buenos Dias!* Where are we? 'Madrid! She said laughing and left.

It was 08:07 by the station clock when I got off the train, so I'd slept for seven hours through all the numerous stops including Albacete, Cordoba and Manzanares. More about Albacete in the next episode.

I checked out the connections to Frankfurt after I'd had a coffee and *Bochadero de Jambon,* (Ham sandwich). After fortifying myself I took the metro to the Prado and spent several hours looking at the exhibits, including both versions of Goya's 'Duchess of Alba' and Picasso's 'Guernica'. Shortly after 18:00 I caught the train to Paris. Once again I had a bunk in a six bed compartment and slept like a dead man until we were all rudely woken by the alarm clock at 05:30 belonging to one of the other individuals. It took him 5 minutes to find this in his luggage.

So for the last ninety minutes of the journey I was wide awake. After a quick trip on the Metro to Gare du Nord I soon had a connection to my final destination, Frankfurt/Main.

THE GRAEFIN (The Contessa)

Sunday 16th June 1991. Woke up some time, climbed down from the loft-bed, went to the kitchen and put on some water for coffee. When it was ready I took two cups up to the loft-bed. Linda was also awake and after we'd drunk our coffees we cuddled and made love again. After a long lazy breakfast, we went for a walk into town because I hardly knew it myself, as I'd spent most of my time working in the school. We went to the *Domplatz* (Cathedral Square) and strolled through derelict streets in the so-called *Altstadt* (Old Town). Just like I'd done with Renate, the photographer in the Dutch Quarter in Potsdam the previous summer!

By 14:00 we were both feeling a bit hungry so we stopped and had a late lunch of braised rabbit with red cabbage and boiled potatoes in an old restaurant called *'Feuerkugel'* (Fireball). The food was excellent. After we'd eaten we went back to my WG and Linda packed her bag and drove back to Niederjosbach because she didn't like driving at night and she seldom drives faster than 100 km/h. In fact, she told me at later date that when she's on the motorway she tucks in behind someone who is travelling around about this speed and stays behind them until the vehicle exits the motorway. Mike said he would like to stay until Monday and take some photos in town.

Silke came back from her weekend so I gave Mike the keys to the school, as there wasn't a spare room left where he could pitch his rucksack. He left sometime on Monday afternoon and I set about trying to get one piece of very important equipment organised, namely a functioning telephone line. I spent the rest of the week putting finishing touches to toilet in the stairwell after painting some patches of the walls with damp-proof paint.

Friday 21.06.91 12:00 or thereabouts a man from *Telekom* came to check the lines. He told me that the new telephone in-house switchboard was installed but the lines hadn't been connected yet. However, he said that the old lines were still active. So I asked him if he could connect up the line to the old wires. He hummed and ahed and said he would have to run a line to be able to do it. So I told him that if he could do it today I would give him ten DM. He agreed at once and twenty minutes later he came back up from the cellar, checked the line and wished me a *Fröhes Wochenend* (Have a nice weekend) as he took the promised ten DM and left.

I had told Linda that I would come and visit her on the Friday evening after I'd done all that was necessary in the school. So I was able to catch a relatively early train to Frankfurt/Main. However, at the time it meant changing trains three times between Erfurt and Frankfurt and took about five hours. Plus, thirty-five minutes on the S Bahn to Niederjoshbach. So it was almost 21:00 when she picked me up at the train stop. There were no buildings just two platforms with ticket dispensers and a barrier-controlled level crossing. Linda had already completed her daily bathing rituals when she came home from Hoechst. She works in the accounts department as an invoicing clerk. It only took two minutes to drive to her house in a quiet side street at the upper end of the village, which was to become my second home, and partial justification for my existence for the next four years or so?!

She made us some food while I was having a good scrub in her bath; on her request, because she said that I smelled like a Billy goat. This was, to some extent true, when you've been working and travelling for hours in the clothes you put on at 07:30 in the morning you don't necessary smell l like the Garden of Eden 14 hours later! When I'd had my bath I put on the towelling bathrobe that she had given me to use on our second rendezvous, two weeks after our first encounter at the end of April. We ate the supper on her large balcony and watched the sun setting over the Taunus foothills.

After we'd eaten I rolled a Spliff and drank a light white wine. Linda refrained from smoking this time and only drank wine. It was a very warm and pleasant evening so I said,

"Why don't you get some cushions from the living room so that we can enjoy the sunset out here on the balcony?"

"That's a great idea, Alan!" She answered, jumping up and almost running into the adjacent living room. I cleared away our dinner dishes and made space for the large, thick cushions.

She returned promptly with the aforesaid cushions and a quilt from her bed. We laid the four cushions together and we both lay down on them then Linda covered us with the quilt and cuddled up to me. All I was wearing was the bathrobe and it wasn't long before she started massaging my chest vigorously, occasionally pushing the robe aside and biting me. She just had thin cotton leggings on and a light summer sleeveless blouse with a camisole underneath so I was able to return the favour.

I soon freed her from her clothes as she undid the belt of the bathrobe and rubbed and pressed her small, firm breasts and nipples across my chest slowly making her way down my stomach where JT was standing to attention, having attracted hers. She then started rubbing him and scraping him with her aroused nipples and sucking him deep into the back of her throat until neither her, nor I could resist the tension.

So I said taking her face in my hands and releasing JT from her lips, *"Gräfin"* (Countess, my pet name for her because her maiden name is Burggraf), I don't want to come in your mouth. What does your thermometer say?"

"My period finished two days ago, so it should be alright for you to come inside me, and I'd like that, too!" she said still clasping JT in her well-manicured fingers, his helmet glowing like Rudolf's nose. "Ok, would you like to ride me?" I asked kissing her and reaching down to gently squeeze her quim lips.

"Oh yes! But can I ride side-saddle like the last time you were here?"

"Sure, just help yourself!" I answered as she sat up without releasing JT from her grasp and straddling my groin fed him into her juicy quim emitting a gasp of pleasure as he sank into his full length, tickling her kidneys from the inside as the old proverb goes. She soon started riding me and JT, rubbing her clitoris on the sinews of my inner thigh.

She then changed up to a canter, her firm buttocks massaging my balls with each downward stroke until clasping my knee she cried out in relief as her climax kicked in causing JT to erupt in her quim, my glans knocking on her vulva as the cushions slipped from under us due to our convulsions, depositing us on the still warm balcony tiles ripping JT from her quim - the life-line of our combined juices the only connection now between us.

Linda tried to stuff him back inside her minge, to no avail and I sat up laughing, pulled a cushion under my backside and said as I caressed her slender back,

"Let him recover awhile, Gräfin. Sir John has done his duty for tonight."

"Your right!" she said laughing too. Let's go straight to bed and cuddle." as she stood reaching down to give me her hand. I took it and followed her into the bedroom picking up the sofa cushions on the way. When we were finally in bed she snuggled up to me and she fell asleep almost at once with JT nestled between the cheeks of her bum. Before I disappeared into the Land of Nod I thought maybe the reason for her maiden name of Burggraf was because someone on her father's side had once worked as a stable boy at the local castle!

E-MAILS TO CLAUDIA

Von: claudia <ckue@web.de>

An: Alainwalker <walker@yahoo.de>

Gesendet: Dienstag, den 24. February 2004, 20:04:29 Uhr Betreff: Re: Reformation day?

Beloved Alain,

unfortunately, the entrance in the Allerheiligenstrasse is closed and we had to choose the way through Pergamentergasse - so you might not be able to find us. I feel this makes me a bit sad. So we should find time to sorrow.

At 11am I'm in Johannesstr. for shiatsu and half past 3 pm at Silvia Winzer's

(My homoeopath).

Got your postcard today, so Claudia

Alain <walker@yahoo.de> schrieb am 18.02.04 13:55:10:

Dearest, I was surprised to read your e-mail because I just wanted to send you a greetings card.

Lots of loving and kissing when I return.

LOL, Alain

SPANISH SIESTAS III

The first person I ran into the day after I returned from Spain in August was Liz, the photographer. She was in a hurry as she was driving to Brittany for three weeks that evening, and said I should give her a ring when she got back. The next weeks soon passed as I got back into the work mode. It was about this time when my relationship with Heidi, who was my *Delabe, (Derzeitigelabensabschnittbegleiter)*, current live-in-lover, at the time, started to go apart at the seams. We'd been living together for three years in a large flat with my two sons. Everything was fine until our landlord said that he needed the flat for himself and his fiancée when they got married. This meant that we had to look for somewhere else to live. It also coincided with the fact that my sons, J&L had both started apprenticeships in the town where we were living. So we decided that I would rent a flat in the neighbour-hood that they could share and I would pay half the rent until they had finished their training. With a low-cost loan from the bank where she worked and a cash loan from her father Heidi was able to buy a 'Yuppie' loft apartment in the West End, one of the prime locations in Frankfurt. When I say Yuppie, the bathroom alone cost as much as a middle class Mercedes and the rest of the apartment had solid wood- block parquet flooring. About three weeks, later after a soul-searching session with Heidi and she'd gone to bed early I went to a little wine bar that we occasionally frequented and did a bit of navel-gazing when I realised that maybe Liz would be back from Brittany. This was 1988, long before mobile phones became our comfort blankets. Unfortunately, there was a pay-phone in the bar so I dialled Liz's number. It turned out that she had returned that afternoon and if I liked I could come by as she was going to have a hot bath and open a bottle of wine. I thought, 'What the Fcuk!' finished my wine, walked to Heidi's Loft, where she was fast asleep. I left a brief note saying I was going to see Liz - the photographer who'd taken the publicity 'photos for the theatre group where I had played one of the lead characters in Luigi Pirandello's, 'Six Characters in Search of an Author.' (See Thespian dreams). I grabbed the car keys and drove to Liz's second floor, Gründerzeit, Baroque flat, with 3.50m ceilings. After she'd buzzed me in the door to her flat stood open as

I reached the top of the wide stairwell. I went in and called out, 'Liz, I'm here.' *'Hier bin ich,* 'she replied from her studio, which was simply a darkened living-room without the furniture and numerous cameras on tripods and ladder-back, Tonet chairs. Liz stood there in the middle of the room dressed in a long silk T-shirt, a glass of wine in one hand and an open bottle of Rioja in the other. *'Komm 'rein, Mein liebster, Alain!'* in her Rheinische dialect. thing lead to another, so I will leave the conclusion of this encounter to your obvious imaginations.

WHY?

This is not a dissertation about the meaning of life. No, it's the account of one man's search for the answer to the following question: Why, after thirty years as a serial bigamist did I suddenly feel the need to make a further contribution to the human gene-pool? Was it caused by a short-circuit in the galaxy of my hard-drives? Maybe the following will give some inkling. I've already sired two alpha males - I'm an alpha-beta male by the way - in the meantime I have three beautiful granddaughters.

Shortly after our second son Leo was born Alexis, my first wife commented that she didn't relish the idea of taking the pill for the next thirty years; she was twenty-five at the time. We'd even contemplated the vasectomy, which however didn't become reality, otherwise I wouldn't be writing this. I didn't realise it at the time but this was a sublimated desire to have more children. Which she was able to fulfil a few years later with her second husband.

Until Easter 1978 we, that is Alexis and our two sons Jacob and Lukas, all lived in the family compound in Riyadh, the capital of Saudi Arabia where I worked as a technical trainer.

We came to the UK on leave for 21 days' holiday, via a week on Crete When it came for us to return she dropped the bombshell and said that her and the two boys would not be returning, and that after thirteen years of wedded, blissful ignorance of each other's needs, she wanted a divorce.

I had to return to Saudi to fulfil my contract obligations wind things up. This took two months, and when I returned to the UK at the end of May I rented a bed-sit in Filton, Bristol, where the British Concorde was built and had her maiden flight. It was an old Edwardian terraced house that had been converted into six self-contained furnished bed-sits with a large shared kitchen and two bathrooms with gas meters, which had to be fed with 20 pence pieces - three were necessary for one had a half hot baths. And it was only 10 miles by car to where Jake and Luca lived with Alexis in Sodding Chipbury.

Once I'd moved into the bed-sit I set about getting wheels. A spot of luck and connections I was able to attain an ex Bristol Flying Squad, black, jelly-mould, Mk II Jaguar 2.4 with a V6 aluminium engine, twin overhead camshafts and a stiffened suspension. The car shone like a black diamond after a weekend with cutting paste and chrome cleaner.

At the time I had a cache of around DM 30,000 and US $ 1,000. They were the ill-gotten earnings from distilling and distributing 'White Lightning', known colloquially as '*Sideki*' (Arabic for friend), - more about this later. I'd bought the German currency on the advice of a colleague who liked to speculate; AKA as gambling. He told me that the Deutsch Mark was going to be re-valued.

I supplemented this by contracting at East Midlands Airport then known as Castle Donnington where the work involved converting DH Heralds, 4 engine turbo-prop medium haul passenger 'planes to freighters; and with my winnings from playing Blackjack at various casinos in Bristol.

Sometime in early July I received a letter from Joe, a friend and colleague from Singapore, when we both were attached to 205 SAR Squadron.

I'd contacted him and told him and his wife Barbara about the breakup with Alexis. The gist of the letter was that they were sorry to hear about the divorce. They were leaving at the end of the month to go to their 19th century farm labourer's cottage in the Gironde, which they had been renovating for the last three years, and that I was more than welcome to visit them and help with the restoration if I was at a loose end. In addition, he said that I could also bring some British products that were either very expensive or impossible to get, in France, i.e. baked beans, tea-bags etc., and my tool-box. He must have had a premonition, because he also included a sketch of how to find 'Les Gallineaux', their residence in Le Grande Nation.

His final words were a quote from a Carly Simon song from the film 'They Shoot Horses, don't they?' It went something like this:

"You've gotta keep on dancing, even when the Mafia has broken your legs."

THE SUMMER OF '78

Around the end of July, I sent Joe a postcard at Les Gallineaux telling him to expect me sometime after the beginning of August. I told my agent at EMA that I wouldn't be available until after my birthday at the beginning of September.

When I finished work on the last Friday in July I drove to me Mam's and spent the night there. Early on the Saturday morning I drove to Ruislip, cashed my pay-cheque with Jane, 'my accountant' and current squeeze. We picked up my two sons in Sodding Chipbury. Then we drove to Minehead a resort on the north Somerset coast and stayed the night in a B&B. The weather was pretty inclement so we couldn't go to the beach. However, we made the most of it and I delivered them safely to Alexis on the Sunday afternoon.

The following Thursday I packed my meagre possessions into the jelly-mould, clothes, music cassettes; there were only three, 'Street Legal' by Dylan, 'Baker Street' the album by Gerry Rafferty and the best of 'The Eagles', including 'Take it Easy'. I left my few books and winter clothes with my neighbour, Tom, an electrician with British Rail.

The other inhabitants of the WG, *Wohngemeinschaft'* (shared house) were; Brian, an ex-army lorry driver, who missed the camaraderie and had therefore joined the TA; Dennis, a free-lance taxi driver with a Kevin Keegan Afro; The fifth member of our commune was hardly ever seen, we suspected that she was a part-time sex-worker. This was Hilary, a well-built young woman from Liverpool, who occupied the attic flat and functioned as a go-between with our landlord. She also worked occasionally as a barmaid in the Disco club, which was owned by our landlord, the well-known small-time crook and scrap metal dealer, Willy Blair.

I set off after midday heading east and negotiated the South Circular round London, (in case you don't know pre M25 mayhem) without incident and arrived at the Hover port in Ramsgate 15 minutes before the last Hovercraft of the day left for Boulogne was due to depart. I pulled up at the check-in booth, bought a one-way ticket and was only on board a couple of minute when the ramp closed and we lifted off. The smooth flight only took 35 minutes. At the exit to the hover port in Boulogne I picked up two Australian girl back-packers and headed for Paris.

Claudine and Jacques, a French architect couple who we'd met in Saudi Arabia had said that we could visit them any time. I took them at their word and it didn't take me long to find their apartment in a side street only 500 meters from Port Autoille on the *'peripherique'*. They offered the girls the floor of their living room for their sleeping bags. They declined, however and left.

The following morning, we drove in convoy to their country house in a little village 60 kilometres south of Paris, which I think was called Janvry. I spent the rest of Friday and Saturday relaxing and eating. I took my leave early on Sunday morning with a terrible cold and headed south on the A71 bypassing Orleans and Limoges. I was able to forego the *'Peage'* because they wouldn't or couldn't take DM or US$ and I couldn't use my Amex, Diner's Club or Barclaycard. Luckily the petrol stations accepted Barclaycard. Sometime around mid-afternoon I located Les Gallineaux, which turned out to be a hamlet of six houses and various outbuildings at the end of a 500 metre one track road. The sketch had included the annotation to turn left just after the sign for La Roquille on the road from Ste Foy le Grande to Duras. I pulled into the large grassed area between two buildings and parked next to what appeared to be a brightly coloured crusader's tent complete with pennants. This turned out to be my domicile for the next 2-3 weeks. I decided that the house on the right was the most likely candidate for my destination because the central part had a newly laid wall and roof. I tried all doors on the adjacent buildings to no avail. I was on my way back to the car when a young woman's voice shouted, *'Messieur, Messieur! Arête, si vous plait.'* I turned slowly and was confronted with three B's, Buxom, Brown Brigitte, the farmer, Msr. Charbonier's 18-year-old daughter, whom I got to know more intimately after Joe and Barbara returned to the UK! I smiled and said *Bon jour.* After she'd got her breath back she explained that J & B had gone to lunch in a restaurant in Duras *avec* their Eenglish *Amis.* I discovered later that the French Sunday lunch can take up to three hours. Indeed, I had the pleasure of such a lunch also after J&B

had returned to the UK. Brigitte's parents invited me to '*Midi*' the Sunday after they had left. Ten courses with the obligatory *Eau de Vie* and flirting with Brigitte.

About 20 minutes later they pulled up in their Citroën Dyane. Joe's first words were: 'Fucking Coonmobile, Man!' After hugs and introductions to their friends, Elaine and Jim, two of Joe's colleagues from the tech college in Colchester where he taught Business Studies and Drama. The next three weeks went by like a dream.

We spent the rest of the day, eating, drinking, smoking, and reminiscing. All we drank was water, coffee and wine, which Joe bought in 20 litre plastic cans at the local Cave Cooperative in La Roquille for two Francs/litre. I think the exchange rate at the time was nine Francs to the pound!

We all slept late and were awoken by Monsr. Laconte, a local carpenter who had come to lay the framework for the new cement floor in the middle barn. Coffee was made and Joe had a con-flab with Monsr. Laconte and after the obligatory glasses of *Eau de Vie* we all dived in and by 13:00 it was done. Monsr Laconte left after a final *Eau. De Vie.* We were unable to do anything for the next two days because we had to wait for the cement mixer that Joe had rented to be delivered. So we went for a swim in Le Lac du Gaillard just south of Duras. It was an artificial lake which served as a fresh water reservoir for the surrounding villages. There was a small sandy beach and a paved area with a shower.

On a similar occasion the following week once again we all went to the lake, this time with the jelly-mould and the Ugly Duckling's big sister, Joe's Dyane. This was because Joe, Barbara, Elaine and Jim wanted to see the Château du Duras. In my time I'd seen enough castles from the inside and out. I'd even enjoyed the iniquities of medieval plumbing. Whilst we were there I was attracted to a buxom teenager who kept smiling at me. Egged on by the others I plucked up my courage and went over and spoke to her. It turned out that she was indeed English, but lived in the neighbourhood with her parents and her 10-year-old younger brother. She told me she was there mainly to keep an eye on her brother and his two friends and that her name was Hermione. Sometime later J, B, E and Jim left for their castle viewing. Shortly after Hermione asked me if I had a car, and if yes, I could drive her, her brother and his friend's home because the sky had become overcast and it was getting cooler. I agreed. When I got back to Les Gallineaux some three hours later I was greeted by the following:

Joe as Doctor with improvised stethoscope: *'Big Breaths!'*

Elaine as girl: *'Yeth and I are only Thixteen!'*

"Chance would be a fine thing!" I retorted, "She was only fourteen." One-day Joe borrowed the Jelly-mould and took Elaine and Jim to see the festival in Bergerac before their return to the UK.

It was about then when the first aquarelle course arrived. They were run by Joe's neighbour Jahn, a Dutch art teacher. However, there were no pickings there. It was a party of Dutch and Belgian couples in their 40's and 50's. Joe and I created an outdoor dining area and built a barbecue pit out of natural stone that we dug up on his property and scrap metal from the local rubbish dump.

On the last week in August the final aquarelle course arrived and it was more promising: four young women, early twenties and two older Dutch couples. I can't remember all their names except for Bea, Zhuli Li, Grit and Hildegard were participants in summer '78. One afternoon after they'd arrived I drove to the lake in the jelly mould and practised Backgammon against myself. By chance half of the painting course was also there enjoying the sun. It was easy to say hello. They invited me to join them for a drink and to play Backgammon that evening in their dining room - a converted cow barn. Which I did, and after a very pleasant evening I was about to take my leave when Bea, a blonde, chubby 20-year-old veterinary student with a toothy grin from Genk in Belgium, although she was Dutch, said she would leave with me as there was no street lighting on the track her chalet and it was on my way. When we got outside there was a full august moon so I said,

"You won't need me now."

"Why?" she asked innocently.

"Just look up there." I replied.

And as she did her pale slender neck was too much so I went into my werewolf mode and kissed and nibbled on her jugular. She almost fainted, but recovered sufficiently to meet my mouth and exchange DNA's. We snogged a bit and she told me she was still a virgin. I told her that Joe and Barbara were leaving after my birthday in two days' time and that she was invited to my party at Joe 's. I also invited Zhu Li, Grit and Hildegard and Joe's other neighbours.

The following day Claudine and Bogdan arrived. She was the daughter of Monsr Professor Surete-Canale, a retired teacher who had been part of the French civil service in Algeria. Claudine was a talented illustrator of children's books. Her husband, Bogdan was an up-coming Polish artist - later he became Professor of Fine Art at the Sorbonne. So I invited them as well. We became friends and I visited them later several times, either in Paris or in Les Gallineaux.

My birthday was two days later. Joe said I could invite anybody from the village. Brigitte made a brief appearance to wish me good luck and left shyly after 20 minutes. The two Belgian girls had previous plans. I'd bought an additional 20 litres of '76 La Roquille and Joe and I barbecued the dead animals that we'd found on the road, or we'd bought at the market in Ste Foy le Grande, on the pit we'd made of junk. Sometime during the evening Claudine's brother, Laurent arrived with his Spanish girlfriend, Penelope.

When Bea came over in the evening, after Joe and Barbara had left for Calais I was sitting in the kitchen-living room drinking wine and smoking a spliff. She seemed nervous so I gave her a glass of wine. This appeared to relax her so I took her by the hand and led her to the sleeping area above the kitchen. She asked me to switch off the light while she undressed. I complied with her wish, did the same and when she had slipped under the bed-cover I lit a candle, placed it on the floor and got under the covers myself. She had put her T-shirt back on and had retained her panties. I kissed and caressed her under the t-shirt and went through the erogenous zone check-list until she was ready to receive JT, who was champing at the bit. After she had got past the minor pain of the loss of the remnants of her hymen - they ride bikes a lot in the Low Countries - she soon started to enjoy the experience until I extracted JT and deposited my gene code on her stomach. After she'd cleaned up we cuddled until she got dressed and went back to her chalet. Subsequently she visited me every evening until she departed. Even when I invited Zhu Li to come and listen to the Dylan 'Street Legal' on the stereo in my limo the night before they were due to leave.

We sat in the back in order to get the best from the hi-fi system. Bea sat on my right and Zhu Li on my left and I was 'Piggy in the middle'.

I first kissed and caressed Bea, and then I turned and kissed Zhu Li who responded so I said we could listen to the cassette on the Hi-fi in the bedroom. We trooped upstairs and I put the tape on and lay down between them on the double bed. After five minutes of 'Ping pong' Bea got up and left saying that she didn't understand. I continued with Zhu Li for a further five minutes and she said it was too soon. As I walked Zhu Li back to her chalet I noticed Bea slouched on the back seat of the jelly-mould which was parked behind the house. I made my farewells with Zhu Li; we'd already exchanged addresses and telephone numbers, and walked back to my car. I coaxed her out and back to the bed where I licked and nibbled her clitoris until she had a massive orgasm and doubled up almost squashing my head between her plump thighs. I freed myself, sat up and held JT up to her lips. She greedily gobbled him down gagged a little as she swallowed my gene code. We cuddled a while until she got dressed and went to her chalet.

The next morning, I drive Bea and Zhu Li to the station in Ste Foy le Grande and said Adieu, with the suspicion that we'd all meet again.

I was alone in the house; Joe had said that I could stay there over winter if I wanted. I had the germ of an idea to look for work with Airbus in Toulouse. Another of Joe's neighbours, Msr Charbonier, Brigitte's father, a small-holder who had a small vineyard said that I could help out during the 'Vintage'. This was not to be. It rained heavily the week after Joe and Barbara left. Msr Charbonier said that the harvest would not be before the first week in October.

In the meantime, I was passing the time and picking up some pocket money picking 'Pruneaux ', large plums that were mainly used to make a fortified wine of the same name, similar in strength to Sherry. As mentioned earlier Brigitte came by one Sunday morning to invite me to have lunch with them. It turned out to be the

10 course lunch mentioned earlier, the last course being a glass of the aforesaid Pruneaux. Brigitte flirted with me when she thought her parents and 10-year-old brother weren't watching. A few days later on my way home from Pruneaux picking I saw a poster advertising a circus in Duras. When I got back I mentioned it to Brigitte and said that I could take here and her brother Louis to see it. Apart from the clowns the performance was abysmal.

When we got back I parked up behind the house and asked Brigitte if she'd like to listen to Bob Dylan from the back seat. She changed places with Louis and I got in the back seat with her and we had a preliminary reconnoitre until Louis said that he was bored and said that he was going home. At which, Brigitte said, 'I can't stay because my parents may still be awake,' taking a deep breath she continued in a whisper, 'Tomorrow evening I go to the Technical Lycee in Ste Foy le Grande until 21:00 and my parents expect me by 22:00. I'll leave early and park my moped down the lane. I must go now, *Bon Nuit, Mon Cheri!*' as she kissed me goodnight. As I mentioned earlier Brigitte was a stocky, brown 17-year-old farm girl with a broad Gallic smile who was studying at the local Lycee.

The following evening, I was lying in bed reading when at just before 21:00 when I heard the kitchen door open. Seconds later her careful footsteps preceded her broad smile as she climbed the stairs. Putting her finger to her lips she whispered,

'Bon soir, Mon Cheri! 'and came over to the bed and kissed me demandingly as she took off her leather motor-bike jacket - Hell 's Angel 'came to mind as she lay down next to me on the bed. 'Kiss me, Cheri,' she demanded as she stroked JT through the bed sheet. I succumbed to her wishes and after I'd discovered her pert, dark nippled breasts and caressed them she moaned with delight, pulled back the sheet covering JT and started massaging him enthusiastically, so I undid her jeans and pulled them down so that I could caress her Mons. After a while I said, thinking of cricket, 'I think we'd better stop,'

'You're right Cheri; we'll have more time at the vintage. Then I can get le 'Bon bon ', because I 'll be 18! 'she replied.

'*Oui*,' I said, as she rearranged her clothes and left.

Over the next few days before I spontaneously left Le Gallineaux she found some excuse to visit me, telling her Mama she was bringing me some vegetables and help her with her English homework. It wasn't to be.

The following Saturday I went to the lake for a final swim and met a 25-year-old English girl, Jennifer, who worked for a British export company in Bordeaux. She was staying the weekend in her parent's one-bedroom flat in Duras. She told me that she played Backgammon so I invited her to dinner and a game that evening in Duras. She agreed so I turned up neatly spruced at the restaurant overlooking the town square. After we'd eaten we went across the plaza to her apartment to play backgammon and the inevitable occurred.

The ensuing morning after I'd kissed her goodbye I drove back to Le Gallineaux, packed my belongings, said adieu to Brigitte and her parents, saying that I would return in time for the wine harvest and left just after 18:00. I drove through the night to Cherbourg. It was just after 05:30 when I got there only to discover that the next ferry to Weymouth was at 17:00 that evening. I dozed on the back seat for a couple of hours, went for a walk and had lunch at a 3-star restaurant on my Amex card.

The dice were rolled again when I got back to my bed-sit in Filton and spent some time with Jacob and Luc. I decided it was time to top up my bank account and called an old acquaintance from Carey Aviation. He told me that Carey was recruiting for a three-month contract with Lufthansa at Frankfurt/Main airport refurbishing 747's that Lufthansa was selling or leasing to the Korean Airlines. I called the number he gave me and found out that the money was good with medical insurance and accommodation in a Pension hotel close to the airport. The agent still had my details on file and said that I should report to the Lufthansa check-in for the 17:30 flight to Frankfurt on the 1st October where a ticket would be waiting. I told him that I would prefer to drive and if I could claim for petrol. He laughed and said OK and told me the name of the Pension in Kelsterbach, where the site coordinator would meet us.

I took Jacob and Lawrence out for a meal before I left. Once again I packed most of my possessions into the jelly-mould and set off about midday for Ramsgate, the Hovercraft crossing to Calais and Boulogne. With 10 minutes to spare I arrived at the loading gate, bought a ticket and drove on board. Forty minutes later we docked in Boulogne. With the aid of a poor road map and my inborn sense of orientation skills I found the route to Bea's student Bed-sit in Genk, Belgium where she was studying veterinary medicine, although she was from Utrecht in the Netherlands, where her father had a small engineering factory.

She was overjoyed when she opened the door and saw me standing there. We spent a delightful night in her narrow student bed. I left late the next morning telling her that I would write, and took a leisurely drive in time to meet the agent in Kelsterbach.

There were seven other technicians, even a couple of Trenchard's Brats, like myself. For the next few weeks we worked from 07:00 until 16:00, with appropriate breaks. On Fridays we finished at 13:00. However, we could work for 5 hours on Saturday mornings if we wanted, until it was cancelled one weekend. I packed a few things and drove to Genk in just over three hours, and spent 3 nights with Bea and left early on the Monday morning.

The following weekend I met Angelika, my first stewardess, who the following week moved into a 'mansard' flat in Niederrad close to the racecourse with Dagmar, a fellow trainee, aka Moerchen - who later became the second in the 'Boeing, Boeing' trilogy.

Before long we were lovers and often spent the nights together in her mansard room after I'd organised a 1.20m divan bed for her. One Thursday afternoon I was helping one of my colleagues, Pete, aka 'Ratty' move into an apartment - he'd brought his wife, a hair dresser to Frankfurt and she already had a job in a salon at the airport - when Bea turned up out of the blue in her two-year-old Mini. I hadn't replied to her letters since the relationship with Angie blossomed. Fortuitously that afternoon Edgar La Motte, Dagmar's French fiancée and social worker from her home town of Hamburg arrived to help move her things back, because she'd been kicked off the training course two weeks before it finished. I took Bea to Angie's flat in Niederrad where we had dinner with Edgar, Dagmar and Angie. An old school friend of Angie's had made her a 2m square double bed with planks from a cowshed. So when the time came I suggested that Bea share the big bed with Dagmar and Edgar and I would sleep with Angie on the divan. I left early next morning and dropped Angie off at the Lufthansa training centre before I went to work and worked until 13:00. I drove to Niederrad and Bea was still there.

Dagmar and Edgar had loaded up and already left. I made us a coffee and we made love one last time until she left before Angie came home at 14:00.

Two weeks later I received a very bitter letter saying that I'd used her. I sent her a postcard with the sentiment that we had both used each other for very different purposes. Nevertheless, I never misused or abused her.

Angie was already on her maiden flight, in a DC10 on a 12-day trip to Osaka and Tokyo, with a stop-over in Anchorage, when one evening while I was cooking my evening meal, Dagmar turned up. Since she got kicked off the course she'd been shacked-up with a German border guard, who was stationed at the airport - he even loaned me his 1100 BMW coupe to find a solenoid for my jelly mould - in Moerfelden, a satellite town of Gross Gerau.

I shared my dinner with her and after she'd showered we lay on the divan watching Angie's black and white 12" TV. In order to be close enough to discern the flickering screen one had to lay on one's stomach about a metre from the set, which sat on a stand under the eaves.

Before long the foreseeable occurred and in the second round Dagmar rode me and banged my head on the IKEA wardrobe as she came, rubbing her firm, full breasts in my face, crying, *'Beiss Mich'.*

We eventually fell asleep on the divan. Sometime in the night I woke with an erection between her well-formed buttocks. Reaching round I pulled JT between her legs rubbed him along her still juicy minge and in her sleep she pushed him inside her and started thrusting until we found a mutual rhythm and came together. Five minutes later we were fast asleep.

I woke at 06:00, kissed Dagmar awake and said as I got dressed, 'It might be a good idea to go into the other room because I'm picking up Angie from the airport at 07:30.

In addition to flying DC10's Angie also flew 737-400's. These were primarily used for domestic and inter European flights, such as London, Paris, and Vienna etc.

When Dagmar finally left I took over her mansard flat. Shortly after I started working for Pan-Am Angie and I moved into a one room first floor flat with a balcony in the same house. It also had a small kitchen and bathroom/toilet only 10 minutes by bus to the airport. In May '79 we went on holiday to Le Gallineaux in Angie's Citroen 2CV for three weeks with the objective of getting married in the local Marie, the council mayor's office in Ste Foy le Grande. However, we soon found out that this was not possible without a residence permit.

Nevertheless, we just relaxed and spent a night in a B&B in Pyla sur Mare, close to the huge sand dunes on the Atlantic coast. We left after a late breakfast and after a lunch of Moule Marnier we went for a stroll on the beach. We had a quick dip in the sea and took shelter from the wind in the dunes where we got out of our wet swimsuits. Angie was not impartial to 'Al fresco' so the inevitable ensued. In addition, we had two more open-air encounters. One day at the lake we'd swam and were lying on our beach towels in the long grass only five metres from the beach in the warm May sunshine.

The other occasion was one Monday a few weeks later when Angie was at home for four days and I didn't have to be at work in time for the night shift until 22:00. It was a warm summer's day so after a long, lazy breakfast in bed we got dressed and drove to Koblenz a medieval town on the confluence of the Rhine and Mosel. We visited Burg Ehrenbreitstein which overlooked the town. It was late morning when we arrived so we decided to 'do' the Burg before lunch. After we'd paid our entrance fee we explored the castle. At the end of the 'Great hall' was a steep ladder leading to the ramparts. We both climbed up and to our surprise the whole roof was a lawn and the battlements were overgrown with vines. It was a beautiful day and when we'd taken the obligatory holiday snaps it happened.

Due to the differences in our height I couldn't enter her standing up and the grass was still damp with dew, so she turned round and bent her knees and leant against the battlements. Lifting up her skirt I slipped JT between the leg of her French knickers and the rutting began. After a few minutes I thought'

'What the fuck!' and withdrew JT, released her grip on the battlements' turned her round and said,

'Ride me!' as I lay down on the damp lawn, pulling her down on top of me. She slipped off her French knickers squatted and fed JT into her Docking Module, etc., etc.

Once while Angie was on a 20-day tour to Sydney I had a brief snogging session with a petite South African stable hand who was employed at the nearby race-course. She lived in the block of flats opposite ours adjacent to the heavily guarded Russian Delegation. One weekend that summer Angie and I flew to Bordeaux via Paris to go to Dagmar and Edgar's wedding party in a small village, Campagne Charente, 50 kilometres south of Angouleme. The flight to Paris was in a Lufthansa 727 and the Air Inter flight to Bordeaux was Sud Aviation Caravelle, Frances' answer to the BAC 111. We hired a car at the airport, a clapped out Renault 5 and drove the 100 kilometres or so and arrived at the destination after asking for directions at the village tavern. It was a hedonistic weekend! On the way back to Bordeaux we dropped in on Joe and Barbara in Les Gallineaux. I gave him the money I'd borrowed the previous year. The return journey was strenuous. Due to a go slow by baggage handlers we missed our connection to FfM from Orly so we took the 19:30 LH flight to Dusseldorf. We once again rented a car. I called in to Tech control to tell them that I would be late and drove back to our flat in Hoechst.

After I quick wash and I coffee I reported in at 23:00.

We'd been married 6 months when I became aware of Angie's infidelities. Believe it or not I was nonplussed. We'd moved into a 3 room flat in Unterliederbach, a suburb of Hoechst. And early in 1981 she went for 5 days to Monaco with a Lufthansa co-pilot, Klaus who was 10 years younger than me.

MARIE-THERESE

Until I met Marie Therese I had seldom had the experience of two women fighting over me. The day after they left I went to the Irish Pub in Sachsenhausen, the 'Ebbelwöi' tourist quarter of Frankfurt south of the river. Before long I got in conversation with two attractive, young French women, Chantal and Marie-Therese. As the evening drew on the chemistry between Marie-Therese and me improved. She was a stocky 20-something young woman from a small town in the French Alps. Her thick dark hair was pulled back, which highlighted her dark amber eyes. It turned out that she was also a stewardess with Lufthansa flying 747's and 727's. Her friend, Chantal, from the same town was in the process of getting a divorce from her husband who worked for Ford in Cologne, and was soon a little tipsy. Marie-Therese suggested that I drive behind her car to her 2 room second floor flat in Offenbach. When we got there she put Chantal to bed and before long we were snogging and petting on the sofa in the living room until Chantal wandered in half asleep as I was removing Marie-Therese' bountiful bra.

'Let's all go to bed now.' said Marie-Therese to both Chantal and me as she adjusted her clothing.

And that's how it was to be as all three of us snuggled up like three commas in the 1.40m bed with Marie-Therese in the middle and JT snug between her ample posterior. The next morning while Chantal was making breakfast Marie-Therese and I consummated our friendship. After breakfast I drove to my flat in Unterliederbach to feed our two cats, Buggsy and Samson, did some laundry and went back that evening and spent the next two days with Marie-Therese, sometimes without Chantal.

Marie-Therese had noticed my wedding ring on the first evening and asked me if I was married. To which I replied,

'Not anymore.' as I had already written off my marriage to Angie. On the Monday evening after dinner she said that it was a pity that we didn't have much time because she was leaving for Buenos Aires on the Tuesday afternoon. So I suggested that I could call in sick.

Marie-Therese thought this was a good idea and at 21:30 I gave her the number of the Tech Control at Pan-Am. 'Who shall I say is calling?' she asked as she waited for the connection.

'My wife,' I replied with a guilty grin, like the cat that got the cream. When she'd done the dirt I told her about Angie and her co-pilot and that we were breaking up. There was a slight 'Boeing, Boeing' feeling to the situation, however I wasn't juggling three stewardesses from three different airlines. I was juggling two stewardesses from the same airline, who, as I already mentioned, flew on different aeroplanes.

Marie-Therese's trip meant that she'd be away for two and a half weeks so I told her that I would visit her when she came back.

Two days later Angie returned from Monaco and we had a heart to heart. I told her about Marie-Therese, including the fact that she was French and flew 747's and 727's with Lufthansa.

Two weeks later I was somewhat taken aback when I visited Marie Therese a few hours after she'd got back to her flat. When she let me in I could tell that she had been crying. We sat on the sofa and she showed me the letter that she'd found in her company mailbox that morning. It was from Angie thanking Marie-Therese for taking care of me in her absence, but I was her husband so back off.

However, before long I was able to convince Marie-Therese that it was really over between Angie and me.

Later that year I went to Fort Worth in Texas to take my FAA exams.

Marie-Therese requested a tour to Mexico City with stopover in Dallas. I arrive two days earlier and started my studies. (See Texas Time). She also met Jacob and Lawrence when they visited me in the Easter holidays.

We were lying naked in bed one evening in the afterglow when the question arose. Marie-Therese said somewhat broodingly,

'Mach mir ein kind, Cheri!'

'Kinder wird nicht gemacht, ma cher'

I answered, 'Sie wird geboren. '

'Dann bohr mir eine, bitte!' she said as we both broke out in a grin.

Angie visited me a couple of times when she was off-duty and when Marie-Therese was out of town as well as Klaus...On one occasion, not long after Jacob and Lawrence had come to live with me. She turned up one Saturday afternoon still in her elegant, if somewhat rumpled Lufthansa uniform, I've always had a hard spot for a uniformed woman, after a five day short-haul tour. I made fresh coffee while she had a shower.

We were sitting on the IKEA sofa half-heartedly watching TV when she turned to me and whispered in my ear,

'Have you got any porno magazines? '

I confess in dry times I have seldom refrained from self-help with visual or mental stimulation.

So I said, 'I think I have a story somewhere.' and got up and soon found the aforesaid book in my sparsely filled bookshelf. I gave it to her and she flicked through its well-thumbed pages, reading intensively until she sat up and said suddenly,

'I'm going to have a lie down.' and swept into the adjacent bedroom where our 2 metre square marriage bed stood and closed the door behind her. Five minutes later when Jacob came into the kitchen and said somewhat concerned,

'I think Angie's not well. She's groaning. Is she ill?'

I put my cup down and said, nonchalantly, 'She's suffering from jetlag and probably having nightmares. I'll look in on her in a couple of minutes.' as we made our way back to the living room. Sure enough she was clearly audible so I said to the boys, 'I think she needs some quiet. Turn off the TV. Why don 't you two go and have a kick-about? Here 's a couple of Marks for an ice-cream each.'

They instantaneously disappeared faster than a milli-second, which is, incidentally the time between red and amber and the first horn in the Middle East.

After they'd gone I peeped round the door and said, 'How are, Buggsy, (my nickname because of wriggling her nose when she was feeling good) 'Are you all right? And went in without further ado.

The room was darkened and Angie was reading the book, propped up on the pillows; her bathrobe was open and with her free hand she was caressing her engorged lips and clitoris.

CLITORIS AND COHORTS.

'You don't have to do that yourself, Buggsy, 'as I dropped my trousers, knelt between her thighs. She took her hand away when I started, nibbling, stroking and kissing her clitoris she put the book down and started squeezing her firm young breasts. After she'd had her first orgasm she said, *'Fick mich, Alain, Bitte!'*

'Only from behind, 'I replied in my alpha male mode. She turned over and presented her ample rump, etc., etc.

The divorce process with Angie ran its course. And shortly after Marie-Therese left Lufthansa and started flying for Air France based at the new Paris airport, Charles de Gaulle north of the capital.

As I mentioned in Lin-Fout Jacob and Lawrence came to live with me in Unterliederbach. It was during this autumn that I met Barbara, (See she who eats little).

***

Betreff: WG: pix

Von: melvyn <maevewalker@yahoo.de>

An: schnellmel@web.de

Datum: 05/08/1010:27:19

Anlagen: PICT0583 .JPG, PICT0271

JPG, PIGT0375.JPG, PICT0582.JPG

Von: Bianca <cosmo@web.de>

An: maevewalker@yahoo.de

Gesendet: Dienstag, den 11. November 2008,3:41:00 Uhr

Betreff: pix

Hi there,

here come the kids and your arrival pic...

The 5th day that I haven't seen the sun. The sky is a leaden blanket. Everything is moist - the humidity crawls into everything, books, clothes, wood. My towels just don't dry for days and I'm having increasing troubles with my doors and windows - every time a big bang. How spoiled I am I get a notion of how it feels like being stuck in the rainy season in Ranong. It's not too bad having lots of good stuff to read, to watch and to write. Just had a breakthrough with my story line. Chaptered it out, created the major characters, etc. The dialogues seem to flow out of my fingers naturally. Well, let's see how I consider them in a few weeks' time when I start revising. I think it even possible to accomplish this while I'm working. This term is quite relaxed and there are hardly any people here who could distract me.

Please send me the details concerning Krabi ASAP. I might wanna go there the coming weekend.

Take care, BB

IN FUTURUM VIDERE
(To see into the future)

We can all see into the future; it's a scientific fact; the surface skin of the eyeball, known as the Conjunctiva, has hundreds of nerve endings, which register the speed and velocity of an object thrown at us 1/30,000 of a second before the retina can send a signal to the brain, via the optic nerve in time for us to take the appropriate action. Otherwise we wouldn't have sports, ball sports in particular. This ability has developed, and is still developing ever since we started to try being masters of our environment.

Some of my friends call me 'Elephant-Eye', because I see things others don't, and I remember the majority of what I've seen and heard. But mostly I remember when I do something myself. I heard something the other day on 'Look North'; it was some member of a Yorkshire Chamber of Commerce, to quote, 'Businesses need to make more profit.' unquote.

Can anyone tell me why businesses have to make more profit each year?

What happens to the 'more profit'? Who benefits from it? Maybe some people get an even larger bonus than last year? Which means that they can afford more un-necessaries? Some of this filters down and everybody can take two or three holidays and complain about everything when we're not getting bamboozled by the Media and their lackeys.

In my opinion True happiness is; 'Wanting what you have and not having what you want!' Don't be fooled.

'ear all see all, say nowt, eat all drink all, pay nowt, if tha' iver does owt fir nowt, allus do it fir thisen '.

DESINFORMATION

A STUDY by North Staffordshire academics has rejected a link between smoking cannabis and an increase in mental illness.

The research found there were no rises in cases of schizophrenia or psychoses diagnosed in the UK over nine years, during which the use of the drug had grown substantially.

Pro-cannabis campaigners seized on the results as supporting the legalising of cannabis, and claimed the report had been suppressed. But the leading expert behind the study said it could be too low-key to re-ignite the debate on whether restrictions should be removed from soft drugs.

From their base at the Harplands Psychiatric Hospital in Hartshill, the four experts reviewed the notes of hundreds of thousands of patients at 183 GP's practices.

The work had been set up to see if earlier forecasts from other experts had been borne out, that the mental disorder would soar through the growing popularity of cannabis.

Published in the Schizophrenia Research journal, a paper on the study said: "A recent review concluded that cannabis use increases the risk of psychotic outcomes

"Furthermore an accepted model of the association between cannabis and schizophrenia indicated its incidence would increase from 1990 onward.

"We examined trends in the annual psychosis incidence and prevalence as measured by diagnosed cases from 1996 to 2005 and found it to be either stable or in decline.

"The casual models linking cannabis with schizophrenia and other psychoses are therefore not supported by our study."

The research was conducted by Dr's Martin Frisher and Orsolina Martino, from the department of medicines management at Keele University. Its findings come shortly after the Government reclassified cannabis from Class C to Class B, which invokes heavier penalties

Yet Dr Frisher revealed last night that the study had been partly commissioned by the Government's advisory committee on the misuse of drugs. He said: "We concentrated on looking into the incidence of schizophrenia during those years and not specifically at cannabis use. "It was relatively low-key research so I don't believe it will re-ignite the debate on whether the drug should be legalised." Hartshill-based Dilys Wood, national coordinators of the Legalise Cannabis Alliance, said that so far the report had been published in medical journals and would have a far-reaching reaction if it surfaced more widely. She added "I believe that if it had found a causal link between cannabis and schizophrenia it would have been all over the press. "The public needs to know the truth about drugs; not more Government-led propaganda." And Alliance press officer Don Barnard said: "It is hard to believe the then Home Secretary Jacqui Smith did not know of this very important research when deciding to upgrade cannabis to Class B."

The team said a number of alternative explanations for the stabilising of schizophrenia had been considered and while they could not be wholly discounted.

DEATH IN THE AFTERNOON

No, this isn't about Ernest Hemingway or Bull fighting, it's about a near death experience. It was just a usual Thursday midday in Riyadh sometime at the end of March 1978. I'd finished work on time because the last sortie of the day had been cancelled. On the way home from work I stopped off at a local bakery to buy extra European sliced bread. This was because we, that is my wife, Alexis and our two sons, were planning to have a picnic with a couple of friends at the Camel race that was scheduled to start later that afternoon 10 kms east of the capital. We had been told that this was something not to be missed. Having made my purchases, I put the bread in the pannier, mounted my 350cc Yamaha off-road bike, kicked it into life, selected first gear, dropped the clutch and opened the throttle.

An indeterminate time later I woke up on an operating table in what transpired to be the King Faisal hospital. When my vision had returned to normal I looked up to see an Egyptian doctor cleaning the centimetre hole in my right foot. He had already dressed the grazes on my arms and legs. Standing at the foot of the bed, and looking extremely concerned, was a Yemeni dressed in the typical Thobe - Arab dress and a dirty looking cloth on his head. After he had dressed the wound the doctor explained in excellent English, that as far as he could establish, the man standing at the foot of the table had driven out of a side street in his Toyota pick-up truck without looking and cut me off. The doctor then asked me to stand up, which I did. After I'd recovered from the momentary dizziness he said that the Yemeni would drive me home. When I'd managed to hobble outside with his assistance, he took me to his pick-up truck - which to my surprise had my bike on the back - I noticed a large dent in the side; obviously the part I 'd collided with. By means of hand gestures and my basic Arabic I managed to direct him to our house in the company compound. With difficulty I helped him unload the bike, which seemed to have survived the mishap with only negligible damage. Once inside I removed my crash helmet, something the doctor had neglected, or had not had the foresight to do. It was obvious that Alexis and the boys had left with our friends for the Camel race because by now it was already 16:00, which meant I had been unconscious for almost 3 hours. As I was still feeling dazed I decided the best thing to do was sleep. The dressing on my foot was already blood soaked. I pulled a plastic sandwich bag over it and secured it with a rubber band, took off my torn dusty trousers and shirt, got into bed and fell into a deep sleep almost immediately. I was awoken some hours later by my wife's scream when she came into the bedroom and saw me lying on a blood-stained pillow. She thought that either someone had slit my throat or that I'd committed suicide. Because the doctor had failed to remove my helmet the wound on my head had gone undetected and had bled profusely whilst I was asleep. I later came to the conclusion that the hole in my ankle had been caused by the brake lever as I sailed over the handlebars, and the one on my head by my impact with the load bed of the truck. Without the helmet I wouldn't be writing this.

HOME OF THE SLAVE & LAND OF THE CREE

OR

SLAVERY IN THE USA TODAY

Many people have the mistaken impression that slavery was outlawed or abolished in the United States after the civil war by the passage of the Thirteenth Amendment. Unfortunately, that was not the case. The Thirteenth Amendment reads: "Neither slavery nor involuntary servitude, except as punishment for crimes whereof the party shall have been duly convicted, shall exist within the United States, or any place subject to their jurisdiction."

The effect of the Thirteenth Amendment was not to abolish slavery but to limit it to those who had been convicted of a crime.

The reality was made apparent in the aftermath of the civil war when large numbers of newly freed Black slaves found themselves "duly convicted" of crimes and in state prisons where, once again, they laboured without pay. It was common practice for state prisons to "lease" prison labour out to private contractors in a modern form of chattel slavery. This situation led the Virginia Supreme Court to remark in an 1871 case, Ruffin v. Commonwealth, that prisoners were "slaves of the state." All that has changed since then is that the state is less honest about its slave-holding practices. Until the 1930s most state and federal prisons were largely self-sufficient, producing most of the goods and food they consumed and even producing a surplus, for sale, of food and some industrial products. In many states prisoners even served as armed guards (until the mid-1970s the state of Arkansas held some 3,000 prisoners with only 27 civilian employees) and many other functions which required minimal investment by the state. Prison self-sufficiency and excess production for profit largely ended during the mid-1930s when the U.S. was in the midst of the depression and both unions and manufacturers complained about competing against prison-made products on the open market. One of the laws passed was the Ashurst-Sumners Act (1935) which prohibited the transport in interstate commerce of prison-made goods unless the prisoners were paid at least minimum wage.

Prison labour did not start to become a major issue again until the 1980s. Until then most prison-produced goods were either for use within the prison system or sold to other state agencies, license plates being the most familiar example. This began to change with the massive prison building and incarceration binge. In a 1986 study designed to reduce the cost to the government of its prison policies, former Supreme Court Justice Warren Burger issued the call for transforming prisons into "factories with fences." In essence, prisons should once again become self-sustaining, even profit-producing, entities requiring minimal financial input from the state. While some think that slavery, i.e., unpaid, forced labour-offers enormous profit potential for the slave owner, there are historical reasons slavery is no longer the dominant mode of economic production. First, the slave owner has a capital investment in his slave: regardless of whether the slave is working or producing profit he must be fed, housed, and so on, in minimal conditions to ensure the slave's value as a labour producer remains. With the rise of industrial capitalism in the 18th and 19th century capitalists discovered that capitalism has its boom and bust cycles characterized by over-production. Thus idle slaves would become a drain on the owner's finance because they would still require feeding, housing, etc., regardless of whether they were working. However, if the slave were "free" he could be employed at low wages and then laid off when not producing profit for the employer, the wage slave was free to starve, free to be homeless, and so on, with no consequences for the owner.

Another reason chattel slavery was inefficient compared to wage slavery was that the slaves would occasionally revolt, destroying the means of production and/or killing the slave-owner. More common and less dramatic were the acts of sabotage and destruction that made machinery, with its attendant capital investment, impractical for use by slaves. So by the middle of the 19th century wage slaves employing machines could out produce, at greater profit for the factory owner, chattel slaves using less easily damaged, more primitive machinery. The problem slave owners of old faced was what to do with non-producing slaves. Today's slave owner-the state faces the opposite problem of having idle slaves who must be fed, clothed and housed whether or not they produce anything of value. The current thinking goes that any potential profit produced by prison slaves is better than none. Some of the proponents of prison slavery try to disguise it as a "rehabilitation" or "vocational" program designed to give prisoners job skills or a trade which can be used upon their release. This is not the case. First, almost without exception the jobs available in prison industries are labour intensive, menial, low skill jobs which tend to be performed by exploited workers in three places: Third World dictatorships, and in the U.S., by illegal immigrants or prisoners. Clothes and textile manufacturing are the biggest example of this. Second, because the jobs don't exist in the first place the job skills acquired are hardly useful. Does anyone expect a released prisoner to go to Guatemala or El Salvador to get a job sewing clothes for the U.S. market at a dollar a day? Third, if its rehabilitation then why not pay the prisoner at least minimum wage for his/her work? Fourth, it ignores the reality that the U.S. has at least 8 or 9 million unemployed workers at any given time, many of them highly skilled, who cannot find jobs that pay a meaningful wage to support themselves.

So-called "job retraining" programs are a failure because all the training in the world won't create jobs with decent wages. In pursuit of higher profits-by paying lower salaries – the U.S. and transnational corporations have transferred virtually all labour intensive production jobs to Third World countries. The U.S. has little problem condemning the export of prison-made goods from China. What makes this blatant hypocrisy is the fact that the same criticisms levelled by the U.S. government against Chinese prison made goods can be levelled at U.S. prison-made goods. Prison-made goods from California and Oregon are being exported for retail sales. In a supreme irony, the California DOC is marketing its clothing lines in Asia, competing against the sweatshops of Indonesia, Hong Kong, Thailand and of course, China. The Prison Blues brand of clothes, made by prisoners in Oregon, has annual projected sales of over $1.2 million in export revenues. U.S. State department officials were quoted saying they wished prison-made goods were not exported by state DOC's because it is being raised as an issue by other governments. Namely the Chinese, which have cited U.S., practices in response to criticisms. For their part, the

Chinese have announced a ban on their export of prison-made goods while the U.S. is stepping up such exports. California prisoners making clothes for export are paid between 35 cents and $1 an hour. The Oregon prisoners are paid between $6 to $8 an hour but have to pay back up to 80 per cent of that to cover the cost of their captivity. As they are employed by a DOC-owned company this is essentially an accounting exercise where the prisoners' real wages are between $1.20 to $1.80 an hour. Still competitive with the wages paid to illegal immigrant sweatshop workers here in the U.S. and wages paid to garment workers in the Far East and Central America.

Fred Nichols, the administrator of Unigroup, the Oregon DOC prison industries, has said: "We want them to work in the same environment as on the outside" in terms of hiring interviews and such. Yet obviously this does not include the right to collective bargaining and union representation.

While the particulars may change, the trend continues towards increased exploitation of prison slave labour. Some states, especially those in the South-such as Texas, Arkansas, Louisiana-still have unpaid prisoners labouring in fields supervised by armed guards on horseback, with no pretence of "rehabilitation" or "job training." In those states the labour is mandatory, refusal to work brings harsh punishment and increases prison sentences served. In 1977 the Supreme Court decided Jones v. North Carolina Prisoner's Labour Union, which removed court protection for prison union organizing. Efforts to obtain the minimum wage for prisoners through litigation have been largely unsuccessful, with courts bending over backwards to read exemptions (which are not written) into the federal Fair Labour and Standards Act (FLSA). In Washington the state offers a lot of incentives for private businesses to employ prison slaves. Class I venture industries pay no rent, electricity, water or similar costs. They are exempt from state and federal workplace safety standards and pay no medical, unemployment or vacation/sick leave to slaves who have no right to collective organizing or bargaining. In a case like this we are seeing welfare capitalism where private business is getting a hand-out from the state at taxpayer expense. One which will largely swallow the profit paid back to the state under guise of taxes, room and board, etc., by the prisoner. To the extent that prison slaves are forced to pay state and federal taxes there arises the question, linked to the right to vote, of taxation without representation. If forced to pay taxes like any other citizen, under the guise of rehabilitative or vocational employment, then why not the right to vote given other workers and taxpayers?

Workers on the outside should also be aware of the consequences that prison slave labour poses for their jobs. Ironically, as unemployment on the outside increases, crime and the concomitant incarceration rate increases. It may be that before too long people can only find menial labour intensive production jobs in prisons or Third World countries where people labour under similar conditions. The factory with fences meets the prison without walls. I didn't write this, I just copied it from Google.

THE 51st. STATE

OR

LANDING STRIP ONE?

When I refer to the 51st. State I don't mean the film starring Samuel L Jackson and Robert Carlyle, nor do I mean Heathrow, Gatwick, Stansted, or any other UK airport when I mention Landing Strip One, as William Burroughs called the UK in his book Neuromancer.

To give him credit Aldous Huxley called Britain Airstrip One. Yes, that's right the US administration regards the UK as no more than a transit base in their bid to dominate the world.

After spending the majority of my adult life away from this 'Septic Isle', what I refer to is US American imperialism.

Did you know that there between 700 and 750 US military bases around the world? If you don't believe me just look it up on Wikipedia or Google.

For anyone who is a free-thinker, and who doesn't blindly put up with the insidious destruction of the British way of life including the bastardisation of the English language, this must be a priority.

Do you dress, speak, eat and behave like your children, because that is what you do if you accept the American way of life. This entails eating so-called 'fast-foods', ready meals, falling for the tricks of the numerous 'coffee shops', whose main endeavour is to relieve you of as much of your hard-earned money as possible.

Do you think it's cool and modern if you wear a baseball cap, or consider it increases your self-esteem if you dress in your favourite football club's colours and logo because it cost a lot of your hard-earned money? Do you carry a half litre bottle of French or other brand name 'mineral' water around with you wherever you go, not realising that it is costing you £ 2000/ cubic litre? Is your name Rockefeller or Roth-schild (pronounced Red Shield)?

Did you know 'Evian' is an anagram of 'Naïve'? British tap water is subject to more stringent controls than bottled water. Don't allow yourself to be fooled; ignore what the TV tells you. Why do you think Hitler promoted the production of 'Volks Radio in the 1930's? Mind control, that's purpose of television today...A recent observation at a well-known supermarket in Yorkshire: two weeks ago rhubarb from the Netherlands was on sale - bad but not terrible; last week it was from Germany; also acceptable. Three days ago I almost had an epileptic fit because the rhubarb on offer was from, believe it or not, New Zealand!

All I can say is; 'Every little helps the shareholders!

LETTER TO THE PRIME MINISTER

As a British citizen, who took the Queen's Shilling when I was sixteen, and who has never voted in the last forty years, I am appalled at the state of the country.

Don't get the wrong idea, it's not because I am politically disinterested; indeed, whilst living in another country in the European Union I was asked to stand as a listed candidate in the local government elections for the Green party; believe it or not I received some 170 votes at the election. Unfortunately, it transpired that I had left myself open for a criminal prosecution because I was not a national of that country. However, the situation was resolved when I agreed to give my votes to another party candidate.

Whether it is obesity, or the incidence of violent crime, the nauseous obsession with so-called celebrities and their clothes, the imitation of US vernacular, the fact we throw away 30 % of our food, and the absurd belief that we live in a democracy. Who is to blame for the uncontrolled spread of this malady? None other than the media, whose sole objective is to increase circulation, or advertising revenue, and the advertising agencies, whose sole aim is to awaken unnecessary desires, at the same time keeping the general public anesthetised with irrelevancies, just as all previous totalitarian Empires have done in the past.

How can we break away from this state of affairs?

First of all, we must abandon this misguided concept that 'Economic Growth' is the answer to all that ails Britain. In addition, we must accept the fact that 'Sustainable Growth' is in itself an oxymoron. We must first strive to attain a 'Steady State Economy' as proposed by Herman Daly, Dr King M Hubbert and even Adam Smith.

How can we achieve this? First of all, accept the premise that GDP is a false measure of prosperity. A more reliable yardstick for affluence is per capita income.

As most informed people know Britain, as well as the other EU states, has a negative population growth rate, which means that we have to appeal to people to emigrate to this country.

The only reason why any government tolerates immigration, limited or not, is not only to perform the menial tasks that we are no longer willing to do, but also to be consumers of the increased production. What happens when this enlarged capacity cannot be sold? If you would like an answer to this question take a trip down the M5 past Avonmouth and you will see thousands of vehicles waiting patiently for prospective buyers. A few years ago there were more than 2 million cars produced and left unsold in Europe.

This situation applies to almost all articles produced today. That's why we have the BOGOF offers we see in the shops. If you would like more information about this read the theories of Herman Daly, Dr King M Hubbert and even Adam Smith.

Whenever you or the other people's representatives try to justify your toadying to the U.S. of A......., with regards to our involvement with the so-called war on terrorism, you quote the 'Special relationship' with this imperialist nation. So can you clarify for me and the other uninformed citizens of the UK what this 'special relationship' entails? It can't be the language because, as I believe, Oscar Wilde once commented so succinctly; Britain and the U.S. of Abominations 'are two nations separated by a common language, and furthermore the U.S of A doesn't have a national language. In addition, it can't be that we are in debt to U.S. of A, because if I remember correctly, the obligation incurred during World War II was settled a couple of years ago.

Aldous Huxley and George Orwell were not merely writers; they were visionaries, who predicted the future we are living today. 'Big Brother' wasn't the Soviet Union, nor was it a mindless worthless television programme. I'll leave it to the reader to decide who the culprit is.

Enough about me and the past, it's time we started looking to the future. Some facts you must, or should be aware of as Fuehrer of our country:

Per capita income in Saudi Arabia has fallen by three quarters over the past twenty years. They only have one commodity; Oil. In the Gulf States women can't get contraception. When oil prices were rising population grew; now oil prices are falling and it is growing just as fast. The population is doubling every twenty years. If the population doubles over the next twenty years, per capita income could drop by as much again. The population of the Gulf needs high or rising prices. The U.S. of A, Europe, Japan, India and China need stable or falling prices. It's irreconcilable. There's no work. Large numbers of young men face a lifetime of unemployment.

The rat cage is now too small.

Rising population and falling income fuel anti-western movements: couple that with Islamic fundamentalist Wahhabism and you have a time bomb.

Now, to misuse a well-known saying, for some something completely different. I recently read the following in a work of fiction:

'Kuwait has no public services, there never has been; all there is, is money and power, and those who have it and those who don't. The people there live as people have lived throughout history, as the cattle of stronger men.

Government exists solely for the benefit of the governors. The law of enforcement is force only. There are no duties, only taxes to be avoided and no freedoms, only privileges to be taken.'

It doesn't require a great deal of imagination to see the parallels with the UK.

Introduce legislation to coerce the producers of all beverages and the manufacturers of the relevant containers to limit the number of materials used in order to make the recycling simpler; in addition, impose a surcharge on all drinks bottles and cans of 25 pence/ up to half a litre and 50 pence for all larger containers. This could kill the proverbial two birds with one stone, reduce waste and help to keep our streets cleaner; maybe even three if the surplus recycled plastic was exported to China, which would reduce China's need to build new power plants.

Cut the £10 billion plus we are spending annually on the war against terrorism in Iraq and Afghanistan, and the prospective £130 billion cost of the Trident renewal/ replacement, supposedly to make the streets of Britain safe could be used more effectively at home.

Repeal the smoking law; allow anyone over the age of 21 to cultivate sufficient cannabis for personal use, Decriminalise the possession of small quantities of controlled substances.

Finally make sure you and your cabinet and advisers stop talking out of the wrong end of your alimentary canals. Make a blanket cut of 10% on all public servant salaries over £60,000/annum.

Of course you won't do any of the above because; all you and your fellow People's representatives are worried about is maintaining the status quo.

Sincerely yours,

A Freethinking Citizen.

WOMENS LIB

I have been a feminist for the past fifty years. A little over thirty years ago McDonald's opened their first outlet in London. It was about then that I read 'Women's Room' by Marilyn French.

THE WORLD IS A STAGE

It must have been a Friday in autumn sometime in the early 50's. Our class teacher had taken us to the old village hall to watch the dress rehearsal of 'Holme Player's rendition of 'Oklahoma'.

If I remember correctly I was probably about 8 or 9 years old, and according to my class teacher somewhat ebullient, so I was not surprised, but a little bit apprehensive when she called me from the row where I was sitting with my fellow conspirators.

I thought, 'Ok, why me?' I wasn't the only one who wasn't taking an interest in the performance.

As it transpired it wasn't because of my misbehaving, but more to do with my size. I was maybe just over a metre tall and weighed about 35kgs. She took me to meet the director of the play who wanted to ask me to participate in the musical. He didn't want me to sing. That would have been a fatal mistake because a few years later I was politely asked to leave the church choir. He told me that when the curtain closed for the scene changes between the acts, two older boys came on stage in front of the curtain and had the following short dialogue,

1st boy, 'Why are you crying Michael?' upon which Michael replied, showing his black eye, 'Jimmy Brown did this!'

This was repeated after Act 2. However, this time Michael had two black eyes. And once again Jimmy Brown was the culprit.

Cut to the final curtain; one after another the cast came on stage and took their bows. My role was to wait until they were all assembled and then to saunter on and end up down stage centre, upon which the leading man asked me, 'Who are you?' And as innocently as I could, I replied, 'Me? I'm jimmy Brown!'

You can imagine this resulted in a round of applause and raucous laughter, because Michael was a strapping 14-year-old and who was at least twice my weight.

In retrospect I believe that it was this that subconsciously aroused in me my love of the theatre, especially much later the Theatre of the Absurd.

A few years later I attended Market Weighton secondary school where I took part in several Gilbert and Sullivan operettas, including Pirates of Penzance and Trial by Jury.

Quite a few years later, whilst serving in the Royal Air Force in Aden, I played one or two minor roles in the Khormaksar drama club. When I returned to the UK I was posted to RAF Lyneham. Because we didn't know anyone there my wife, Alexis and I joined the 'Lyneham Players'. Both of us were active members for three years until I was posted to RAF Tengah in Singapore. Alexis and I had agreed that we would give the theatre a break because she was expecting our second child, who was, coincidentally born in Changi hospital.

Instead we regularly went to the base Folk club. It was here where I was approached by a young radio technician. He told me that the Tengah Drama club had become dormant since several active members had returned to the UK and he asked me if we would be interested in reactivating it. Apparently word of our involvement with the theatre at RAF Lyneham had come down the RAF grapevine. I had a heart to heart with Alexis and we agreed that I should take on a role until after she had had the baby. The role I was given was Stanley in Harold Pinter's Birthday Party. This was to be a one off, because six months after my arrival the squadron was disbanded and I was posted to 205 Squadron at RAF Changi. Because the Birthday Party won the inter-services drama festival and I was awarded the best actor accolade, we were not unknown when we arrived at Changi. It wasn't long before I was approached by a squadron Air Electronics Operator, Joe, who later became my close friend. He wanted to try his hand at directing and asked me to play a leading role in a one-act play by Edward Albee.

By this time our second son Lucas had arrived and Alexis was also asked if she would be interested in playing the role of the American stewardess in 'Boeing. Boeing ', a French farce. There was no question of either of us declining the offers because we had employed a Chinese 'Amah' after Lucas was born. So for the next 2 1/2 years we took an active part in the theatre club, not only acting, but also properties, prompt, scene painting etc. I was even able to make my debut as a director when Joe played the part of Ben in

Pinter's 'The Dumb Waiter'.

My theatrical activities were curtailed until I was sacked from my job as an applications technician in Offenbach/Main. Because the sacking was illegal I was awarded compensation by an Industrial Tribunal. This meant that I was entitled to unemployment benefit immediately. I used the money from the court to train to be a teacher. I therefore had the time to follow my theatrical leanings once again.

I answered an advertisement in the Frankfurter Rundschau from a local amateur dramatic society. This turned out to be a mistake. Because as I was the oldest member of the company, apart from the Czech director, I was offered the role of the father in Pirandello's 'Six Characters in Search of an Author '. Apart from being a very demanding character I was also presented with the task of club chairman, wherein my main chore was to keep tabs on our alcoholic, Czech 'Artistic Director'. After one play I regretfully made my farewells to the ensemble, several of whom had become close friends. A few months later one of the young women members of the ensemble asked me if I knew a humorous monologue for women because she was auditioning for a drama school and had to perform a classical, a tragic and a funny monologue. As I didn't, I decided to write one myself. That was when 'Martha' was born; she was an elderly lady prone to malapropisms, e.g. Pie-Ella, Flamingo dancers, etc., who runs into an old friend in the supermarket and starts reminiscing about the time when they went to the Costa Brava with the WI. I tried it out myself in a small bar one evening and it was received with moderate success. So shortly afterwards I used it for an impromptu audition for the English Theatre in Frankfurt as I knew the American woman, Judith Rosenbauer who was the driving force and part owner. However, she told me that although I'd impressed her, she could unfortunately only employ actors who were members of Equity, the British performing arts union.

My next excursion on the stage was brought about after I heard an advert on AFN, the American Forces Network, another Amateur dramatic club run by and for the American forces and families in the Frankfurt area. They were looking for people to perform in their production of 'Nuts', the stage play of the film which starred Barbra Streisand in the leading role. I went along for the auditions and was given the role of the prosecuting District Attorney. An ex-pat English woman got the part of the main character. We both had some difficulties adapting our English accents to the American vernacular. After 2 months' rehearsal we did six performances. The following year I plucked up the courage and wrote a couple of new sketches. In addition, I adapted several 'Monty Python' sketches and sketches from the 'Two Ronnie's'. Then with the help of friends and acquaintances from my Squash clique, some of my students and the son of one of the members of the now defunct German theatre club, who took responsibility for sound and lights I produced, directed and acted in 'Stop Press', an Evening of English Humour and Drama 'in a small theatre in the Gallus Quarter of Frankfurt am Main. Once again this was reasonably successful as we managed to fill the 100 seat theatre even though we only performed two night's midweek during a Women's Theatre week. After spending six weeks, following this gruelling undertaking at a friend's Finca in Andalucía, I returned to FfM fully re-energized, and inspired by my new quarters - a garret in a church vicarage, courtesy of a colleague's husband - I started on my next theatrical adventure. This as 'A Sleep of Prisoners' by Christopher Fry. The play takes place in a church where the four characters are interned for an indefinite period. On this occasion I was able to get Four different nationalities; Doug, a banker and fellow Brit, Petros, a Greek student, Ndako, a lab technician from Namibia and Andreas a Lufthansa steward. My next excursion into theatre was delayed somewhat due to the fact that in January 1991 I was given the task of setting up and running a language school in what was the German Democratic Republic, where I spent the next 18 years. A year later things eased off and I was able to turn my attention to theatrical thoughts once again. In 1992 with my students and new acquaintances I produced an English theatrical evening in a residence where Goethe once held court. Since then I have only had one occasion to practice my love of theatre and that was in 2008 when I worked at a summer school in Hatfield.

PARENTHOOD

When Alexis unexpectedly sent our two sons, Jacob and Lawrence to live with me in the summer of 1981, my marriage to Angie, and my first Lufthansa stewardess was already in tatters. The divorce was finalised the following May. I'd booked two weeks' holiday from Pan-Am, where I worked at the Rhine-Main airport. I was under the impression that they would be staying for the two weeks. However, Jacob had a letter from Alexis stating that it was now my turn to look after the boys as she was remarrying and joining her new husband in Saudi Arabia.

After I'd recovered from the shock I told the boys that it will only work if we work as a team. The nearest school was just a five-minute walk from my three room attic flat in Unterliederbach a suburb of Hoechst, one of the German chemical giants. It took pupils from 6 to 14. It was closed for the summer holidays until the end of August, so before I went back to work I bought a 'Teach yourself German' book. We worked through the book whenever my shift duties permitted. In addition, I told them to watch TV as much as possible, especially children's programmes.

In my free time we played a lot of Boule. I also took them to the tenpin bowling alley regularly because it was in the Main-Taunus shopping centre at the other side of the A66, autobahn, known by the locals as 'Route 66', and within walking distance of our flat. We also played pool in squash club in Zeilsheim, another suburb of Frankfurt/Main.

When school reopened I registered Jacob in a year below his age. At the time he was a polite, almost shy 13-year-old. I registered Lawrence, who had turned ten in May in his age group. They only attended this school until the Christmas break - as you can read in, Lin-Fout, I changed jobs in January 1982, shortly after I'd joined the Ransburg Corporation in the Glass-Mate department, in Heusenstamm, a small town south of Offenbach/Main. We moved into a three room flat in Doernigheim, 200 metres from the Main River and a ferry. This saved a 15 kilometre detour and traffic jams. The Glass-Mate department of the company was set up as an independent GmbH, (Limited Company) by a management buy-out in March 1982 shortly after I 'd joined the Ransburg company. When it came to the bottom line GM delivered 30 per cent of the group's turnover, but only ten per cent of the personnel costs. By two directors, an engineer and an accountant with Herr Dieter Nossem as General Manager. All department employees could work for the new company. Herr Trimble, the marketing manager was retiring; - his deputy Herr Hasenstab took over his duties, Frau Buschlebb and Frau Dambrowski, the import/export clerks. In addition, the whole complement of the technical department, Herr Helmut Behrendt, Herr Oswald Frischkorn, Herr Siegfried Sigel and little me. In addition, a part-time book-keeper and an ex-car mechanic/salesman would be employed as store man. After a marathon weekend we moved equipment, furniture, files etc., lock stock and barrel to our new premises on an industrial estate in Offenbach/Bieber.

It was during this phase of physical and mental activity that I met Barbara W, a student in the other Irish Pub in Frankfurt/Bornheim where she was celebrating passing her first civil exam, which was necessary to become a teacher in Germany. We got chatting and it transpired that she was also in the process of getting a divorce, studying to be a teacher and had two young children aged four and six. When she told me that she lived in Bischofsheim, figuratively *'Ein Katzensprung'* a stone's throw from where I lived in Doernigheim; we swapped 'phone numbers.

BARBARA

OR

SHE WHO EATS LITTLE

I was pleasantly surprised the following midday when she called to tell me that her two kids were with their father until bedtime at 19:00, and if she could come over for a coffee later and meet my kids. In the meantime, Jacob was a strapping 14-year-old, suffering from acne and Lawrence was a cheeky 11-year-old.

Barbara was a somewhat skinny 30 something; as tall as me, she had a wide, infectious smile and blonde hair which she kept in a loose pony-tail. She was about five kilos underweight, in view of the fact that she was living on BaFog, the student grant, children's allowance and the alimony from her soon to be ex-husband. In order to run a car, she also did a couple of cleaning jobs.

I said it would be OK if she came round before three o'clock if she wanted to meet Jacob and Lawrence, because since we moved into the flat they'd managed to join football clique with the other kids from the block on the estate. She turned up at 15:05 in her battered 1200cc VW Beetle, (Which she sold to me some time later). I was on the small balcony adjoining the living room and large kitchen, where the remnants of our Sunday lunch lay, still warm on the large table.

Jacob pressed the door release buzzer and went back to watching football on television with Lawrence. I came in from the balcony and greeted her with hug and a peck on the cheek. After I'd made the introductions with brief nods of recognition from the 'Trainer's Bench', we went and sat at the kitchen table. There was half a bottle of Aldi's best so I asked her if she'd like a glass as I topped up mine. 'Only if I can eat something,' she answered looking longingly at the remains of the pork loin, broccoli, carrots, roast potatoes and rich creamy gravy.

'Sure,' I replied, 'I'll warm it up.' I took a clean plate from the cupboard, sliced to two generous portions of the joint, added the vegetables and gravy, and 'pinged' it in the micro-wave for a minute. After she'd demolished her plateful - probably her first square meal she'd had in a long time - I made a fresh pot of coffee. I asked the two football fans if they'd like some bonus pocket money before they went to play. They appeared in the kitchen like two tornados. 'Ok, 'I said, 'How about this? Clear the table, do the washing up and leave the pots to soak.'

By the time we'd drunk our first cup of coffee they'd washed, dried and put the crockery and cutlery away in their respective places. I gave them the promised bonus, DM 2 each and they disappeared. Barbra and I took our second coffees to the living room. I put Dylan's 'Street Legal' on my improvised mini Hi-Fi unit. It consisted of a radio module, a graphic equaliser and cassette deck, all intended for installation in a car. These powered two 8 Watt loud-speakers mounted on bricks.

While we were talking and drinking our coffee Barbra turned to me and said longingly,

'Du warst mir sehr sympathisch gestern Abend, und ich wollte Dich näher Kennenlernen. ' and kissed me gently on the lips.

'She likes me and wants to get to know me better,' I thought returning her kiss. Pretty soon we were exchanging DNA.

TONGUE, TEETH, GENE TRANSFER UNIT AND DOCKING MODULE were in their element.

I broke off and said,

'Maybe we should stop, because Jacob and Lawrence might come back any minute.'

She agreed and suggested the following Saturday at her flat after she'd got her kids to bed. On the respective Saturday I played Backgammon and Blackjack with Jacob and Lawrence until about 21:00; then I told them that I was going to visit Barbara, and might not be back before morning and that they shouldn't stay up too late.

'Que Sera, Sera!'

Over the next six months we grew closer and I ended up spending several nights together at her place, mainly at the weekends, and once or twice at mine when her two kids spent the night with their father. In addition, when I had to go away on business trips she kept an eye on Jacob and Lawrence.

This was all thrown into a form of limbo when I got a call from Zhu Lie, whom I'll call, 'She who looks like a Mouse and walks like an Elephant!'

Zhu Lie was the Dutch/Chinese; girl/woman I'd met in France. (See Summer '78). We'd been communicating by mail and phone ever since my second wife, Angie, the Lufthansa stewardess had visited her in Amsterdam during a layover. She'd even visited us in Frankfurt. Subsequent to my break-up with Angie, Zhu Lie and I consummated our relationship one weekend when I visited her in her two room basement apartment in Amsterdam. I played the 'Gingerman' strategy. After our first night over coffee together the next day Zhu Lie said that she wouldn't be able to look Angie in the eye ever again. This would have been difficult anyway because Angie was 1,76m and Zhu Lie barely made 1,50m in her socks. Apart from that she was very resolute. Her father was a professor at one of the universities and her mother ran a flourishing laundry business. She was 21 and had just successfully achieved a First class degree in History, and in the autumn semester she intended to start studying Law with the intention of a doctorate in Legal History. A further goal was to work at the International Court of Justice in Den Hague.

It transpired that she had been visiting her brother, Feng Lie who was studying in Berlin. She asked me if I could pick her up on the coming Friday at the 02:00 night train at the main station in Frankfurt. I said sure and when I told Barbara that Zhu Lie would be staying until Sunday she wanted to know if I'd been intimate with Zhu Lie. I didn't deny it. Of course she asked the $64,000 question,

'Would I sleep with her when she stays?'

'Sure,' I replied, 'I don't have a spare bed.'

'Nein, ich meine, wirst Du sie Ficken?'

'I just don't know,' I answered, 'I haven't seen her since last summer.'

However, it was not to be. After a couple of months Barbara said that she would like us to move together with me and Jacob and Lawrence. In addition, she could imagine having another child. She even organised a joint holiday in Tuscany with all our kids. I managed to avoid this by claiming unexpected work-load. Shortly after we split up.

I invited Barbara to have dinner with us in the Saturday evening and fortunately she didn't ask any more questions after Zhu Lie's departure.

On one occasion I surprised Zhu Li one Sunday morning on my way back from Muscat in the Oman. I had a full economy ticket so I was able to fly to FfM via Amsterdam at no extra charge, (My boss was totally ignorant).

When I got to her flat at 07:30 we made love and I fell asleep immediately. Zhu Li woke me five hours later to tell me that she had cooked lunch. Then we went for a long walk along the Graachten and ended up at an early evening showing of 'Ten' with Dudley Moore and Bo Derek. Afterwards she said that although she found the film quite amusing it wasn't her usual genre. I'd already booked a seat on the KLM flight to FfM at 07:30, which meant I'd be in the office in Offenbach by 09:00.

It became obvious that we were like chalk and cheese; she came from an academic background with high ambitions, and I was a recently divorced - once bitten, twice greedy - with two growing teenage sons, a demanding job, ex-military, artisan. She claimed to be liberal when she told me that she would understand if I had women friends in FfM. Indeed, as I already mentioned she met Barbara when she came to visit me.

One long weekend in Amsterdam Zhu Li was studying for an exam when I visited her. I took care of the household and shopped and cooked the meals and organised some *Ganja*. After a delicious dinner on the Sunday night she said that when she had completed her second degree she would maybe take time off to have a baby before she started on her Doctorate and thought I would make a fitting father.

A few weeks after my first date with Heidi, Zhu Li called and said she wanted to talk to me and could she come and visit me. I told her that I was taking Jacob and Lawrence to the cinema, which was true, but that she could come the following weekend. She was somewhat aloof when I picked her up at the HbF and drove to my flat in Doernigheim. We made love mechanically after Jacob and Lawrence had gone to bed. While they were doing the shopping on the Saturday, Zhu Li and I had a heart to heart. She said she would be willing to come and live with me and my two sons, to work and continue her studies, but felt that something was holding me back. Which was true; I was restrained and unsure as to commitment for a long time. And a child requires 100% commitment. I'd told Heidi that Zhu Li was visiting so I couldn't see her that weekend. The rest of the Saturday went by in a stony, not wanting to lose face semi silence from both of us. That night Zhu Li kissed me goodnight and turned her back.

The next morning Heidi called and said she would like to come and talk. So I agreed. However, she refused to come up and meet Zhu Li. So we sat outside for an hour smoking and conversing about the situation until she left just before midday. When I went back up to the second floor flat Zhu Li said that she'd like to leave ASAP. I knew the times of the commuter trains to FfM and walked Zhu Li to the local station and made my fare-thee-wells. A few months later I visited Zhu Li when I was on a business trip near Utrecht. We petted but stopped at that when she said confidently, 'What's over, is over!' adjusting her apparel.

"The moving finger, having writ moves on."

I said as I kissed her goodnight and left. A short while later Heidi broached the subject of moving together. (See Whirlwind).

THE WHIRLWIND

I first met Heidi, AKA The Whirlwind when I started hanging out in the bar at the Frankfurter English Theatre that at the time was located in a converted factory building in Frankfurt Bockenheim. I'd been hanging out there after I'd met the proprietor, Judith Rosenbauer, the ex of Hans-Joachim Rosenbauer the presenter of Kulturweltspiegel, the regional TV station's contribution to German TV landscape in the early 80's.

The reason for my frequenting the bar was to give rein to my creative energy and to maybe get an audition. However, this was not to be as Judith explained to me after I'd surprised her at an after show party with a monologue for an elderly woman I'd written. She could only employ actors who were fully paid up members of Equity, the British Actor's Union.

So late one Friday I was sitting at the bar waiting for the final curtain and nursing my first beer. I didn't register Heidi until she deposited her well up-holstered posterior on the bar stool next to mine. Whirlwind, as I came to name her was a chubby 26-year-old secretary in a British bank in Frankfurt, as I later learned.

I glanced over taking in the close cropped Titian red hair noticing her grey eyes, still adjusting to the level of light in the bar. It turned out that she had just come out of the cinema one floor below. I turned to her and said in my best standard English,

'What's your name, Droopy or Sleepy?'

Without hesitating she turned on her bar stool and said in perfect American English, with a Fraenkische dialect,

'Neither, I'm Happy, my name's, Heidi, by the way.'

'Cheers!' I rejoined, 'My name's Alain.'

We got chatting and sometime later I suggested going somewhere else. So we drove in tandem to the Main Ufer and went to a little late-night bar I knew called 'Balalaika' run by an Afro-American women called Anita, who entertained her guests between pulling beers with guitar and standard blues. Her gimmick was that she could hold the last note of a certain song and drink a double Jack

Daniels simultaneously. Whatever!

We made a date for the ensuing Saturday to see the English Theatre's production of Tennessee William's, 'A Street Car named Desire' (Film version with Marlon Brando and Vivien Leigh).

When Heidi arrived at the theatre I was laughing and jokingly flirting with Angie II, a voluptuous blonde, nineteen-year-old. The evening ended with me in Heidi's bed doing what a man's gotta do! When I broached the question of contraception she said it would be Ok because she knew her body. Nature took its course so I told Barbara about Heidi. Mission accomplished.

Several weeks later Heidi raised the concept of moving together. I wasn't entirely averse to the notion, but I stipulated that it would mean that she would have to move out of town, because I didn't want Jacob and Lawrence to change school. Jacob was in the middle of doing his Realschulabschluss, (GCSE's). She agreed and quite soon we found a 4 bedroom 1st floor flat in a recently extended end of terrace house with a large balcony and garden. It was five minutes by bike to the school, five minute to the commuter station, where I dropped Heidi off to catch the 08:18 to FfM and caught the ferry to work. I also picked her up in the evening unless I was working late. Shortly after we'd set up house Heidi told me that she was pregnant and asked if I would support her if she decided to have the child. I could have, I should have, and I would have if I had felt more settled after living in Germany for almost five years. She decided on an abortion and I accompanied her to the doctor's clinic. Some two hours later she demanded that we make love.

After that we became a sort of family; Heidi and I worked, Jacob and Lawrence went to school and played football at every opportunity; we acquired two cats, two mice, (not at the same time!). Heidi knitted in the evenings while watching TV and I worked on my 'Teach yourself to Draw 'correspondence course.

I did most of the cooking. Heidi signed up a Cambridge First Certificate and the Frankfurt VHS, i.e. Adult education centre, and I, after convincing my boss to pay for the course, signed up for an Intensive Italian course. Unfortunately, this had to be terminated due to business commitments.

Between meeting Heidi in 1982 and our break-up on 1987 I had several erotic encounters before Liz arrived on the landscape.

The first was with Ingrid, a 40 something, free-lance driving instructor who was a passive member of the German Am-Dram club that I got involved with in 1987.

The second was Gabi, a Lufthansa stewardess in her late 20's; *Deja Vu!* We met at a party in Bad Vilbel, a small town to the north east of Frankfurt. And after the initial soundings we met regularly when she was at home in Niedernhausen.

Gabi invited Heidi and me to a party in her flat one evening. It was something I would like to forget! Gabi and Heidi slagging each other off in front of the lift at 02:00, causing the neighbours to open their doors and protest noisily. The next occasion was shortly after we'd met.

Mathias, at whose party I'd met Gabi, called and asked if I'd be interested in a double date on the coming Saturday. I said yes. It turned out to be a very pleasant date. My date's name was Inez, a 30 something, attractive, small dark-haired woman from the Black Forest who worked as an office clerk for Cathay Pacific in downtown Frankfurt. She was divorced with a seven-year-old daughter who lived with her parents and ex-husband, a Swedish textile technician. After Inez had dropped off her friends, Sonja and Mathias she said she'd drive me to my car. Can you believe it?!

On another occasion with Zhuli during one of my business trips to the Netherlands and Amsterdam. The final occasion was when I was on my way back from a sales demo in Ulm.

I drove back via Tauberbischhofsheim in order to see the woman with whom I'd had a brief encounter in *'Café Grossenwahn'*. It was shortly after I'd started seeing Heidi regularly.

One Sunday morning we went to have brunch with a friend of Heidi's, Susanna. After we'd eaten I was banished to the bar. So I'm sitting there minding my own business when an attractive woman sitting on the opposite side of the bar starts gesturing. I mouth 'Me?' She shakes her head and points to my right, indicating the slim young man. So I give him a nudge indicating the woman. He looks up and shakes his head at her. She turns her gaze on me and indicates that I should join her. Second best springs to mind, nevertheless I complied and spent the next 25 minutes verbally fencing with Ursula, as she said I could call her until shortly before Heidi caught my eye signifying that she was done with her friend, Sonja and she was ready to leave. The barfly, Ursula took her business card, pressed it forcefully against my groin, stuck it in my top pocket and said, 'Call me if you're ever in Tauberbischhofsheim and I 'll show you that I 'm not afraid of my sexuality!' and left.

So I took up Ursula's challenge. It was late one Friday afternoon and as I mentioned I was on my way back from Ulm when I arrived at her basement apartment in Tauberbischhofsheim.

She was already half tipsy when I turned up unexpectedly. Before long she started dancing and at some point removed her panties and suggested that I should take of my jacket and tie and relax. It wasn't long before I ended on my back, naked with Ursula, who was also naked and in the process of inflating my Gene Transfer Module, from now on GTM, occasionally squeezing it between her breasts, which were too large for her tall, willowy frame. After successfully completing her task she looked up at me and said,

'I think he's ready for me now!' as she rolled over on her back, her long slender legs raised to her breasts. When my GTM had entered her Docking Module, now known as DM she locked her ankles behind my neck, pulling my face down to hers as I thrust into her. When she came she raked my back with her blunt finger nails. It was when she said that the twins, two buxom 16 year olds, one who I'd already met, could join us later that I decided to make a run for the border. She didn't have a phone, so under the pretext of calling my kids I made my escape, jumped into my truck and got home late. I passed off the scratches on my back as an industrial accident after I'd ripped my shirt.

On a later occasion I dropped in at Café Grossenwahn on my way home in Heidi's car in the hope of catching her again.

Fortunately, she wasn't there because I soon got in conversation two well-rounded Abitur (High school) students, called Elke and Elke. Elke One said that Elke Two had dropped a tab of 'acid' and that is why she was occasionally incoherent. The afternoon soon turned into evening. Elke Two was getting amorous so I suggested leaving and having a spliff. Elke One said that her Bed-sit was only five minutes by car. A short while later, Elke Two and I were exploring each other when Elke One said,

'Wenn Ihr Ficken wollen, get a room! '

There was no way round it. By the time we got to my flat Jacob and Lawrence were already in bed reading. They told me that Heidi had rung several times. I said that I would call her and that I probably wouldn't be there in the morning for breakfast and said goodnight. Back in the living room Elke Two and I continued where we had left off. After two bouts Elke Two was readying my GTM for a third round when the phone rang. It was Heidi wanting to know where I'd been and what was I thinking! She'd been worried. I told her that I'd run into an ex-colleague from Pan-Am, Mike Forster and we'd gone on a pub crawl and I'd fallen asleep when we got back to his flat in Frankfurt-Dornbusch. She calmed down and told me to bring her car immediately, or she'd get a taxi and get it herself!

I told her that I'd be there in 30 minutes. I dropped Elke Two off at Elke One's flat. Round three was with Heidi. She had a very satisfied smile when I dropped her off at U-Bahn station the next morning. The flat in Maintal was only on a three-year lease, so sometime later we moved into the Loft apartment that Heidi acquired.

When we moved into Heidi's luxuriously furnished and fitted loft apartment, which had a large roof-terrace just off the spacious living area and was divided into natural spaces due to the open support beams, we threw a party. We fitted our up-market IKEA kitchen. There was a large high ceiling bedroom, a spacious corner bath, a granite wash-basin console and shower stall. In addition, there was a counter-balanced trap door/stairs that opened at the top of the steps.

This led to a carpeted living/guest bedroom.

One of the guests was Günther, the young man who had played my son in the abortive German theatre escapade. He'd brought a young friend with him, Grit a young music student who I'd met once when she was having piano lessons at his flat in the Gallus suburbs. She flirted with me the whole evening until I took her aside and enquired discreetly.

'How long have you had a father complex?'

She looked me directly in the eyes and countered,

'Quite some time. Is that a problem for you?'

'Not at all I,' I replied, 'It's just a question of when and where.' And left her to say goodnight to my agent, Martin and his girlfriend Astrid. When she left with Günther, sometime after midnight she gave me a lingering kiss and pressed her groin against mine.

At the time I was only working 10 or 12 hours a week for Eloquia, so a few days later I was at home when Grit rang to say that she was in the neighbourhood and if she could come by for a coffee. I said that it would be OK and 10 minutes later she arrived out of breath at the door of the fifth floor loft. I was enjoying the life as a part-time houseman, you might say Gigolo, Toy boy was inappropriate because I was 11 years older than Heidi and looked like a poor imitation of Che Guevara. I lived rent free and took care of the household duties such as laundry, shopping, cleaning, cooking etc. I paid as well for the upkeep of the two-year-old VW Golf – a present from her wealthy father, a master baker, in Franconia near Nuremberg. I used it to go to my out of town clients that Martin arranged for me. Grit came and left rather calmer than when she arrived!

SINGAPORE

Can you remember what you were doing, and what were the first words spoken on the moon, and who said them?

You'd be wrong if you said, 'A small step for a man, but a giant leap for mankind, and 'Neil Armstrong.' In fact, it was, 'We have contact', by Buzz Aldrin, the Lunar module pilot as the Eagle touched down on the moon's surface.

'What's that got to do with Singapore, you may well ask?'

Quite simply, when Neil Armstrong uttered those legendary words I was Deputy Crew chief for the night duty at Tengah air force base with 45 Squadron and we had to prep a two aircraft steep dive bombing exercise with take-off at 05:00.

At 01:30 my senior air-frame specialist, Tom, told me that he had found during his pre-flight checks that the hinge attachment screws of the rudder trim-tab were loose and he couldn't tighten them. After inspecting the aforesaid screws, I told him to make up a batch of Araldite epoxy resin, stick a couple of matches coated with the resin in the screw holes. Then leave it for an hour to harden, trim off the excess and tighten the screws. It'll be like new by the time the flight crews arrive at 04:30. Ten minutes later he came back and rejoined the card school.

So in all likelihood I was playing cards with my crew when Neil said those familiar words. Two hours later I checked the screws. They were rock solid so I certified the aircraft as airworthy for the mission. In retrospect Singapore was like a 3 year extended paid working holiday. Our second son Lucas was born in Changi military hospital in May 1970.

Initially I was posted to Royal Air force Tengah. My wife and two-year-old son Jacob flew out with me on the regular VC10 from Brize Norton in Oxfordshire. The first three weeks we stayed in a family guest house with a swimming pool until we were offered a furnished house on the economy, as the US military call privately rented accommodation.

BIGAMY

OR

BETWEEN WOMEN

Bigamy is having one partner too many. Monogamy is the same. Anon.

Consider this:

There was an old lady of Lyme
Who married three men at one time,
when asked: 'Why the third?
'She replied: 'One's absurd,
and bigamy, sir, is a crime.

At the time Heidi was breaking up with me I told her about my night with Liz. She bought a 'last-minute' two weeks' holiday on Corfu with one of her gay, architect friends from Darmstadt; with the codicil that I wasn't to see Liz in her absence. I resisted the temptation until the Saturday before she returned. I went to a theatre performance in the Mousson Turm in Bornheim with an Italian colleague from Eloquia, Eleanora, a large-breasted 40 something woman from Bari on the heel of Italy. After the show I suggested going for a drink in the 'Rotlint' Café just around the corner from Liz's flat, which I knew she frequented. After I'd got our drinks I called Liz and invited her to join us for a glass of wine. She arrived five minutes later somewhat flustered. When we left after an hour, and more than a few glasses of wine, we dropped Eleanora off at her flat, Liz said that she would like to see where I lived, so I drove to Heidi 's Loft apartment, which was where I was ensconced at the time. She was impressed and after a night of unbridled passion we had a bath in the large triangular tub. Liz called her kids, Juliette and David and told them to meet us in Café *Grossenwahn* because she was inviting us to Brunch.

When Heidi returned the following Friday I didn't lie. She gave me a two-week ultimatum to move out with my meagre personal

261

effects, which were few, clothes, books, records, VCR etc. Fortunately, Angie Two, (See English Theatre), whom I was cultivating at the time, said that I could live in her two room flat in Frankfurt/Oberad, because she was sleeping at her boyfriend's during the week, a chubby Art Director at Saatchi & Saatchi agency in downtown Frankfurt, where she was in client relations, and only came home at the weekend to check her mailbox, change clothes, do laundry etc. This worked out fine until I went to Spain again on Boxing Day the 26th December 1987 (See Spanish Siestas IV). I had enough work from Eloquia to enable me to live comfortably. I split the rent and utilities with Angie Two. During the break-up with Heidi I was given the role of the District Attorney in 'Nuts' at the American Playhouse at the US Army admin base in Frankfurt.

In case you don't know, Barbra Streisand played the female lead in the film version. This role was quite a challenge as I not only had to acquire a US American accent, but added this was the fact that I had longer hair than that is normally commensurate with military life. This was taken care of by wearing my hair in a pony-tail before it became *'de rigueur'*, giving me a somewhat Maverick façade. I invited Liz and Angie Two to the ultimate performance on the Saturday evening. Angie Two agreed at once and Liz said she would come to the after show party because her English was not as good as her French, (She grew up on the opposite Rhine bank to the Alsace). I was smoking a last cigarette at the back stage door when Angie Two arrived. We hugged and kissed and were chatting when Heidi pulled up in her Golf II. I greeted her and told her that Liz was coming later. To which she said that, that was OK.

After the show I was chatting with Angie 2 and Daniel, Judith Rosenbauer's son when Liz arrived. At first I was dumbfounded as I introduced her and Heidi, when Heidi said that they had already spoken on the phone. So there I was again, between two women. Angie Two gave me a wink, caressed my thigh, digging in her long, painted nails, kissed me on the cheeks with her squashed grape lips and said smiling as she turned to Liz,

'You were great Alain; you really brought out the undercurrents of incest!'

When I first met Angie Two at the English Theatre she was a

bubbly, curvaceous 19-year-old director 's assistant.

Heidi, as you by now know, was a small, chubby, attractive, intelligent young woman of thirty-one Moons with a natural looking, asymmetric henna red hair style. During our five-year relationship she dropped 10 kilos - thanks to my culinary skills and thrifty housekeeping.

When we'd first met she had been undergoing therapy for her eating disorder.

Liz was a slender, freckle-faced forty-six-year-old, mother of two teenagers and natural auburn hair. She'd recently taken over as studio manager at the trade publishers where she works as a staff photographer

The four of us were standing there in the car park outside the theatre between Liz 's BMW and Heidi 's Golf and Angie Two's Cadet when the question arose; 'Who gets to drive me home?'

If I'd been any less than a gentleman I would have taken the third option and asked Angie Two to drive me to her place and up the ante. Liz and Heidi both knew that I was residing in her flat. Instead I said that as I had invited Liz to the show that I would go with her. Our relationship developed over the next few weeks until Christmas 1987. I spent Xmas Eve and Day with Liz, her kids and mine. On Boxing Day, I got a lift from the Mitfahrzentrale, (A car sharing organisation) in Frankfurt to Barcelona, (See Spanish Siestas).

By the time I returned to Angie Two flat at the end of January 1988 she'd moved out and was living permanently with her art director. She'd kindly packed my belongings, including my latest acquisition and most modern, *'Joyce'* my green-screen PC. So I stayed with Liz for a couple of weeks until Linda Sierra-Evert, a colleague at Eloquia, whom I nicknamed Nevada, said that there was a small bedsit in the Pfaarhaus (Vicarage) where she lived with her husband, the Pfarrer, Johannes. It was perfect; I could eat with them and it was only 15 minutes' walk to Liz's. I stayed there until Ludwig, one of the inmates of the WG below Liz's flat, said I could stay in his room as he was going away somewhere - in retrospect most probably Thailand -for a month.

All I had to do was to pay my share of the utilities and phone bill. So I moved in without telling Liz. When she found out the following day she was to some extent annoyed because I should have told her. She was noticeably mollified the following evening when she came down freshly bathed in a bathrobe and a towel round her wet hair. We lay on the large double bed drinking the wine she'd brought with her watching some crap on Ludwig's TV.

The cards had been dealt so I introduced Liz to the delights of oral pleasure. Her departed husband, Helmut had flatly refused to pleasure her with his mouth. She told me she'd had to wear 15cm high-heels before he was capable of an erection.

When Ludwig returned I got a room in a two man WG in Dornbusch, where I met Mike, (See Mousson Turm). Liz visited me there on a Friday afternoon. She was a little bit tipsy. They'd been celebrating 'Putting the baby to bed', (a publishing expression). It wasn't long before we were naked and entwined on the thin mattress on the floor in my room, when my flat mate came home entered my room without knocking. He took in the scene and gulped, *'Entschuldigung!'* (Excuse me) and closed the door.

That Easter Liz asked me if I was planning to go to Spain that summer, and if yes, could we go together. I was delighted so I said yes. The next few months I took on as much work as possible for Eloquia, teaching translating, etc.

In addition, I had a very lucrative contract from Regina a management consultant and a director of the family construction company, in Königstein. I met Regina at a party of one of Heidi's gay architect friends. She wanted her next speech in English to be polished as well as humorous. DM 1000 for 20 hours work with free lunches.

A month before we were due to leave for Spain Liz had her 316 BMW checked at her local back-street garage. They told her that the gear box bearings and shims were worn, and they couldn't guarantee that it would survive the 5000 Kilometre round trip to Andalucía. A 'new' works replacement would cost DM 2,500 including fitting. When she told me this I made a deal with her. If I could get it done for half the cost, she would pay for all the petrol on the trip. She accepted. It was a win-win situation, because I knew that there was a transmission overhaul workshop in Hanauer Landstrasse. The next day I picked the BMW from Liz's office building, drove to the workshop and got a quote for total overhaul, replacement of all bearings, dismantling, reassembly etc., with a 12 months guarantee and 24-hour service for DM 850 and change. Liz was ecstatic. I soon became a surrogate father for Juliette and David and some of their school friends, Goetz, Sami, Monica, Manuel, Tino and Laura as well. I often had to pick-up 14-year-old Juliette and her friend Monica at the roller disco in Hanau at 23:00 on a Saturday night when Liz was away on a photo assignment.

SPANISH SIESTAS IV

Sometime at the end of June '89 late one Friday evening I set off with Liz, Juliette and Monica in Liz's BMW, which was packed to the gunwales. The plan was for Liz to drive the first leg to Mulhouse on the French border and then for me to take over after a short break for coffee etc. I took the tiller and Liz and the two girls soon fell asleep to the sound of the tyres on the Autobahn, which was clear so I pushed up the speed 180 Kph, and just as dawn was breaking behind us I pulled into the motorway services shortly before the Spanish border at Pont de Livia-Fita. After a lazy breakfast we set off once again with me at the wheel. We were due to drop Monica and Juliette off in Alicante, where Monica's parents had an apartment, before heading on to Conil de La Frontera in Andalucía. However, Liz had said that she would like to go to Andorra in the Pyrenees - in my opinion - a drive-through Aldi. So I took the fork for Andorra and pretty soon we were on a series of serpentine bends. Monica and Juliette were getting queasy in the back, so we stopped at the next village for coffee and to consult the road map. There was an auto-route tunnel that led to Barcelona, where Monica also had relatives. Thanks to her navigational skills and memory, we soon found the suburbs where she found the house in a broad, tree-lined, dusty avenue.

Unfortunately, her relatives could only accommodate Monica and Juliette. Liz and I found a small hotel two streets away and slept till late afternoon. We left early next day and stopped at a small beach so that Liz could cool down.

We arrived at the apartment in Alicante early evening and Monica said that if Liz and I intended staying a couple of days it would be better to put the car in an underground car park nearby. We stayed two nights and on the third day we set off early and by midday Liz said that she needed to cool down, so I took a track to the nearest beach. It was a stony, almost deserted place. Liz had a dip and cooled down and fell asleep under the sunshade. While she was sleeping I swam for a while and then read my book until a large pick-up truck full of immigrant workers with their families and numerous cars ruined the tranquillity. Within 10 minutes the beach was transformed into a Fiesta. They cut reeds to make wind-breaks; fires were lit, food was cooked and they offered some to us. A target was built consisting of a wedding ring suspended on a cord that was stretched between two 3.50m high poles.

When everything was ready the competitors arrived on their chargers. Six young riders whose task was to spear the ring with a stick the size of a chopstick.

After Liz had taken numerous photos of the spectacle we drove down the coast until we found a place to spend the night. TBC.

COSMO@WEB.DE

Zunächst einmal: ich denke an euch alle, auch wenn meine Emails in letzter Zeit ziemlich selten waren. Die Umstände... Aber, ich bring euch mal auf den neuesten Stand.

Am 25. November bin ich mit zwei großen Taschen auf Koh Payam angekommen. Ziemlich alleine. Geplant war ja eigentlich, dass mich Tao mit Sack und Pack in Hua Hin abholt und wir zusammen nach Koh Payam fahren. Ich hatte aber schon einige Tage zuvor ein komisches Gefühl und so war der Nicht-Empfang auf Koh Payam nicht wirklich eine Überraschung. Nur immer mit der Ruhe, dachte ich mir. Ich werde schon herausfinden, was passiert ist.

Dank der Vermittlung (ohne mein Wissen) eines neuen Freundes kam dann auch jemand auf mich zu und klärte mich auf. Tao‚s Frau ist eifersüchtig auf den Wind... Und ich bin ihr bevorzugtes Hassobjekt. Sie hat also einen Riesenaufstand gemacht und wie es aussieht, steht Tao voll unter dem Pantoffel. Naja. Ein Freund von Tao, Polo, ist dann für ihn in die Presche gesprungen und hat mir angeboten, in seiner Bar (Rasta Baby Bar) unterzukommen. Koh Payam Zeit - immer schön langsam. Also habe ich mir die Zeit genommen, die Leute dort kennenzulernen und ihnen ebenso Zeit gegeben, mich zu checken. Schon nach einer Woche fragten die ersten, warum ich denn noch immer im Long Beach Bungalow wohne... Ca. 4 Wochen später bin ich dann in die Rasta Bar umgezogen. Ich wohne und esse für umme und Polo meint, ich kann tun und lassen was ich will: Massage, Unterrichten, etc. Das Geld, das ich damit verdiene, gehört ganz mir. Als Gegenleistung soll ich mich ein bisschen um Neuankömmlinge kümmern, vielleicht auch mal in der Bar aushelfen, ein bisschen Show-Thai-Boxen machen ;). Das kam so: ich habe mit meinem Hawaiianischen Bruderfreund am Strand morgens nach einer Party rumgealbert und da ist dann irgendwer auf die Idee gekommen, dass ich Thaiboxen kann. Wie auch immer...

Kurz nach Weihnachten musste ich Koh Payam dann wieder verlassen, um meinen Pass in Bangkok abzuholen. Das Boot von Koh Payam hält nach ca. der Hälfte der Fahrt an, um Passagiere von

Koh Chang aufzunehmen. Und da stieg dann Mook ein. Ein Film- und Musikproduzent - z.Zt. ohne Beschäftigung. Er gab mir seine Telefonnummer und lud mich ein, ihn in Bangkok zu besuchen. Silvester - der letzte Tag des Jahres und Murphy hatte es auf mich abgesehen. Ich hatte meine Taschen von Tinas Haus mit dem Tuk-Tuk zur Busstation gebracht und wollte sie nach Ranong schicken. Ankunft 12.20. Wann der nächste Bus denn nach Ranong ginge? 12.45 Uhr.

Ok. Busse wie Passagiere kamen und gingen. 3.5h Staub und Abgasen ausgesetzt, fragte ich erneut und diesmal hieß es, dass es keinen Bus nach Ranong gibt. Na super. Da saß ich nun mit meinen Taschen, die ich nirgendwo unterstellen konnte und niemand mit einem Auto verfügbar und noch ein Tuk-Tuk konnte ich mir nicht leisten. Außerdem war ich mit Ines in Bangkok verabredet. Wieder ein Bus nach Bangkok. Habe nicht gezählt, wie viele ich schon ankommen und wieder abfahren gesehen hatte. Also kurzerhand rein in den Bus nach Bangkok mit dem ganzen Krempel. Eine halbe Stunde vor Ankunft setzte sich ein Thai zu mir und wir plauderten nett. Er wollte ungefähr in die gleiche Richtung und so beschlossen wir, uns das Taxi zu teilen. Ich wollte bei einem Freund, Du, unterkommen, der eine Art privates Guesthouse in Bangkok betreibt. Schwer zu finden. 2 Taxifahrten später hatten wir es dann auch gefunden. Die Tür ging auf und ein Fremder teilte mir mit, dass das Zimmer schon belegt sei und Du gegangen sei. Wir hatten noch 5 Minuten zuvor telefoniert... Ich nehme mal an, dass er dachte, ich schleppe da einen wildfremden Typen mit an; was ich gar nicht vorhatte. Ich war nur auf Tragehilfe mit den schweren Taschen angewiesen. Nun denn. Wieder in ein Taxi und zum Guesthaus, in dem Ines abgestiegen war.

Ming, meine "Tragehilfe" benutzte derweil munter mein Handy, um sich mit seinen Freunden zu verabreden. Kein Problem. Ankunft bei Ines. Ming bestellte Essen und Trinken und seine Erzählungen wurden immer ungereimter. Schließlich sagte er, dass seine Freunde ihn abholen kämen und er nur mal eben nach draußen ginge, da sie nicht wussten, wo genau er war. "5 Minuten". Ich hatte ein komisches Gefühl und wollte noch sagen, er solle seinen Rucksack dalassen. Aber, weg war er und mit ihm mein Handy. Stimmung ganz tief. Keiner kann mich erreichen und all die Nummern fort.

Also auf zum 7/Eleven, eine internationale Telefonkarte kaufen. Musste doch dringend meiner Mutsch Bescheid geben, dass es mir gut geht. Einstieg ins Jahr 2008: Zwei Deprimierte vor einem 7/Eleven in Bangkok. "Happy New Year"!

Nach einer durchgepusteten Nacht - ja, ich bin schon wieder erkältet - war das Glück mir wieder hold.

Mook hatte mir seine Telefonnummer auf einen Zettel geschrieben und so konnte ich wenigstens ihn erreichen. Wir verabredeten einen Treffpunkt und checkten aus dem Guesthaus aus. Und da kam er auch schon. Er hat ein wunderschönes 100 Jahre altes Haus an einem Kanal. Mitten in Bangkok und mitten im Dschungel. Kaum zu glauben. Dort sind wir dann die nächsten 3 Tage untergekommen. Mooks Vater, ein Schiffbauer, gab mir schon nach 5 Minuten die Erlaubnis, seinen Sohn zu heiraten - na huch! Am nächsten Tag machte ich mich dann auf Telefonnummern Jagd. Glücklicherweise konnte ich mich an die Adresse von Tuk erinnern. Der Ladyboy, bei dem ich zwei Tage gewohnt hatte. Da ich geldmaessig kurz vor der Pleite stand / stehe, nahm ich das Abenteuer mit den Bangkoker Stadtbussen auf mich. Superguenstig und viel Spass. Natürlich wohnt Tuk am entgegengesetzten Ende von Bangkok. Bei seiner Adresse angekommen, habe ich ihn nicht angetroffen, konnte aber beim Concierge eine Nachricht hinterlassen. Januar: auf zur Botschaft und gehofft, dass mein Pass schon abholbereit ist. Das hat geklappt. Dann auf zur Immigration wegen des Visumstempels. Wann und wo ich denn in Thailand eingereist wäre? Ich hatte keine Ahnung, welchen Grenzübergang ich von Malaysia aus genommen hatte; es war ja alles organisiert mit Minibus etc. Anrufe bei den Grenzübergängen - man konnte mich nicht finden. Die Botschaft hatte nämlich einen Zahlendreher mit meiner alten Passnummer verursacht. Glücklicherweise hatte ich noch eine Kopie der Verlusts Meldung von der Polizei und dort stand die richtige Passnummer. Puh. 2 Stunden später hatte ich dann meinen Stempel in meinem neuen Pass.

Auf nach Hua Hin. Ich konnte meine Freundin Tina nicht erreichen und bin auf gut Glück zu ihrem Haus. Da lag dann ein Zettel: ich hätte wohl meine Pläne geändert etc. und sie müsse zum Arzt. Ich hatte ihr eine E-Mail geschrieben, aber offensichtlich hatte sie die nicht gelesen. Da saß ich also vor ihrem Haus und wartete. Zur gleichen Zeit war Ines auf dem Weg nach Ranong mit meinen beiden Taschen. Ich machte es mir also mit ein paar Bier und der Gesellschaft zweier Hunde bequem. Ein bisschen Musik auf die Ohren und abwarten. Nach dem 2. Song gefror mein MP3-Player. Nichts ging mehr. Na super. Auch das noch. Nach ca. einer Stunde des Wartens kam sie dann.

4th Januar: gegen 11 Uhr rauf aufs Moped und Richtung Süden.

Geplant hatte ich, nur die Hälfte der Strecke zu fahren und eine Übernachtung einzulegen. Doch dann hat es mich geritten und ich dachte, dass ich auch die ganze Strecke fahren könne und noch vor Einbruch der Dunkelheit in Ranong sein könnte. Fast 400km. Mein Hintern eingeschlafen, meine Fußgelenke arg strapaziert.

Dennoch: Die letzten 100km einfach traumhaft. Bergig, waldig, Serpentinen. Das wäre was für Paps gewesen... Ankunft in Ranong bei Sonnenuntergang. Völlig erledigt, aber happy. Und mein mp3Player funktioniert wider - Hurra! Januar (heute): habe einen ganzen Tag in Ranong. Endlich Zeit, ein paar E-Mails zu schreiben und mich ein bisschen umzusehen. Vorhin bin ich zu den heißen Quellen gefahren. Toll zum Relaxen. Außerdem habe ich ein paar Kleinigkeiten einkaufen könne. Ich bin nämlich wieder am

Kunsthandwerkeln - angefangen habe ich mit Rumba Kugeln aus

Kokosnüssen. Morgen früh mache ich dann meinen Visa-Run nach

Burma, lass mein Moped durchchecken (Ölwechsel und neue Lampen) und am Nachmittag sitz ich dann wieder auf dem Boot nach Koh Payam - mit meinen restlichen Sachen und meinem Moped.

Meine Planung hat also super hingehauen!

Dann heißt es ranklotzen: Massage und Unterricht und Basteln! Bin mit der Kohle komplett am Ende. Nun beginnt also das wahre Ueberlebensabenteuer. Unterkunft und Essen ist kein Problem, aber, wenn ich auf Party will, muss ich mir das erst verdienen. Hatte, bevor ich von Koh Payam weg bin, schon 3 Massagen. Unglaublich anstrengend, fast schon Sport. Eine Thaimassage dauert ca. 2.5h.

Außerdem werde ich Englisch, evtl. Deutsch, und hört hört! Thai unterrichten. Auch hier in Ranong habe ich ungemein Glück. Ich kann bei meinen Freunden im Guesthaus umsonst übernachten und auch fürs Essen muss ich kein Geld ausgeben. Gebe wieder mal einigen die Gelegenheit zu guten Taten ;-).

So, das soll's für heute gewesen sein. Viel ist passiert, und nicht alles hat hier Erwähnung gefunden. Wer mich mal anrufen will; hier meine neue Nummer: 0066 (0) 800 746328 - bin jetzt auch auf Koh Payam erreichbar!

Ich wünsch euch alles Gute! Chok dee,

Eure Mala

***

Datum:05/08/2010:27:19

Von: Bianca <cosmo@web.de>

An: maevewalker@yahoo.de

Gesendet: Dienstag, den11.November 2008,3:41:00 Uhr

Betreff: pix

Hi there,

here come the kids and your arrival pic. The 5th day that I haven't seen the sun. The sky is a leaden blanket. Everything is moist - the humidity crawls into everything, books, clothes, wood. My towels just don't dry for days and I'm having increasing troubles with my doors and windows - every time a big bang. How spoiled I am I get a notion of how it feels like being stuck in the rainy season in Ranong. It's not too bad having lots of good stuff to read, to watch and to write. Just had a breakthrough with my story line. Chaptered it out, created the major characters, etc. The dialogues seem to flow out of my fingers naturally. Well, let's see how I consider them in a few weeks' time when I start revising. I think it even possible to accomplish this while I'm working. This term is quite relaxed and there are hardly any people here who could distract me.

Please send me the details concerning Krabi ASAP. I might wanna go there the coming weekend.

Take care,

BB

JUST ANOTHER MONDAY?

Monday 11.04.05 06:45. I woke up a little later this morning because I'd watched TV with Bastian, one of my young cohabitants in our three person WG, until about 23:30 last night. He's a young high school student from Steinach in the mountainous deep south of Thüringen.

As usual I got up and went to the kitchen to micro-wave the left over coffee from the previous evening. Anne, the other member of our humble abode was already having breakfast before leaving for work for the local seed company. We exchanged greetings while my coffee was running its cycle in the micro-wave. I made a roll-up and took them both to my still warm bed and read my latest book until 08:30, occasionally getting up to replenish the coffee and make another spliff. I got up and had a bath, loaded the washing machine and switched it on, checked my e-mails and checked Ryanair flights to Stansted next week, ate my yoghurt, made a couple of phone calls and tried, to no avail, to make Petra change her mind about access to our daughter. She would only agree to the date we had agreed on last Friday. I played Blackjack against my PC for roughly speaking an hour, and as usual I finished with a small gain, unfortunately only a virtual profit – I have better uses for my meagre pittance than tempting fate with money I need to live, although the system I play does give the player a slight edge on the casino (see Blackjack). Over the past ten years I have learnt that it is better to invest any surplus cash in commodities.

In the meantime, the washing was done so I hung it to dry on the washing line on our three square metre balcony. When I'd finished I took the empties to the supermarket and caught the number 2 tram to the Anger, went to the bank and drew some money and got the number 3 tram to BB's. Drank a Bud and smoked a couple of Spliffs and chatted to Andreas, the son of K-D, the landlord. However, it was in vain none of the usual merchants turned up so I made my farewells and decided to take a stroll to one of my favourite spots in Erfurt, the Krämerbrücke.

FRENCH INTERLUDES

Apart from landing in transit from Riyadh early one morning at Charles de Gaulle Airport near Paris, the first time I set foot on French soil was when I went to stay at Joe's cottage to help him renovate the cottage, and for me to come to terms with life after my divorce at the age of 34. (See Summer of '78).

Von: Claudia <@web.de>

An: Alain walker walker@yahoo.de>

Gesendet: Montag, den 30. März 2009, 14:24:42 Uhr

Betreff: Re: my visit

Hi Alain, yes,

would be nice. Great Fotos. M starts to look like you. I like this. See you then in April - spring is coming now. And I ordered the best weather for this week.

Claudia

From:" Alainwalker" maevewalker@yahoo.de>

To: <ckueh@web.de> sent: Friday, March 27, 2009 4:29 PM

Subject: my visit.

Dearest Claudia, I'm coming to Erfurt on the 22nd of April and I'd like to see you. I took these Fotos on Wednesday when I was in York and I had to think of the time when you visited me. LOL

von: Claudia @web.de

An: Alainwalker <walker@yahoo.de>

Gesendet: Freitag, den 29. März 2002, 13:49:54 Uhr Betreff:

happy eastern!

My dear,

I wish you happy Easter days, good meals, nice weather for all your walks with Maeve, meetings with good friends and a lot of good feelings - and fun! Could you already find somebody to move in your flat? I prepared very carefully the lesson I have now with the difficult group. I will do something zum harvesting.

So they will be busy with listening and sorting of text fragments. For next week I sent all my classes to the theatre, so this will be a very welcome week of doing other stuff than preparing lessons and thinking about teaching and whatever. I mean, I still like teaching, but in special this one group makes it stressful. On Tuesday, Wednesday and Friday I will have the workshops I give. Every evening and night I'll go to the theatre, after that may be for a party.

Monday evening start with the welcome party. But as you know: I'm not so strong; probably I will not stand it to be out every night. I need my private quiet lonely hours to relay and refresh. Two guys from Hungary will come, Steffen, who is also lecturer in Szeged, whom I really like, and Bjorn, who is a nice man as well, with his wife and children. I'm looking forward for the, Bjorn does also workshops, and both together play cabaret. I haven't seen them before, I'm very excited, and how it will be. I hope, I will have a good time, will make good experiences and learn a lot. On Tuesday I will have access to the computer again. because Monday is a holiday here. All the best to you!!!

love,

Claudia,

Von: claudia cku@web.de

An: Alainwalker <walker@yahoo.de>

Gesendet: Samstag, den 17. April 2004, 7:21:18 Uhr Betreff: spring time greetings Sweet honey dear, Alain,

it seemed to me like you sometimes check your emails. So why not send you a love letter via wires...?

I got up seven o'clock this morning, had breakfast and a chat with Steffi, they came back last night and I'm now happy to see the green and white bus standing in front of my window.

Makes me feeling more home. I carried Valentine up the stairs and brought the sleeping child in his bed, when they had arrived. I only noticed their arrival because of Rainer, who wanted to visit a girl in our house, but she was not there and so he rang my door bell while I was painting my kitchen door the 4th. time (and it wouldn't be bad to do it once more), and when he left, just in this moment Steffi went in to the house floor.

So sun is really shining another day even though the weather forecast made me afraid by telling the weather for the next days: 10 till 14 degrees. This means to turn on my stove again and as you know the wood is empty. So good bye for today, Claudia

Donnerstag, den 28. März 2002, 13:46:22 Uhr

Re: Re: Re: Re: <no subject>

Von: claudia <ckue@web.de>

An: Alainwalker <maevewalker@yahoo.de>

Dear Alain,

I do write in German only when I'm tired or I feel, I cannot explain in English as well as in German...This week was much better.

Actually there was no chance yet to talk to this terrible German student in my theatre-group, because I was still ill on Monday and after that day she didn't have time. So I still see it coming up to me in the future, but on Wednesday she didn't turn up, so I could work with the group as I wanted to and felt much better. Next week we go in the theatre together and have a rehearsal already on Tuesday. She will than still be in Germany.

I hope this will strengthen, staerken our relations in the group, so that when she turns up again, she has lots power and influence of the students. But still I fight for getting her out of my Project in General.

After our rehearsal I went to the German Stammtisch, gleich in der Naehe. It's fun, because now there is not only the German but also an English Stammtisch - you will like it, when you come to visit me - and lots of people know each other or take part on both of them. So it's a reges Treiben.

Than I could not sleep and had to get up at 6, what is not my time, as you know? The horror will be tomorrow.

I think about more group and partner work for them. May be, it will help.

Today is the first warm day after an endless period of 6 cold days. I will leave soon and visit my bed and have rest in there to be stronger tomorrow. Aber, ich kann Dir sagen, ich bin fest entschlossen, mir das nicht zu nahe gehen zu lassen mit diesem ersten Studienjahr. eine gute Übung darin, nicht alle Verantwortung auf meine Schultern zu nehmen und es ertragen zu können, wenn etwas nicht gut läuft.

Ich wünsche dir viel Spaß bei der kleinen Gruppe und viele liebe

Grüße! Claudia

Von: claudia Kühn <ckue@web.de>

An: Alainwalker <walker@yahoo.de>

Gesendet: Dienstag, den 23. Dezember 2003, 19:29:37 Uhr

Betreff: Re: rainy bad tempered holiday

Lieber Alain,

Süße Weihnachtsgrusse an Dich,

Von Claudia

Donnerstag, den 28. März 2007, 13:46:22 Uhr

Re: Re: Re: Re: <no subject>

Von: claudia <ckue@web.de>

An: Alainwalker <maevewalker@yahoo.de>

My dearest Alain,

I wish you happy Easter days, good meals, nice weather for all your walks with Maeve, meetings with good friends and a lot of good feelings - and fun! Could you already find somebody to move in your flat? I prepared very carefully the lesson I have now with the difficult group. I will do something zum Hörverstehen. So they will be busy with listening and sorting of text fragments. For next week I sent all my classes to the theatre, so this will be a very welcome week of doing other stuff than preparing lessons and thinking about teaching and whatever. I mean, I still like teaching, but in especially this one group makes it stressful. On Tuesday, Wednesday and Friday I will have the workshops I give. Every evening and night I'll go to the theatre, after that may be for a party. Monday evening start with the welcome party. However, as you know: I'm not so strong, probably I will not stand it to be out every night. I need my private quiet lonely hours to relay and refresh. To people from Hungary will come, Steffen, who is also lecturer in Szeged, whom I really like, and Bjorn, who is a nice man as well, with his wife and children. I'm looking forward for the, Bjorn does also workshops, and both together play cabaret. I haven't seen them before, I'm very excited, and how it will be.

I hope, I will have a good time, will make good experiences and learn a lot. On Tuesday I will have access to the computer again. Because Monday is a holiday here.

All the best to you!!! Love, Claudia

Printed in Great Britain
by Amazon